Timothy D. Wilson

Strangers to Ourselves

Discovering
the
Adaptive
Unconscious

The Belknap Press of Harvard University Press
Cambridge, Massachusetts, and London, England · 2002

Library of Congress Cataloging-in-Publication Data

Wilson, Timothy D.
  Strangers to ourselves : discovering the adaptive unconscious /
  Timothy D. Wilson.
    p. cm.
  Includes bibliographical references and index.
  ISBN 0-674-00936-3 (alk. paper)
    1. Self-perception. 2. Subconsciousness. I. Title.
BF697.5.S43 2002
154.2—dc21   2002024088

Contents

Preface

It might seem that self-knowledge is a central topic in psychology. In some ways it is; from Freud onward, psychologists have been fascinated by the extent to which people know themselves, the limits of this knowledge, and the consequences of failures of self-insight. Surprisingly, however, self-knowledge has not been a mainstream topic in academic psychology. There are few college courses on self-knowledge and few books devoted to the topic, if we rule out self-help books and ones from a psychoanalytic point of view.

I think this is about to change. In recent years there has been an explosion of scientific research on self-knowledge that paints a different portrait from the one presented by Freud and his followers. People possess a powerful, sophisticated, adaptive unconscious that is crucial for survival in the world. Because this unconscious operates so efficiently out of view, however, and is largely inaccessible, there is a price to pay in self-knowledge. There is a great deal about ourselves that we cannot know directly, even with the most painstaking introspection. How, then, can we discover our nonconscious traits, goals, and feelings? Is it always to our advantage to do so? To what extent are researchers in academe rediscovering Freud and psychoanalysis? How can self-knowledge be studied scientifically, anyway? These are the questions to which I turn in the following pages. The answers are often surprising and have direct, practical, implications for everyday living.

I have been interested in these questions since I arrived in Ann Arbor to attend graduate school in the fall of 1973, fresh from my graduating class of twelve at Hampshire College (a small, experimental college in Massachusetts then in its third year of existence). The University of Michigan was an amazingly stimulating place, and I am grateful to the many there who helped launch my career in social psychology. I owe a special debt to my mentor, Dick Nisbett, who taught me how to pursue ideas about self-knowledge empirically and to think about them theoretically. Many of the ideas in this book took seed in the stimulating conversations we had at the Institute for Social Research in the mid-1970s. Even more important, Dick showed me that social psychology is not just a profession or academic pursuit, but a way of life that challenges basic assumptions about the world.

I also want to thank the many graduate students I have worked with over the years who helped me investigate the issues discussed here, including Sarah Algoe, David Centerbar, Michelle Damiani, Dana Dunn, Liz Dunn, Sara Hodges, Debby Kermer, Kristen Klaaren, Dolores Kraft, Jaime Kurtz, Suzanne LaFleur, Dan Lassiter, Doug Lisle, Jay Meyers, Nicole Shelton, Julie Stone, and Thalia Wheatley. I can't imagine having pursued these ideas without this impressive bunch to share the fun and hard work.

I also thank John Bargh, Jon Haidt, Angeline Lillard, Jonathan Schooler, Dan Wegner, Dan Willingham, and Drew Westen, who read all or part of the manuscript and provided valuable feedback. Finally, I am grateful to my Harvard University Press editor, Elizabeth Knoll, for her wise, witty, and patient counsel during the seemingly endless time it took to write this book.

The topic of self-knowledge is an intimate one, and in the following pages I draw upon my own and many of my friends' experiences. To avoid any embarrassment I have sometimes changed the names of my friends and the details of their experiences. My own embarrassing experiences are pretty much intact.

Strangers to Ourselves

Freud's Genius, Freud's Myopia

Self-reverence, self-knowledge, self-control,—
These three alone lead life to sovereign power.
—*Alfred Lord Tennyson, "Oenone" (1833)*

What are more important than matters of the heart? Or more difficult to decipher? Some people are blessed by knowing exactly what it is their hearts desire, but are cursed by not knowing how to achieve it. Like King Lear, some stumble into a course of action precisely opposite to the one that would satisfy their hearts and minds. Because of their own pride, stubbornness, or lack of self-insight, their goals remain unfulfilled.

But at least such people know what they want, be it their daughters' devotion, a lover's embrace, or peace of mind. A worse fate is not knowing what it is our hearts desire. Consider Marcel, in Proust's *Remembrance of Things Past*, who is convinced that he no longer loves Albertine and broods and plots and schemes about ways of leaving her, until his housekeeper rushes in with the news that Albertine has left him. At the instant he hears the words, Marcel realizes how much he still loves Albertine: "These words: 'Mademoiselle Albertine has gone!' had expressed themselves in my heart in the form of an anguish so keen that I would not be able to endure it for any length of time. And so what I had supposed to mean nothing to me was the only thing in my whole life. How ignorant we are of ourselves."[1]

Marcel's ignorance of his own feelings is far from rare. Consider Susan, a friend of mine who was once involved with a man named Stephen. Stephen was a very nice guy, kind and attentive and reliable and clearly head over heels in love with Susan. Both he and Susan were social workers and shared many interests. They dated for over a year, and the relationship seemed to be getting quite serious, except for one problem—it was obvious to all Susan's friends that she did not love Stephen. She *thought* she did, but as far as we could see, Susan had convinced herself that she felt something that she didn't. Stephen was a dear friend, yes, but was he someone she deeply loved and wanted to spend the rest of her life with? No way. Eventually Susan realized that she had been mistaken and ended the relationship.

Perhaps Marcel and Susan are exceptions, people who are especially blind to their own hearts and minds. Yet I suspect that most of us can think of times when we were in a similar state of confusion, like Elizabeth in *Pride and Prejudice*, who found that her feelings toward Mr. Darcy "could not be exactly defined":

> She respected, she esteemed, she was grateful to him, she felt a real interest in his welfare; and she only wanted to know how far she wished that welfare to depend upon herself, and how far it would be for the happiness of both that she employ the power, which her fancy told her she still possessed, of bringing on the renewal of his addresses.[2]

Imagine that at such times of confusion we could hook ourselves up to a machine called an Inner Self Detector. After attaching electrodes to our temples and adjusting the dials we could ask questions like "How do I really feel about Stephen (or Mr. Darcy)?" After a few whirs and clicks the machine would display the answer on a little monitor (a more technologically advanced version, perhaps, of the Magic Eight Ball that kids use at slumber parties to tell their futures).

To see how people would make use of an Inner Self Detector, I asked the students in one of my college seminars to list the questions they would ask of it. Like Elizabeth in *Pride and Prejudice*, some of the students wanted to know how they really felt about someone. One person, for example, said her first question would be "How do I truly feel about a couple of people in my life?" How nice it would be to have a machine to tell us the answer to questions like this!

The students also had questions about the nature of their own personalities, including their traits and abilities (e.g., "What is my main objective/motivation in life?" "Why am I socially inept in certain situations?" "Why do I sometimes lack motivation for doing homework?"). Some of these questions, such as those about academic performance and careers, are undoubtedly specific to the uncertainties of early adulthood. Even seasoned adults, however, sometimes wonder about their personalities and abilities. Blindness to one's character can lead people to make poor choices, such as the man who assumes that he has what it takes to lead a fulfilling life as a lawyer when he is better suited to be a teacher, or the woman who turns down an offer to make an important speech because of the mistaken belief that she could never pull it off.

The students also wanted to know why they felt or acted the way they did, such as what it was that made them happy. Understanding the causes of our responses is crucial to avoiding unwanted influences on our feelings and behavior. Consider a lawyer who interviews an African-American applicant for a job as an associate in her firm. She finds the candidate to be cold, unfriendly, and a tad aggressive, and thus recommends that he not be hired. She is a fair-minded person who believes that her negative impression had nothing to do with the applicant's race. But what if she is wrong, and his race did influence her impression without her knowing it? She cannot confront her racism and try to change it if she does not know that it exists and is influencing her judgment.

This book is concerned with two main questions: Why it is that people often do not know themselves very well (e.g., their own characters, why they feel the way they do, or even the feelings themselves)? And how can they increase their self-knowledge? There are undoubtedly many reasons for a lack of self-insight; people may be blinded by their hubris (a favorite Greek and Shakespearean theme), confused, or simply never take the time to examine their own lives and psyche very carefully. The reason I will address—perhaps the most common of all—is that much of what we want to know about ourselves resides outside of conscious awareness.

The idea that a large portion of the human mind is unconscious is not new and was Freud's greatest insight. Modern psychology owes Freud a large debt for his willingness to look beyond the narrow corridor of consciousness. A revolution has occurred in empirical psychology concerning the nature of the unconscious, however, that has revealed the limits of the Freudian conception.

Initially, research psychologists were skittish about even mentioning nonconscious mental processes. In the first half of the twentieth century, the behaviorist onslaught in psychology was fueled by a rejection of mentalism; behaviorists argued that there was no need to take into account what occurred inside people's heads, consciously or unconsciously. In the late 1950s, mainstream psychology took the giant step of rejecting behaviorism and initiating the systematic study of the mind. But the first experimental psychologists to leap off the behaviorism bandwagon said little about whether those aspects of the mind they were studying were conscious or unconscious. This was a taboo question; few psychologists wanted to jeopardize the newfound respectability of the mind as a scientific topic by saying, "Hey, not only can we study what people are thinking; we can study what goes on inside their heads that even they can't see!" In the psychological laboratories of academe, few self-respecting psychologists wanted to risk the accusation that they were, God forbid, Freudians.

But as cognitive and social psychology flourished, a funny thing happened. It became clear that people could not verbalize many of the cognitive processes that psychologists assumed were occurring inside their heads. Social psychologists, for example, were developing models of the way in which people process information about the social world, including how they formulate and maintain stereotypes of other groups, judge other people's personality, and make attributions about the causes of their own and other people's actions. The more researchers studied these mental processes, the clearer it became that people were not aware of their occurring. When researchers debriefed participants about what they must have been thinking during their experiments, they were disconcerted to find that the participants often shook their heads and said, "That's a very interesting theory, professor, but I'm afraid that I don't recall having had any thoughts remotely like that."[3] Most of the mental processes studied by cognitive and social psychologists turned out to occur out of view of the people who had them. This fact became impossible to ignore, and theories of nonconscious processing began to creep into experimental psychology.

Still, many psychologists were reluctant to use the word "unconscious," out of fear that their colleagues would think they had gone soft in the head. Several other terms were invented to describe mental processes that occur outside of conscious awareness, such as "automatic," "implicit," "pre-attentive," and "procedural." Sometimes these terms do a better job of describing a specific type of mental process than the general term "nonconscious." The study of automatic processing has flourished, for example, and a lack of awareness of these processes is only one of its defining features.[4]

But the terms "unconscious" or "nonconscious" now appear with increasing frequency in mainstream journals. A picture has emerged of a set of pervasive, adaptive, sophisticated mental processes that occur largely out of view. Indeed, some researchers have gone so far as to suggest that the unconscious mind does virtually all the work and that conscious will may be an illusion. Though not everyone is prepared to relegate conscious thought to the epiphenomenal refuse heap, there is more agreement than ever before about the importance of nonconscious thinking, feeling, and motivation.[5]

The gulf between research psychologists and psychoanalysts has thus narrowed considerably as scientific psychology has turned its attention to the study of the unconscious. This gap has not been bridged completely, however, and it is clear that the modern, adaptive unconscious is not the same as the psychoanalytic one.

The Adaptive Unconscious versus the Freudian Unconscious

Freud changed his views often, most notably from his topological model of the mind to the structural theory, with the publication of *The Ego and the Id* in 1923. There are also several schools of modern psychoanalytic thought, with varying emphases on unconscious drives, object relations, and ego function. To compare the modern view of the adaptive unconscious with the Freudian unconscious is like trying to aim at moving targets. Nonetheless there are clear differences between the views.

WHAT IS THE NATURE OF THE UNCONSCIOUS?

Freud's topographic model of the mind distinguished between two types of unconscious processes. First, people have a multitude of thoughts that are simply not the focus of their current attention, such as the name of their seventh-grade math teacher. This kind of information is in the preconscious, Freud said, and could easily be made conscious by directing attention to it. More importantly, Freud noted, there is a vast storehouse of primitive, infantile thought that is kept out of consciousness because it is a source of psychic pain. These kinds of thoughts are repressed for a purpose, not simply because our attention is drawn elsewhere. Freud's subsequent structural model of the mind was more complex, in that it allocated unconscious processes to the ego and superego as well as to the id, but he continued to focus on unconscious thought that was primitive and animalistic, and characterized conscious thought as more rational and sophisticated.

According to the modern perspective, Freud's view of the unconscious was far too limited. When he said (following Gustav Fechner, an early experimental psychologist) that consciousness is the tip of the mental iceberg, he was short of the mark by quite a bit—it may be more the size of a snowball on top of that iceberg. The mind operates most efficiently by relegating a good deal of high-level, sophisticated thinking to the unconscious, just as a modern jumbo jetliner is able to fly on automatic pilot with little or no input from the human, "conscious" pilot. The adaptive unconscious does an excellent job of sizing up the world, warning people of danger, setting goals, and initiating action in a sophisticated and efficient manner. It is a necessary and extensive part of a highly efficient mind and not just the demanding child of the mental family and the defenses that have developed to keep this child in check. Nor is the unconscious a single entity with a mind and will of its own. Rather, humans possess a collection of modules that have evolved over time and operate outside of consciousness. Though I will often refer to *the* adaptive unconscious as a convenient shorthand, I do not mean to characterize it as a single entity, as the Freudian unconscious typically is. For example, we have a nonconscious language processor that enables us to learn and use language with ease, but this mental module is relatively independent of our ability to recognize faces quickly and efficiently and our ability to form quick evaluations of whether environmental events are good or bad. It is thus best to think of the adaptive unconscious as a collection of city-states of the human mind and not as a single homunculus like the Wizard of Oz, pulling strings behind the curtain of conscious awareness.[6]

WHY DOES THE UNCONSCIOUS EXIST?

Freud argued that our primitive urges often do not reach consciousness because they are unacceptable to our more rational, conscious selves and to society at large; they "remind one of the legendary Titans, weighed down since primaeval ages by the massive bulk of the mountains which were once hurled upon them by the victorious gods."[7] People have developed myriad defenses to avoid knowing what their unconscious motives and feelings are, some of which (sublimation) are healthier than others (repression, reaction formation, etc.). The therapeutic process involves the elucidation and circumvention of unhealthy defenses, which is difficult precisely because people are so motivated to keep their unconscious motives and feelings hidden.

According to the modern view, there is a simpler reason for the existence of unconscious mental processes. People cannot directly examine how many parts of their minds work, such as basic processes of perception, memory, and language comprehension, not because it would be anxiety provoking to do so, but because these parts of the mind are inaccessible to conscious awareness—quite possibly because they evolved before consciousness did. If we were to ask people to tell us exactly how they perceive the world in three dimensions, for example, or how their minds are able to parse a continuous stream of noise emitted by another person into comprehensible speech, they would be quite tongue-tied. Consciousness is a limited-capacity system, and to survive in the world people must be able to process a great deal of information outside of awareness. Carl Jung acknowledged this point in the 1920s:

> The unconscious has also still another aspect: within its compass are included not only the *repressed* content but also all such psychical material as does not reach the threshold of consciousness. It is impossible to explain the sub-threshold character of all this material by the principle of repression, otherwise a man, at the release of repression, would certainly achieve a phenomenal memory that forgot nothing.[8]

Freud undoubtedly would agree, saying something like "Yes, yes, but this kind of unconscious thinking is the small stuff; nuts and bolts, low-level thinking that is much less interesting than matters of the heart and mind, such as love, work, and play. Of course we do not have conscious access to such things as how we perceive depth, just as we do not have conscious access to how our digestive tracts operate. The fact remains that repression is the reason why more important, higher-order mental processing is unconscious. People *could* directly access their primitive urges and desires, if repression and resistance were circumvented, but generally we do our best to keep such thoughts and feelings outside of awareness."

In contrast, the modern view of the adaptive unconscious is that a lot of the interesting stuff about the human mind—judgments, feelings, motives—occur outside of awareness for reasons of efficiency, and not because of repression. Just as the architecture of the mind prevents low-level processing (e.g., perceptual processes) from reaching consciousness, so are many higher-order psychological processes and states inaccessible. The mind is a well-designed system that is able to accomplish a great deal in parallel, by analyzing and thinking about the world outside of awareness while consciously thinking about something else. This is not to deny that some thoughts are quite threatening and that people are sometimes motivated to avoid knowing them. Repression may not, however, be the most important reason why people do not have conscious access to thoughts, feelings, or motives. The implications of this fact for how to gain access to the unconscious cannot be underestimated and are a major topic of this book.

The Non-Freudian Unconscious

To illustrate further how the adaptive unconscious differs from the Freudian version, let's engage in a bit of counterfactual history, in which we imagine how ideas about the unconscious would have developed if Freud had never proposed his theory of psychoanalysis. To do so, it is necessary to consider briefly the status of pre-Freudian thinking about unconscious processes.

In the nineteenth century, the long shadow of Descartes influenced thinking about the nature of the unconscious. Descartes is best known for his sharp division of the mind and the body. So-called Cartesian dualism, or the "mind-body" problem, has occupied philosophers and psychologists ever since. Many have rightly objected to the idea that the mind and the body are separate entities that obey different laws, and few philosophers or psychologists today would identify themselves as dualists; in fact Antonio Damasio has dubbed the "abyssal separation between body and mind" as "Descartes's error."[9]

Descartes made a related error that is less well known but no less egregious. Not only did he endow the mind with a special status that was unrelated to physical laws; he also restricted the mind to consciousness. The mind consists of all that people consciously think, he argued, and nothing else. This equation of thinking and consciousness eliminates, with one swift stroke, any possibility of nonconscious thought—a move that was called the "Cartesian catastrophe" by Arthur Koestler and "one of fundamental blunders made by the human mind" by Lancelot Whyte.

Koestler rightly notes that this idea led to "an impoverishment of psychology which it took three centuries to remedy."[10]

Despite Descartes's blunder, a number of nineteenth-century European theorists, such as Pascal, Leibniz, Schelling, and Herbart, began to postulate the presence of nonconscious perception and thought. Especially noteworthy were a group of British physicians and philosophers who developed ideas about nonconscious processing that were openly anti-Cartesian and remarkably similar to current thinking about the adaptive unconscious. These prescient theorists, especially William Hamilton, Thomas Laycock, and William Carpenter, can rightly be called the parents of the modern theory of the adaptive unconscious. They observed that a good deal of human perception, memory, and action occurs without conscious deliberation or will, and concluded that there must be "mental latency" (Hamilton's term, drawing on Leibniz), "unconscious cerebration" (Carpenter's term), or a "reflex action of the brain" (Laycock's term).[11] Their description of nonconscious processes is remarkably similar to modern views; indeed, quotations from some of their writings could easily be mistaken for entries in modern psychological journals:

- *Lower-order mental processes occur outside of awareness.* Hamilton, Carpenter, and Laycock observed that the human perceptual system operates largely outside of conscious awareness, an observation also made by Hermann Helmholtz. Though this view seems obvious today it was not widely accepted at the time, largely as a result of the legacy of Cartesian dualism. It was not widely accepted by modern psychologists until the cognitive revolution of the 1950s.
- *Divided attention.* William Hamilton observed that people can consciously attend to one thing while nonconsciously processing another. He gave the example of a person who is reading aloud and finds that his or her thoughts have wandered onto some other topic altogether: "If the matter be uninteresting, your thoughts, while you are going on in the performance of your task, are wholly abstracted from the book and its subject, and you are perhaps deeply occupied in a train of seri-

ous meditation. Here the process of reading is performed without interruption, and with the most punctual accuracy; and, at the same time, the process of meditation is carried on without distraction or fatigue."[12] Hamilton foreshadowed the influential theories of selective attention that were developed a century later.

- *Automaticity of thought.* The nineteenth-century theorists argued that thinking can become so habitual as to occur outside of awareness with no conscious attention, an idea that was not formally developed in psychology until the 1970s. William Carpenter, for example, noted that "The more thoroughly . . . we examine into what may be termed the Mechanism of Thought, the more clear does it become that not only an *automatic,* but an *unconscious* action enters largely into all its processes."[13]

- *Implications of nonconscious processing for prejudice.* One of the most interesting properties of the adaptive unconscious is that it uses stereotypes to categorize and evaluate other people. William Carpenter presaged this work more than a century ago, by noting that people develop habitual "tendencies of thought" that are nonconscious and that these thought patterns can lead to "*unconscious* prejudices which we thus form, [that] are often stronger than the *conscious;* and they are the more dangerous, because we cannot knowingly guard against them."[14]

- *Lack of awareness of one's own feelings.* A controversial claim about the adaptive unconscious is that it can produce feelings and preferences of which people are unaware. Carpenter argued that emotional reactions can occur outside of awareness until our attention is drawn to them: "Our feelings towards persons and objects may undergo most important changes, without our being in the least degree aware, until we have our attention directed to our own mental state, of the alteration which has taken place in them."[15]

- *A nonconscious self.* Do central parts of our personalities reside out of view, such that we do not have access to important aspects of who we are? William Hamilton wrote extensively about the way in which habits acquired early in life become an indispensable part of one's personality.[16] These mental processes were said to constitute a kind of "automatic self" to which people had no conscious access—an idea that was not to reappear in psychology for more than 100 years.

Why has Hamilton, Laycock, and Carpenter's work largely been forgotten? The answer, in no small part, is that the very different kind of unconscious proposed by Freud prevented these views from ever making it to the center stage. To my knowledge Freud never quoted or referred to these theorists. If he was aware of their writings, he probably viewed their ideas as irrelevant to the dynamic, repressive Unconscious with a capital *U*.

But what if Freud had never proposed his theory of psychoanalysis? Imagine that the anti-Semitism of nineteenth-century Vienna had not blocked Freud's budding career as a university professor studying physiology, and he had continued to investigate the spinal cords of fish. Or imagine that he had become addicted to the cocaine he experimented with in 1884, or had never met Josef Breuer, with whom he began his seminal studies of hysteria. As with any life, there are an infinite number of "what ifs" that might have changed the course of Freud's career.

Imagine that experimental psychology began as a discipline uninfluenced by psychoanalytic thinking in two key respects. First, researchers felt no need to distance themselves from difficult-to-test ideas about a dynamic unconscious. They were free to theorize about nonconscious thinking in the same way that Laycock, Carpenter, and Hamilton had, namely as a collection of efficient and sophisticated information-processing systems. Second, they were free to investigate the mind, even the parts that were unconscious, with experimental techniques. An important part of the Freudian legacy was a rejection of the scientific method as a means of studying the mind. The complex nature of unconscious processes could not be examined in controlled experiments, Freud believed, and could be uncovered only by careful clinical observation. Astute clinical observation can be quite illuminating, of course, but psychologists might have turned sooner to the experimental study of mental processes without this methodological limitation.[17]

Even in a Freudian vacuum, researchers interested in the unconscious would still have had to contend with the behaviorist movement, which regarded the mind as unworthy of study by any method. One reason behaviorism flourished in the early and mid-twentieth century, however, was that it provided a scientific alternative to what was viewed as the fuzziness of psychoanalytic concepts and methods. Without this back-drop, it is possible that psychology would have discovered sooner than it did that the mind, including the nonconscious mind, can be studied scientifically.

Thus, in my counterfactual fantasy, cognitive and social psychologists applied their well-honed experimental techniques to the study of the sophisticated, adaptive unconscious sooner than they actually did. Un-deterred by the theoretical and methodological obstacles psychoanalysis created for experimental psychology, research and theorizing on the adaptive unconscious flourished.

This counterfactual history is sure to offend those who find Freud's views indispensable in theorizing about the unconscious. Some theo-rists, such as Matthew Erdelyi and Drew Westen, have argued persua-sively that psychoanalysis was crucial to the development of modern thinking about the unconscious, and that, indeed, modern research has largely corroborated Freud's major insights about the nature of uncon-scious thought.[18]

I agree that Freud's greatest insight was about the pervasiveness of unconscious thinking and we owe him a tremendous debt for his dogged, creative pursuit of the nature of the unconscious mind. It is hard to deny the importance of an infantile, dynamic, crafty, Freudian unconscious, in part because the psychoanalytic narrative is so seductive and explains so much. My counterfactual exercise is meant simply to illustrate that it is not the only narrative about the unconscious, and that we might have reached the current one more quickly if psychoanalysis had not so dominated the intellectual stage.

The narrative of the adaptive unconscious might appear to remove all that is interesting about unconscious processing. The reader with a psy-choanalytic bent might find the adaptive unconscious, with its emphasis on automatic information processing, to be dry, emotionless, and, perhaps worst of all, boring. The Freudian unconscious is ingenious, clever, and sexy and has been the topic of great literature at least since Sophocles. There are few great plays or novels on the automatic pilot of the mind, and focusing exclusively on the adaptive unconscious may seem like talking about romantic love without passion and sex.

This view is misleading, however, because it underestimates the role that the adaptive unconscious plays in all the important and interesting things in life, including Freud's *arbeiten und lieben* (work and love). As we will see, the adaptive unconscious is not involved in just the small stuff, but plays a major role in all facets of life. The failure to find great literature on the adaptive unconscious may say more about the pervasiveness of psychoanalytic thinking than about anything else.

Yet the modern view of the unconscious is not anti-Freudian. To say that we possess a sophisticated and efficient set of nonconscious processes that are indispensable for navigating our way through the world is not to deny that there may also be dynamic forces at work keeping unpleasant thoughts out of awareness. There will be times, in the chapters to come, when we encounter phenomena that have a Freudian hue to them, whereby it seems that the forces of repression are at work. Some readers might react by saying, "Hey, didn't Freud say that?"—and the answer might well be that he, or one of his many followers, did. The question to keep in mind, though, is "Do we *need* Freudian theory to explain that? Are there simpler explanations for the kinds of unconscious phenomena he discussed?"

Sometimes the answer may be that Freud was right about the dynamic, repressed nature of the unconscious. On other occasions the answer might be that although Freud did not say it, one of his many followers did, particularly those who have moved beyond an emphasis on childhood drives and stressed the role of object relations and the ego functioning. Often, however, we will see evidence for a vast nonconscious system quite different from what Freud imagined.

Furthermore, Freud and his followers often disagreed about key points, and over his long career Freud himself changed his mind about key concepts such as the nature of repression. The question thus arises of how we know which of these many ideas are true. A tremendous advantage of the modern psychological approach is a reliance on the experimental method to investigate mental phenomena. There has been an explosion of research on the adaptive unconscious because of the development of some quite clever experimental techniques to study it, many of which we will discuss here. Clinical observations and case histories can be a rich source of hypotheses about the nature of the unconscious, but in the end we must put such ideas to the test in a more rigorous and scientific manner. Thus, even if the answer is "Yes, Freud did say that," he or his followers might also have said something entirely different, and it is only through the work of empirically minded psychologists that we can tell the true nuggets from the fool's gold.

Implications for Self-Insight

Another key difference between the Freudian and modern approach lies in their views of how to attain self-insight. Psychoanalysis shares with many other approaches the assumption that the path to self-knowledge leads inward. Through careful introspection, the argument goes, we can penetrate the haze that obscures our true feelings and motives. No one claims that such introspection is easy. People must recognize the barriers of repression and resistance and remove them. But when such insight is accomplished, often with the aid of a therapist, people have direct access to their unconscious desires. "It is the task of the analyst," wrote Anna Freud, "to bring into consciousness that which is unconscious"—an assumption made by all forms of insight therapy.[19]

But here's the problem: research on the adaptive unconscious suggests that much of what we want to see is unseeable. The mind is a wonderfully sophisticated and efficient tool, more so than the most powerful computer ever built. An important source of its tremendous power is its ability to perform quick, nonconscious analyses of a great deal of incoming information and react to that information in effective ways. Even while our conscious mind is otherwise occupied, we can interpret, evaluate, and select information that suits our purposes.

That's the good news. The bad news is that it is difficult to know ourselves because there is no direct access to the adaptive unconscious, no matter how hard we try. Because our minds have evolved to operate largely outside of consciousness, and nonconscious processing is part of the architecture of the brain, it may be not be possible to gain direct access to nonconscious processes. "Making the unconscious conscious" may be no easier than viewing and understanding the assembly language controlling our word-processing computer program.

It can thus be fruitless to try to examine the adaptive unconscious by looking inward. It is often better to *deduce* the nature of our hidden minds by looking outward at our behavior and how others react to us, and coming up with a good narrative. In essence, we must be like biographers of our own lives, distilling our behavior and feelings into a meaningful and effective narrative. The best way to author a good self-story is not necessarily to engage in a lot of navel-gazing introspection, trying to uncover hidden feelings and motives.

In fact there is evidence that it can be counterproductive to look inward too much. We will see evidence that introspection about feelings can cause people to make unwise decisions and to become more confused about how they feel. To be clear, I am not disparaging all kinds of introspection. Socrates was only partly wrong that the "unexamined life is not worth living." The key is the kind of self-examination people perform, and the extent to which people attempt to know themselves solely by looking inward, versus looking outward at their own behavior and how others react to them.

2

The Adaptive Unconscious

I do not hesitate to maintain, that what we are conscious of is constructed out of what we are not conscious of—that our whole knowledge, in fact, is made up of the unknown and incognisable.
—*Sir William Hamilton (1865)*

Outside consciousness there rolls a vast tide of life which is perhaps more important to us than the little isle of our thoughts which lies within our ken.
—*E. S. Dallas (1866)*

Consider for a moment how hard it is to describe the nature of conscious experience. It is difficult for the simple reason that we cannot observe conscious states directly in anyone but ourselves. How can I be certain that my subjective experience is like yours? We can try to describe our thoughts and feelings to each other, of course, but we have no way of knowing whether the words we use are referring to the same thing, as in the classic enigma of whether my experience of the color red is the same as yours.

Despite these conundrums, we can at least agree that there is a phenomenon to be understood. We know that there is such a thing as consciousness because we have all experienced it firsthand. Moreover, we can reach consensus about some of the contents of consciousness. Most of us would agree that emotions are an important part of conscious experience, because we have all felt love, anger, and fear. We would agree that consciousness can involve a mental projection of images, because if someone said, "Think of a dachshund," we could easily do so. True enough, I have no way of knowing whether your mental image of a dachshund is anything like mine, but we could at least agree that we can both project such images in the theater of consciousness.

It is much more difficult to describe the adaptive unconscious, precisely because we do not experience it firsthand. If you said to me, "Think about the last time you made a nonconscious assumption about what another person was like," the best I could give you would be a blank stare. Describing the parts of our mind that are out of view is as difficult as describing the operation of our kidneys or pineal glands. Even more difficult, actually, because we do not have magnetic-resonance-imaging machines that can take pictures of the adaptive unconscious. Thus, the best way to begin describing the parts of our minds we cannot observe directly is perhaps to describe what it would be like to lose our nonconscious minds.

The Unconscious Takes a Holiday

Consider a man who awoke one Saturday morning with a terrible malady: the unconscious parts of his mind had stopped functioning, and he had only his conscious mind to guide his thoughts, feelings, and actions—an Aware Head, so to speak. How would he fare? If we had posed this question to René Descartes three centuries ago, he would have replied that this man's day would be like any other; what we are aware of is what we think, because there are no other mental processes. A surprising number of early twentieth-century psychologists (and even a few stubborn holdouts today) would agree, arguing that there is no such thing as unconscious thought. In honor of Descartes, we will call the person who has lost his nonconscious mind "Mr. D."

It would be immediately apparent that Descartes was wrong and that Mr. D.'s day would not be like any other, beginning with his attempt to get out of bed. Humans have a "sixth sense" called proprioception, which is the sensory feedback they constantly receive from their muscles, joints, and skin, signaling the position of their bodies and limbs. Without knowing it, we constantly monitor this feedback and make adjustments to our bodies; for example, when we lift our left arm, we subtly shift some weight to the right side of our bodies to maintain our balance. If we didn't, we would list dangerously to one side.

In rare cases people lose their sense of proprioception, with grave consequences. The physician Jonathan Cole documented the case of Ian Waterman, a man who suffered nerve damage when he was nineteen and lost all proprioception. Mr. Waterman was like the straw man in the Wizard of Oz, newly released from his pole. If he tried to stand, he ended up in a heap of tangled limbs on the floor. As long as he focused on his arm or leg he could keep it still, but as soon as he looked away, it would start moving uncontrollably. With a great deal of courage and hard work, Mr. Waterman was able to regain some control of his body, by replacing his unconscious proprioception with conscious attention. He learned to walk, to dress himself, and even to drive a car by watching himself carefully with fierce concentration. He literally kept an eye on himself at all times, because he was in trouble if he lost sight of his body. One day he was standing in the kitchen and there was a sudden power failure, casting the room into darkness. Mr. Waterman immediately fell to the floor. Because he could not see his body, he could no longer control it.[1]

We are completely unaware of this critical sensory system. We can stand and close our eyes and keep our balance, with no awareness of how much mental work is involved. It is only the loss of the hidden proprioceptive system, as in Mr. Waterman's case, that demonstrates how important it is.

Proprioception is but one of many nonconscious perceptual systems. An important role of the nonconscious mind is to organize and interpret the information we take in through our senses, transforming light rays and sound waves into the images and noises of which we are aware. We see that the chair in our bedroom is closer to us than the bureau, with no idea of how our brains transformed the light rays striking our retinas into a perception of depth. If these nonconscious computations were to cease, the world would look like a confusing jumble of pixels and colors instead of cohering into meaningful, three-dimensional images.[2]

In fact it makes little sense to imagine what it would be like to have only a conscious mind, because consciousness itself is dependent on mental processes that occur out of view. We couldn't *be* conscious without a nonconscious mind, just as what we see on the screen of a computer could not exist without a sophisticated system of hardware and software operating inside the box. Nonetheless, it is worth illustrating the importance of nonconscious thinking by pursuing our thought experiment a little further, exploring in more detail what it would be like to be Mr. D. Let's grant him the use of his perceptual system and see what else would be affected.

Suppose Mr. D. turned on the television and heard a newscaster say, "Jones threw his hat into the ring last night, a year before the first presidential primary." When you read this sentence, you did not have to pause after each word and look it up in your mental dictionary; the meanings came to mind immediately. Mr. D., though, does not have this lightning-fast ability to "look up" words; he would have to search laboriously for the meaning of each word as he encountered it. It is not even clear that he could access his mental dictionary without the aid of nonconscious processes, but for the sake of the example let's suppose he could.

When you read the words "threw his hat into the ring," you undoubtedly interpreted them to mean that Jones announced that he was running for president, without consciously considering alternative meanings. You probably did not entertain the possibility that Jones was at the circus and decided that one of the dancing elephants would look nice in his fedora.

Of course not, you might think, because it's obvious what the newscaster meant. But why is this obvious? The part about the presidential primaries came after the part about throwing the hat. There was no way you could have known what the newscaster meant when you first read about hat-throwing; you must have read the entire sentence and then gone back and attached the most likely meaning to the words. All this was done quite rapidly and nonconsciously, with no awareness that you were interpreting what was, in truth, an ambiguous sentence. Alas, poor Mr. D. would have to pause and consider the different meanings of the words and how they might apply in the context in which they were used. By the time he figured it out, the newscaster would be well into the next story about a massive heat wave approaching New England—prompting Mr. D. to wonder whether a tsunami was about to strike Massachusetts.

In short, the mental processes that operate our perceptual, language, and motor systems operate largely outside of awareness, much like the vast workings of the federal government that go on out of view of the president. If all the lower-level members of the executive branch were to take the day off, very little governmental work would get done. Similarly, if a person's perceptual, language, and motor systems stopped working, people would find it difficult to function.

But what about the higher-order functions that make us uniquely human—our ability to think, reason, ponder, create, feel, and decide? A reasonable portrait of the human mind is that lower-order functions (e.g., perception, language comprehension) operate out of view, whereas higher-order functions (e.g., reasoning, thinking) are conscious. Pursuing our executive-branch analogy, the lower-level employees (the nonconscious mind) gather information and follow orders, but it is the high-level employees, such as the president and the cabinet officers, who ponder information, make decisions, and set policy. And these "mind executives" are always conscious.

This portrayal of the mind vastly underestimates the role of nonconscious processing in humans. To illustrate this point, let's make a final concession and give Mr. D. the use of all his "lower-order" perceptual, motor, and language abilities (a quite generous bequest, given the complexities of language and the vast capacity of humans to communicate quickly and efficiently with the written and spoken word). Would the absence of any further nonconscious processes impair him in any way? Or would he now have a fully equipped human mind?

Mr. D. would be at a severe disadvantage in all aspects of his life. Some very important tasks that we usually ascribe to consciousness can be performed nonconsciously, such as deciding what information to pay attention to, interpreting and evaluating that information, learning new things, and setting goals for ourselves. When we see a truck careening toward us as we are crossing a street, we know instantly that we are in danger and quickly jump out of the way, without having to deliberate consciously about the truck. Mr. D. would not experience that sudden fear in the pit of his stomach, at least not until he had time to retrieve laboriously from memory what he knew about trucks and their effects on unwary pedestrians. Similarly, when meeting someone for the first time we quickly make assumptions about the kind of person she is and experience a positive or negative evaluation—all within seconds or less.

Further, much of what we think of as Mr. D.'s personality—his temperament, his characteristic way of responding to people, his distinctive nature that makes him *him*—would no longer exist. An important part of personality is the ability to respond in quick, habitual ways to the social world. It also means having a healthy psychological defense system, warding off threats to the self in reasonable, adaptive ways. Much of this personality system operates outside of awareness.

Defining the Unconscious

A simple definition of the unconscious is anything that is in your mind that you are not consciously aware of at a particular point in time. However, we quickly run into problems here. Suppose I asked you for the name of your hometown. Presumably you did not have any trouble bringing the name of this city into consciousness, even though this city was probably not in your consciousness before I asked you to think about it. Does this mean that the name of your hometown is unconscious most of the time?

This argument would seem to be stretching things and highlights the problem of equating consciousness with attention or short-term memory, as some theorists prefer to do.[3] I, for one, would not want to say that I am unconscious of "Philadelphia" when I am not thinking about it. Philadelphia may not be in my working memory or the object of my current attention, but it is not unconscious, at least in my conception of the term. It is one of the thousands of things I can retrieve from long-term memory when needed—Philadelphia, W. C. Fields's joke about it, the starting lineup of the 1966–67 Philadelphia 76ers, the words and music to "South Street" by the Orlons. Freud described thoughts such as these as residing in the "preconscious," the mental anteroom in which thoughts remain until they "succeed in attracting the eye of consciousness."[4]

What is more interesting is the part of my mind that I cannot access even when I try. A better working definition of the unconscious is *mental processes that are inaccessible to consciousness but that influence judgments, feelings, or behavior.* No matter how long I tried, I could not access my proprioception system or the way in which my mind transforms light rays that strike my retina into three-dimensional vision. Nor do I have direct access to many of my higher-order mental processes, such as the way I select, interpret, and evaluate incoming information and set goals in motion.

The unconscious is notoriously difficult to define, and my definition is but one of many that have been offered. I don't like getting bogged down in definitional issues and will not dwell on the many alternatives.[5] It is more interesting to take a look at what humans can accomplish outside the spotlight of consciousness.

The Adaptive Unconscious, or What Mr. D. Cannot Do

The term "adaptive unconscious" is meant to convey that nonconscious thinking is an evolutionary adaptation. The ability to size up our environments, disambiguate them, interpret them, and initiate behavior quickly and nonconsciously confers a survival advantage and thus was selected for. Without these nonconscious processes, we would have a very difficult time navigating through the world (much less standing up without constant attention, like Ian Waterman). This is not to say that nonconscious thinking always leads to accurate judgments, but on balance it is vital to our survival.[6]

Consider that at any given moment, our five senses are taking in more than 11,000,000 pieces of information. Scientists have determined this number by counting the receptor cells each sense organ has and the nerves that go from these cells to the brain. Our eyes alone receive and send over 10,000,000 signals to our brains each second. Scientists have also tried to determine how many of these signals can be processed consciously at any given point in time, by looking at such things as how quickly people can read, consciously detect different flashes of light, and tell apart different kinds of smells. The most liberal estimate is that people can process consciously about 40 pieces of information per second. Think about it: we take in 11,000,000 pieces of information a second, but can process only 40 of them consciously. What happens to the other 10,999,960? It would be terribly wasteful to design a system with such incredible sensory acuity but very little capacity to use the incoming information. Fortunately, we do make use of a great deal of this information outside of conscious awareness.[7]

LEARNING: THE ADAPTIVE UNCONSCIOUS AS PATTERN DETECTOR

Suppose you were introduced to a person who suffered from amnesia due to brain damage. Organic amnesia can result from a number of traumas to the brain, such as injuries suffered in car accidents, brain surgery, Alzheimer's disease, and Korsakoff's syndrome (brain damage resulting from chronic alcohol abuse). These disorders lead to somewhat different kinds of memory deficits, depending on the exact areas of the brain that are affected. In all of them, however, people lose the ability to form memories of new experiences.

If you were to encounter such a person, you probably could not tell right away that he or she suffered from amnesia. People with these disorders usually retain their level of intelligence and their general personalities. Suppose, however, that you were to chat with an amnesiac for awhile, leave the room, and return an hour later. You would find that the person had no memory of having met you before. Everyone, of course, has occasional memory lapses, such as failing to remember the name of someone he or she has just met. What is striking about amnesiacs is that they have no conscious recollection of any new experience.

Note my key use of the word "conscious" in the previous sentence. It is now clear that amnesiacs can learn many things nonconsciously. A famous (and devilish) demonstration of this fact was performed by a French physician named Edouard Claparède. Each time he visited a woman suffering from amnesia, she had no recollection of ever having met him before. He would have to introduce himself anew at each visit. One day, Claparède reached out and shook her hand, as usual, but this time he concealed a pin in his hand. The woman withdrew her hand quickly, surprised at the painful prick. The next time Claparède visited the woman, she showed no sign of recognizing him, and so he reintroduced himself and held out his hand. This time, however, she refused to shake his hand. She had no conscious recollection of ever having met Claparède but somehow "knew" that she shook this man's hand at her own risk. Claparède observed several other examples of such nonconscious learning in this patient; for example, she had no conscious memory of the layout of the institution in which she had lived for six years. When asked how to get to the bathroom or the dining hall, she could not say. However, when she wanted to go to one of these locations, she would walk directly to it without getting lost.[8]

There are by now many other examples of people's ability to learn new information nonconsciously. People are even able to understand and retain some of what occurs when they are under general anesthesia. When patients are given suggestions during surgery that they will recover quickly, they subsequently spend less time in the hospital than patients not given the suggestions, despite having no conscious memory of what was said while they were under anesthesia.[9]

Cases such as these illustrate the difference between two types of learning, implicit and explicit. Explicit learning is the effortful, conscious kind of memorization we often dread. When we think about the prospect of learning something difficult—a foreign language, how to assemble our new gas grill—we often groan and anticipate a lot of painful work. To accomplish such tasks we need to engage in prolonged concentration, devoting all of our conscious attention to learning vocabulary lists or figuring out how to attach the hose in Figure A11 to the burner in Figure C6.

It should thus come as good news that we are capable of learning a great deal of complex information implicitly without any effort at all, such as Claparède's patient's knowledge of how to get to the dining hall. Implicit learning is defined as learning without effort or awareness of exactly what has been learned. Perhaps the best example is a child's ability to master her native language. Children do not spend hours studying vocabulary lists and attending classes on grammar and syntax. They would be hard pressed to explain what participles are, despite their ability to use them fluently. Humans learn to speak with no effort or intention; it just happens.

Implicit learning is one of the most important functions of the adaptive unconscious. Again, let us not oversimplify. The precise nature of implicit learning and its relationship to explicit processing is the topic of much debate and research.[10] Nonetheless, it is clear that the adaptive unconscious is capable of learning complex information, and indeed, under some circumstances it learns information better and faster than our conscious minds.

A striking demonstration of implicit learning is a study by Pawel Lewicki, Thomas Hill, and Elizabeth Bizot. The participant's task was to watch a computer screen that was divided into four quadrants. On each trial, the letter X appeared in a quadrant, and the participant pressed one of four buttons to indicate which one. Unbeknownst to the participant, the presentations of the X's were divided into blocks of twelve that followed a complex rule. For example, the X never appeared in the same square two times in a row; the third location depended on the location of the second; the fourth location depended on the location of the preceding two trials; and an X never "returned" to its original location until it had appeared in at least two of the other squares. Although the exact rules were complicated, participants appeared to learn them. As time went by their performance steadily improved, and they became faster and faster at pressing the correct button when the X appeared on the screen. None of the participants, however, could verbalize what the rules were or even that they had learned anything.

That they learned the complex rules nonconsciously was shown by what happened next in the experiment. The researchers suddenly changed the rules so that the clues predicting where the X would appear were no longer valid, and the participants' performance deteriorated. They took a very long time to identify the location of the X and made several mistakes. Although participants noticed that they could no longer do the task very well, none of them knew why. They had no awareness that they had learned rules that no longer applied. Instead, they consciously searched for other explanations for their sudden poor performance.

Incidentally, the participants were psychology professors who knew that the study concerned nonconscious learning. Despite this knowledge, they had no idea what they had learned or why their performance suddenly deteriorated. Three of the professors said that their fingers had "suddenly lost the rhythm," and two were convinced that the experimenters had flashed distracting subliminal pictures on the screen.[11]

The kinds of rules people learned in this experiment are notoriously difficult to learn consciously. The Lewicki, Hill, and Bizot study may be a case in which the adaptive unconscious does better than our conscious minds. To return to our example of Mr. D., it is becoming clear that without a nonconscious mind, he would not be able to learn complex patterns in his environment quickly and efficiently.

ATTENTION AND SELECTION: THE NONCONSCIOUS FILTER

As noted, our senses are detecting about 11,000,000 pieces of information per second. As you read this book you can probably hear many sounds, such as the ticking of a clock or gusts of wind outside your window. You can see not only the words on this page, but also the page number and the surface against which the book is resting, such as a desk or piece of clothing. You can feel the weight of the book on your hands and the pressure of your foot against the floor. Let's not forget smell and taste, such as the aroma from a cup of coffee or the faint aftertaste of the tuna sandwich you had for lunch.

All of this assumes that you are sitting in a quiet spot by yourself as you read. Should you happen to be on a subway or in a public park, the amount of information reaching your senses is of course much larger. How, then, can you possibly read and comprehend the words on this page, with all this competing information striking your senses? How do we make sense of the "blooming, buzzing, confusion" that reaches our senses, in William James's oft-quoted words?

We are able to do so because of a wonderful thing called selective attention. We are equipped with a nonconscious filter that examines the information reaching our senses and decides what to admit to consciousness.[12] We can consciously control the "settings" of the filter to some degree, by deciding, for example, to stop listening to the song on the radio and scan the side of the highway for our favorite fast-food joint. The operation of the filter, however—the way in which information is classified, sorted, and selected for further processing—occurs outside of awareness. And that's a very good thing, because it allows us to concentrate on the task at hand, such as finding a place for lunch instead of singing along with Smokey Robinson on the radio.[13]

The nonconscious filter does more than allow us to focus our conscious attention on one thing at a time. It also monitors what we are *not* paying attention to, in case something important happens that we should know about. At a crowded cocktail party, for example, we can block out the many conversations going on around us except for the one we happen to be in. This alone is no small feat and is a tribute to our capacity for selective attention. But what happens when Sidney, standing ten feet away, mentions your name to his companion? Suddenly your attention shifts; you hear your name, and your ears begin to burn. As commonplace as this example is, think of the amazing implications it has for how the mind operates. The nonconscious mind is kind of like computer programs that scan the Internet, out of sight, and send us an e-mail message when it comes across information that is of interest to us. Part of our minds can scan what is *not* the focus of our attention and alert us when something interesting happens. When the nonconscious filter hears Sidney droning on about his gall bladder operation, it decides to ignore it. But when it hears him mention our name—presto, it sends it directly to our conscious attention. Without such an ability to monitor and filter information nonconsciously, our worlds, like Mr. D.'s, would be a "blooming, buzzing, confusion."[14]

INTERPRETATION: THE NONCONSCIOUS TRANSLATOR

A few years ago I met a man named Phil at a parent-teachers' organization meeting at my daughter's school. As soon as I met him, I remembered something that my wife had told me about Phil: "He's a real pain at meetings," she had said. "He interrupts a lot, doesn't listen to people, and is always pushing his personal agenda." I quickly saw what she meant. When the principal was explaining a new reading program, Phil interrupted and asked how his son would benefit from it. Later in the meeting, Phil argued with another parent about how the PTO should conduct a fundraiser and seemed unwilling to consider her point of view.

When I got home that night I said to my wife, "You sure were right about Phil. He's rude and arrogant." My wife looked at me quizzically. "Phil isn't the one I was telling you about," she said. "That was Bill. Phil is actually a very nice guy who regularly volunteers in the schools." Sheepishly, I thought back to the meeting and realized that Phil had probably not interrupted or argued with people any more than others had (including me). Further, I realized that even Phil's interruption of the principal was not so clear-cut. What I saw as rude and belligerent may actually have been a zealous attempt by a caring parent to make his viewpoint known—something I have certainly been guilty of. My interpretation was just that—a nonconscious construal of a behavior that was open to many interpretations.

It is well known that first impressions are powerful, even when they are based on faulty information. What may not be so obvious is the extent to which the adaptive unconscious is doing the interpreting. When I saw Phil interrupt the principal I felt as though I was observing an objectively rude act. I had no idea that Phil's behavior was being interpreted by my adaptive unconscious and then presented to me as reality. Thus, even though I was aware of my expectations (that Phil would be overbearing), I had no idea how much this expectation colored my interpretation of his behavior.

One of the clearest demonstrations of such nonconscious interpretation is an experiment by John Bargh and Paula Pietromonaco, in which people did not even know that they had an expectation about a person. The researchers activated a personality trait by flashing words to people at subliminal levels, and found that people used this trait when subsequently interpreting another person's behavior. As part of a study on perception, participants judged whether flashes on a computer monitor occurred on the left or right side of the screen. Unbeknownst to them, the flashes were words shown for very brief durations (1/10 of a second) and followed immediately by a line of X's. Because the words were flashed so quickly and were "masked" by the X's, people were unaware that words had been presented.

In one condition, 80 percent of the flashed words had to do with hostility, such as "hostile," "insult," and "unkind." In a second condition, none of the words had to do with hostility. Next, people took part in what they thought was an unrelated experiment on how people form impressions of others. They read a paragraph describing a man named Donald, who acted in somewhat ambiguous ways that might be construed as hostile, such as "A salesman knocked at the door, but Donald refused to let him enter."

Those who had seen flashes of hostile words judged Donald to be more hostile and unfriendly than did people who had not seen flashes of hostile words—just as I judged Phil's behavior to be rude and belligerent, because my wife's impression of him was on my mind. We can be certain that this process occurred nonconsciously in the Bargh and Pietromonaco study, because people had no idea that they had seen hostile words earlier in the study. They believed that Donald was an objectively hostile man, with no realization that they had interpreted his ambiguous behavior as hostile because of the words they had seen earlier. (This experiment raises the specter of subliminal influence, such as whether people's attitudes and behaviors can be influenced by flashes of words in advertisements. We will take up this question in Chapter 9.)

The adaptive unconscious is thus more than just a gatekeeper, deciding what information to admit to consciousness. It is also a spin doctor that interprets information outside of awareness. One of the most important judgments we make is about the motives, intentions, and dispositions of other people, and it is to our advantage to make these judgments quickly. The Phil example shows that sometimes these interpretations are based on faulty data (the Bill-Phil mix up) and are thus incorrect. Quite often, however, the adaptive unconscious does a reasonably accurate job of interpreting other people's behavior.[15]

FEELING AND EMOTION: THE ADAPTIVE UNCONSCIOUS AS EVALUATOR
So far, the adaptive unconscious may seem like a rather cold, emotionless interpreter of the world that keeps track of the information impinging on our senses, selects some of this information for further processing, and does the best it can at interpreting the meaning of this information. This portrayal is accurate as far as it goes, except that it makes the adaptive unconscious look like a Vulcan, the *Star Trek* species that is devoid of human emotions. Actually, nothing could be further from the truth. Not only does the adaptive unconscious select and interpret; it feels.

In many hackneyed works of science fiction, human emotions are treated as excess baggage that get in the way of efficient decisionmaking. Invariably there is an android that is a much better thinker and decisionmaker than its human counterparts, because it has no emotions to muck up things. By the end of the story, we come to realize that we would never trade our lives for the android's. Even though emotions cause us to act irrationally and to make bad decisions, we are willing to sacrifice precision and accuracy for the richness of love, passion, and art. Who would want to live the stark, emotionless life of an android?

The irony of these stories is that they underestimate how valuable feelings are to thinking and decisionmaking. It is now clear that feelings are functional, not excess baggage that impedes decisionmaking. Yes, there are times when emotions blind us to logic and lead to terrible decisions. In a fit of passion, people do sometimes abandon their families and run off with the drug-addled leader of a motorcycle gang. More commonly, though, our feelings are extremely useful indicators that help us to make wise decisions. And a case could be made that the most important function of the adaptive unconscious is to generate these feelings.

Consider an experiment by Antoine Bechara, Hanna Damasio, Daniel Tranel, and Antonio Damasio. Participants played a gambling game in which they selected cards from one of four decks. The cards in decks A and B resulted in large gains or losses of play money, adding up to a net loss if played consistently. The cards in decks C and D resulted in small gains or losses of money, adding up to a net gain if played consistently. The question was, how long did it take people to figure out that it was to their advantage to select cards from decks C and D? And how did they do so? To find out, the researchers measured three things: which cards people chose, their reports about why they chose the card they did, and their level of skin conductance while making their choices. (Skin conductance, measured with electrodes on the skin, is a measure of minute levels of sweating and is a good indicator of people's momentary levels of arousal or emotion.)

After sampling cards from all four decks, normal participants learned to select cards from decks C and D and avoid cards from decks A and B—without being able to verbalize what they were doing. That is, they did not seem to recognize consciously that two of the decks were superior to the others. How, then, did they know to avoid decks A and B? After several trials, participants showed a marked increase in their skin conductance while pondering whether to choose a card from deck A or B, signaling them that something was wrong with this choice. Their adaptive unconscious had learned that decks A and B were risky and triggered a quick "gut feeling," before their conscious minds knew what was going on.

The researchers also included participants who had damage to the ventromedial prefrontal region of their brains. This part of the brain, which is a small area located behind the bridge of the nose, is associated with the production of gut feelings. The people with damage to this area never showed an increase in skin conductance when thinking about decks A and B. They continued to make poor choices (and lose money). Antonio Damasio and his colleagues argue that damage to the prefrontal cortex prevents the nonconscious mind from learning from experience and signaling people how to respond. Tragically, the loss of this ability has far more important consequences than failing to learn the payoffs in a laboratory gambling task. Damasio documents several cases in which people's lives have become quite dysfunctional after damage to this area of their brains, because their nonconscious minds have lost the ability to generate gut feelings that guide their judgments and decisions.[16]

NONCONSCIOUS GOAL-SETTING

Suppose you are playing tennis with your ten-year-old nephew. You need to decide whether to try as hard as possible to win the match (and thereby satisfy your desire to be athletic and competitive) or to let your nephew win (and thereby satisfy your desire to be gracious, kind, and avuncular). How do you choose between these competing goals? One way is to make a conscious, deliberative choice: you think it over and decide that in this situation, being gracious is more important than playing like Andre Agassi.

Sometimes this is exactly what we do. One of the most important features of consciousness is goal-setting; we are probably the only species on Earth that can deliberate consciously about ourselves and our environments and make long-term plans for the future. But is consciousness the sole agent in goal-setting?

John Bargh and Peter Gollwitzer and their colleagues argue that events in the environment can trigger goals and direct our behavior completely outside of conscious awareness. Just as other kinds of thinking can become habitual, automatic, and nonconscious, so can the selection of goals. Perhaps you have played so much tennis in the past that you can choose your goal on automatic pilot. You decide to let your nephew win without ever thinking about it consciously. As with other kinds of thought, there are tremendous advantages to such automatic goal-selection in terms of efficiency and speed. You do not need to spend time before every tennis match deliberating about how hard to try; your automatic goal selector does the job for you (e.g., "If playing younger relative, don't ace every serve; if playing obnoxious Oglethorpe from down the street, play as though it's the finals at Wimbledon").

But efficiency and speed come with a cost. The adaptive unconscious can choose a different goal from the one we would if we thought it through consciously. You might find yourself making great passing shots and lobs against your frustrated nephew because your competitive goals had been triggered without your realizing it. Even more ominously, people's adaptive unconscious might acquire goals of which they are completely unaware and would not act on deliberately, such as the desire for sex as a means of satisfying the need for power.

Bargh and his colleagues have shown, for example, that some men have a nonconscious association between power and attraction to women. They conducted a study in which they primed the concept of power in male college students, to see if this influenced how attractive they found a female college student to be. The male participants had no idea that the study concerned power or sexual attraction. They thought they were participating in a study of visual illusions with a female partner, who was actually an assistant of the experimenter. As part of this study they filled in the blanks of sixteen word fragments to make complete words. Six of these fragments could be completed only with words that had to do with power, such as BO_S (boss), _ _ NTROL (control), AUT_ _ R _ T _ (authority). This was the priming task; completing the word fragments made the concept of power more accessible in people's thoughts. Following the word-completion task, the participants rated the attractiveness of their female partner. For some men—namely, those who had scored highly on a measure of sexual aggression—priming the concept of power increased how attractive they found the woman to be (for other men, there was no relation between priming "power" and their attraction to the woman). Further, these men had no idea that there was such a link between the word fragments they had completed and how attractive they found the woman to be.

Men are often said to just "not get it" when it comes to understanding sexual harassment. Generalizing from the research by Bargh and colleagues, this might literally be true: men likely to engage in sexual aggression are unaware that they have a nonconscious association between sex and power, and unaware that this association is triggered automatically. This lack of awareness makes it more difficult to prevent sexual aggression. Men in a position of authority may believe that their behavior toward female subordinates is motivated by good intentions, because they are unaware that their feelings were triggered by their position of power.[17]

What's the Agenda?

The adaptive unconscious thus plays a major executive role in our mental lives. It gathers information, interprets and evaluates it, and sets goals in motion, quickly and efficiently. This is a wonderful set of mental abilities to have, and if we were to lose them, like Mr. D., we would find it very difficult to make it through the day. But how does the adaptive unconscious decide *what* to select, *how* to interpret and evaluate, and *which* goal to set in motion? In short, what is its agenda?

Clearly, in order to be adaptive, nonconscious processes have to be concerned with making accurate assessments of the world. As Charlotte Brontë wrote in *Jane Eyre*, "The passions may rage furiously, like true heathens . . . and the desires may imagine all sorts of vain things: but judgment shall still have the last word in every argument, and the casting vote in every decision."[18] All organisms have to represent their worlds accurately enough to find food, avoid danger, and produce offspring, or they will perish. An early primate who appraised tigers as "fun to pet" and edible plants as "scary, icky things" would not have survived for very long. Those who can spot dangers and opportunities fastest are at a huge advantage. In the Bechara card game study, for example, people seemed able to figure out which decks had the best payoffs quickly and nonconsciously, without being able to verbalize why they preferred decks C and D. Think of the advantage such an ability gives us in everyday life. Our conscious mind is often too slow to figure out what the best course of action is, so our nonconscious mind does the job for us and sends us signals (e.g., gut feelings) that tell us what to do.

Though it is a wonderful thing that our nonconscious minds are so quick to make accurate judgments of the social world, people cannot live by accuracy alone. There is a lot of information out there to analyze, and it is clearly to our advantage to prioritize it, recognizing what we should focus on and what we can safely ignore.

Consider a college basketball player who is dribbling the ball up the court in the closing seconds of an important game. There is a lot to analyze—possible openings in the opposing team's defense, the sight of her teammate setting a pick on the right baseline, the knowledge that her center has always played well against the opposing player who is guarding her. It is by no means easy for people to process such complex information quickly and decide on a good course of action. We tend to take for granted, however, that at least people can narrow their attention to the most important task at hand. Think of all the other things that the basketball player could focus on, if she so chose: what the fans in the first row are shouting, the new routine being performed by the cheerleaders, the fact that she is thirsty and would like a drink of water, the knowledge that she has a history paper due the next day. Instead of thinking about these things, her attention is like a spotlight at the theater, able to focus narrowly on what is happening on center stage and keeping everything else in the dark.

People with damage to the prefrontal cortex find it difficult to know where to point the spotlight of attention. A college basketball player with damage to this area of the brain might be very skilled athletically but would be quite frustrating to watch. In the last seconds of a close game, she might decide to put the ball down and tie her shoes more tightly, or chat with the fans in Row 3. Damasio relates the case of a businessman whose prefrontal cortex was damaged during surgery for a brain tumor.

This man retained much of his intelligence, such as his ability to read and analyze complex business reports. But he couldn't judge the relative importance of different tasks. He might spend all day at the office organizing his desk drawers, believing that this should take priority over finishing a report that was due that day.[19]

How do normal people focus on relevant information and screen out everything else? The cocktail-party example I gave earlier, in which we were able to ignore Sidney's account of his operation but pay close attention when he mentioned our name, suggests that the more relevant to us a piece of information is, the more likely it will be on the nonconscious filter's "A" list of information to notice. Damasio's businessman seemed unable to judge the self-relevance of the different tasks with which he was faced—he did not recognize that it was more to his advantage to finish the report than to put his paper clips in their proper place.

It turns out, though, that self-relevance isn't quite the right way to describe how the adaptive unconscious decides what is important and what is not. Rather, the decision rule is how accessible a particular idea or category is. "Accessibility" is a somewhat technical psychological term that refers to the activation potential of information in memory. When information is high in activation potential it is "energized" and ready to be used; when it is low in activation potential it is unlikely to be used to select and interpret information in one's environment. Accessibility is determined not only by the self-relevance of a category but also by how recently it has been encountered. In the Bargh and Pietromonaco study mentioned earlier, for example, the concept of hostility was accessible in people's minds because of the words that had been flashed a few minutes earlier, not necessarily because this concept was self-relevant.

Another determinant of accessibility is how often a concept has been used in the past. People are creatures of habit, and the more they have used a particular way of judging the world in the past, the more energized that concept will be. Our nonconscious minds develop chronic ways of interpreting information from our environments; in psychological parlance, certain ideas and categories become chronically accessible as a result of frequent use in the past. The college basketball player has been in hundreds of games similar to the current one and has learned what information to attend to and what to ignore. She notices that the forward is late getting around the pick and that the center just cut toward the basket, a half-step ahead of the defender—without having to decide whether this information is more or less important than what the cheerleaders are doing.

The adaptive unconscious is not governed by accuracy and accessibility alone. People's judgments and interpretations are often guided by a quite different concern, namely the desire to view the world in the way that gives them the most pleasure—what can be called the "feel-good" criterion. Jane Eyre observed this motive in her aunt, Mrs. Reed, when she visited her on her deathbed: "I knew by her stony eye—opaque to tenderness, indissoluble to tears—that she was resolved to consider me bad to the last; because to believe me good would give her no generous pleasure: only a sense of mortification."[20]

One of the most enduring lessons from social psychology is that like Mrs. Reed, people go to great lengths to view the world in a way that maintains a sense of well-being. We are masterly spin doctors, rationalizers, and justifiers of threatening information. Daniel Gilbert and I have called this ability the "psychological immune system." Just as we possess a potent physical immune system that protects us from threats to our physical well-being, so do we possess a potent psychological immune system that protects us from threats to our psychological well-being. When it comes to maintaining a sense of well-being, each of us is the ultimate spin doctor.[21]

People who grow up in Western cultures and who have an independent view of the self tend to promote their sense of well-being by exaggerating their superiority over others. People who grow up in East Asian cultures and have a more interdependent sense of self are more likely to exaggerate their commonalities with group members. That is, people who grow up in cultures with an interdependent view of the self may be less likely to engage in tactics that promote a positive self-view, because they have less investment in the self as an entity separate from their social group. Nonetheless, nonconscious spin doctoring occurs in order to maintain a sense of well-being, though the form of the doctoring differs. *What* makes us feel good depends on our culture and our personalities and our level of self-esteem, but the *desire* to feel good, and the ability to meet this desire with nonconscious thought, are probably universal.[22]

To what extent is the psychological immune system part of the adaptive unconscious? Sometimes we act on the "feel-good" motive quite consciously and deliberately, such as avoiding an acquaintance who is always criticizing us, or trying to convince ourselves that we failed to get a promotion not because we were unqualified, but because the boss was an insensitive ox. Given that the adaptive unconscious plays a major role in selecting, interpreting, and evaluating incoming information, though, it is no surprise that one of the rules it follows is "Select, interpret, and evaluate information in ways that make me feel good." Furthermore, there is reason to believe that the adaptive unconscious is a better spin doctor than the conscious mind. As Freud noted, psychological defenses often work best when they operate in the back alleys of our minds, keeping us blind to the fact that any distortion is going on. If people knew that they were changing their beliefs just to make themselves feel better, the change would not be as compelling.

A key question concerns how the accuracy and "feel-good" criteria operate together, because they are often incompatible. Consider Jack, who failed to get an anticipated promotion. If accuracy were his only criterion, Jack might well conclude that he did not have the experience or ability to handle the new position. Instead, he uses the "feel-good" rule and concludes that his boss is an idiot. But is it really in his best interests to pat himself on the back and blame his boss? If he does not have the experience or ability to do the job, wouldn't he be better off to swallow his pride and work harder?

The conflict between the need to be accurate and the desire to feel good about ourselves is one of the major battlegrounds of the self, and how this battle is waged and how it is won are central determinants of who we are and how we feel about ourselves. The best way to "win" this battle, in terms of being a healthy, well-adjusted person, is not always obvious. We must, of course, keep in touch with reality and know our own abilities well enough to engage in self-improvement. But it turns out that a dose of self-deception can be helpful as well, enabling us to maintain a positive view of ourselves and an optimistic view of the future.[23]

Mr. D. Revisited

It should now be clear that Mr. D.'s loss of nonconscious processing would be incapacitating. Not only would he lose his lower-order mental capacities, such as his perceptual abilities, but his higher-order cognitive processing would also be severely impaired. The adaptive unconscious is actively involved in learning, selection, interpretation, evaluation, and goal-setting, and the loss of these abilities would be devastating.

But the fact that nonconscious processes are adaptive does not mean that they always produce error-free judgments. One reason for this is that it is not always to people's advantage to see the world accurately; a dose of congratulatory self-deception can be useful as well.

Further, just because a trait or process has evolved due to natural selection does not mean it is a perfect system that cannot be improved. The human visual system confers a survival advantage; in our evolutionary past, people who could see extremely well were more likely to survive than those who could not. Human vision is not perfect, however; surely we would be even better off if we had the night vision of an owl, or 20/5 vision instead of 20/20. Likewise, though generally beneficial, nonconscious mental processes are not perfect.

Second, many advantageous traits come with a trade-off: though generally beneficial, they have by-products that are not. The human visual system suffers from predictable optical illusions, not because these illusions are themselves adaptive, but because they are by-products of a system that is. Similarly, the advantages conferred by many types of nonconscious mental processes (e.g., the ability to categorize objects and people quickly, correctly "filling in the blanks" when we encounter ambiguous information) can have negative consequences (e.g., the tendency to overcategorize people, leading to stereotyping and prejudice). Further, because much of our mental life resides outside of consciousness, we often do not know how we are sizing up the world or even the nature of our own personalities. We will see many examples of the cost in self-insight we pay for having such an efficient and sophisticated adaptive unconscious.

First, however, we should consider how the nonconscious and conscious minds differ. Many of the nonconscious processes we considered, such as evaluation and goal-setting, can be performed by our conscious minds as well. If the nonconscious mind is so sophisticated and extensive, what is the function of consciousness? Do the conscious and nonconscious systems differ in fundamental ways, or do they perform the same tasks?

3

Who's in Charge?

The more of the details of our daily life we can hand over to the effortless custody of automatism, the more our higher power of mind will be
set free for their own proper work.

—William James, *Principles of Psychology (1890)*

Few would disagree with William James's observation
about the division of mental labor. People would never get
anything done if they had to attend constantly to their
breathing, comprehension of language, and perceptions of
the physical world. A key question, though, is what we
are able to "hand over" to the nonconscious mind. James
seems to imply that we delegate the mundane tasks of living, much as chief executive officers rely on their staffs to
attend to the details while they address the truly important
questions. It is better for a CEO to plan the long-term fate
of the company than to sweep the office floors.

But our nonconscious minds are not just the janitorial
staff or even low-level managers. As we have seen, what is
typically thought of as the "proper work" of consciousness—goal-setting, interpretation, evaluation—can be performed nonconsciously. Once we acknowledge that people
can think in quite sophisticated ways nonconsciously, however, questions arise about the relation between conscious
and nonconscious processing. Exactly what is the division

of labor between these two parts of the mind? Is consciousness really the CEO? Who's in charge, anyway?

Perhaps the nonconscious and conscious systems operate in the same way according to the same rules. By this view, humans are blessed with two redundant systems, like modern jet liners that have backup systems in case one fails. Maybe we have two information-processing systems for the same reason that we have two kidneys and two lungs. Effective thinking is so critical to our well-being, this argument goes, that we have developed two redundant minds that are capable of performing exactly the same duties. If one stumbles, the other is there to take up the slack.

But surely this can't be right. Although Freud underestimated the sophistication and adultlike nature of the unconscious, he was correct that it has a different character from the conscious self. Two information-processing systems have evolved that differ in interesting ways and serve different functions.

Consciousness, Evolution, and Function

Few would disagree with the premise that selection pressures operate on the mind/brain as well as the body. The fact that humans have brains so similar to other primates' is surely not a coincidence but a result of similarities in our evolutionary past. And the fact that the frontal cortex is proportionately largest in humans, second largest in the great apes, and smallest in prosimians such as lemurs and tarsiers, is surely due to the forces of natural selection.[1]

What are we to make of this fact when we try to understand the nature of the mind, such as the roles of conscious and nonconscious thinking? It is reasonable to assume that the adaptive unconscious is older, in evolutionary terms, than consciousness. That is, consciousness may be a more recent acquisition than nonconscious processing, and hence has different functions. Nonconscious processing shares the features of all biological systems that evolved early in the organism's history. For example, older systems are less easily disrupted or damaged than newer systems, they emerge earlier in the individual organism, and they are shared by more species than newer adaptations. Each of these properties is true of nonconscious processing.[2]

If people could think efficiently without being conscious, why did consciousness evolve? It is tempting to conclude that it conferred a marked survival advantage, to explain why it has become a universal feature of the human mind. Although on the face of it this might seem obvious, it is actually an unsettled question that is the topic of much debate.

Now that it is accepted that Descartes was wrong on two fronts—the mind is not separate from the body, and consciousness and the mind are not the same thing—there has been an explosion of interest in the nature of consciousness, both in the popular press and in scholarly circles. *Discover* magazine recently dubbed this question as one of the most important mysteries yet to be solved. Dozens of books, journals, and professional conferences are devoted solely to the topic. A few years ago the philosopher Daniel Dennett declined an invitation to review recent books on consciousness, for the simple reason that there were too many (thirty-four, by his count).

Philosophers are wrangling, with renewed energy, over age-old questions: How can the subjective state of consciousness arise from a physical brain? What is the nature of conscious experience? Can we ever hope to understand what it is like to be another species or even another human? Are humans the only species that possess consciousness? Does consciousness have a function, and if so, what is it?

These questions are of two types: how consciousness *seems* versus what consciousness *does*.[3] We are making more progress on the second question than on the first, at least in a scientific sense. It is telling that there are as many theories about the nature of consciousness (how it "seems") as there are philosophers studying it, and it is not at all clear how to address this question scientifically.

The function of consciousness is a more tractable question and is the one with which I will be most concerned. Before considering how best to obtain self-knowledge, we need to make at least some headway on such questions as whether it makes any difference to know ourselves. Does gaining insight (becoming conscious of previously unknown things about ourselves) change anything? Does the person who has limited insight into the reasons for her actions, for example, behave any differently from the person who has great insight?

A standard analogy is that consciousness is the president in the executive branch of the mind. In this conception, there is a vast network of agencies, aides, cabinet officers, and support staff who work out of view of the president. This is the adaptive unconscious, and a smooth-running government could not exist without it. There is simply too much for one person to try to do, and a president could not function without his or her many (nonconscious) agencies operating out of view. The president is in charge of this vast network, setting policy, making the major decisions, and intervening when serious problems arise. Clearly, consciousness plays a crucial function in these activities. The adaptive unconscious is subservient to consciousness (the president) and reports to it. At the same time, the president who becomes too out of touch is in trouble. If he or she is ignorant of what is occurring out of sight (lacking in self-insight), then the agencies of the adaptive unconscious may start to make decisions that are contrary to the wishes of the president.

Others have questioned the consciousness-as-chief-executive analogy, arguing that consciousness may not play such a crucial role. At one extreme are philosophers who argue that consciousness does not serve any function at all. This position, dubbed "conscious inessentialism" or "epiphenomenalism," holds that consciousness is an epiphenomenal by-product of a skilled, nonconscious mind that does all the real work. Consciousness is like the child who "plays" a video game at an arcade without putting any money into it. He moves the controls, unaware that he is seeing a demonstration program that is independent of his actions. The child (consciousness) believes he is controlling the action, when in fact the software in the machine (nonconsciousness) is completely in control.[4]

The philosopher Daniel Dennett notes that this view equates consciousness more with the press secretary than with the president. The press secretary can observe and report on the workings of the mind but has no role in setting policy and is not privy to many of the decisions made behind the closed doors of the Oval Office. It's an observer, not a player.[5]

How can this be, you might ask, when it so often feels as though we are consciously controlling our actions? Recent work by Daniel Wegner and Thalia Wheatley suggests an answer: the experience of conscious will is often an illusion akin to the "third variable" problem in correlational data. We often experience a thought followed by an action, and assume it was the thought that caused that action. In fact a third variable, a nonconscious intention, might have produced both the conscious thought and the action. My decision to get up off the couch and get something to eat, for example, feels very much like a consciously willed action, because right before standing up I had the conscious thought "A bowl of cereal with strawberries sure would taste good right now." It is possible, however, that my desire to eat arose nonconsciously and caused both my conscious thought about cereal and my trip to the kitchen. The conscious thought might have been completely epiphenomenal and had no influence on my behavior, just as consciousness appears to be unnecessary in lower species in order for them to seek food and survive. Even humans sometimes behave in seemingly intentional ways in the absence of relevant conscious thoughts, such as when I find myself getting off the couch to get a bowl of cereal without ever consciously thinking about what I am doing or willing myself to do so.[6]

Wegner and Wheatley acknowledge that conscious will is not always an illusion, just that it *can* be. The most reasonable position, I believe, is between the extremes of consciousness-as-chief-executive and consciousness-as-epiphenomenal-press-secretary. If consciousness were purely epiphenomenal, then a book on self-insight would not be very satisfying. It might give people a better seat from which to observe the action, but these observations could not change the course or outcome of the game. On the other hand, we have already seen that the adaptive unconscious is quite extensive and includes such higher-order, executive functions as goal-setting. Thus, I think the analogy of consciousness-as-chief-executive or head coach is also misleading. We may have the impression that we, our conscious selves, are in complete control, but that is at least in part an illusion.

The philosopher Owen Flanagan notes that different U.S. presidents have exerted differing amounts of control over governmental policy, and that a more accurate view of the role of consciousness may be consciousness-as–Ronald Reagan. According to many historians, Reagan was more of a figurehead than most presidents and did not exert very much control over the government. In Flanagan's words, "Reagan was the entertaining and eloquent spokesperson for a cadre of smart and hardworking powers (actually layers of powers), some known to outsiders, and some unknown. This is not to deny that Reagan felt as if he were in charge in his role as 'The Great Communicator' . . . The point is that one can feel presidential, and indeed *be* presidential, but still be less in control than it seems from either the inside or outside."[7]

In other words, we know less than we think we do about our own minds, and exert less control over our own minds than we think. And yet we retain some ability to influence how our minds work. Even if the adaptive unconscious is operating intelligently outside our purview, we can influence the information it uses to make inferences and form goals. One of the purposes of this book is to suggest ways this can be done.

In a memorable *Saturday Night Live* skit from the 1980s, President Reagan was portrayed as a brilliant, cunning leader whose "Great Communicator" persona was all a shtik. In public, he was the fatherly, slightly bumbling Hollywood actor the voters knew and loved. Behind the scenes, he was a ruthless visionary who could think circles around his aides and negotiate brilliantly with foreign leaders. (In one scene, he gets tough with an Iranian leader over the phone—while speaking Farsi.) The goal of this book is to make us all more like the Ronald Reagan in the skit—an executive who knows and manipulates, at least to some extent, what is going on behind the scenes.

Properties of the Adaptive Unconscious versus Consciousness

But what is going on behind the scenes, and how does this differ from conscious processing? It is useful to map out the different functions of these mental systems, which are summarized in the table.

The adaptive unconscious versus consciousness

Adaptive unconscious	Consciousness
• Multiple systems	• Single system
• On-line pattern detector	• After-the-fact check and balancer
• Concerned with the here-and-now	• Taking the long view
• Automatic (fast, unintentional, uncontrollable, effortless)	• Controlled (slow, intentional, controllable, effortful)
• Rigid	• Flexible
• Precocious	• Slower to develop
• Sensitive to negative information	• Sensitive to positive information

MULTIPLE VERSUS SINGLE SYSTEMS

As already noted it is a bit of a misnomer to speak of *the* adaptive unconscious, as there are a collection of modules that perform independent functions outside of conscious view. One way we know this is through studies of brain-damaged patients; different areas of the brain seem to be associated with quite different aspects of nonconscious learning and memory. Damage to some areas can impair explicit memory, for example (the ability to form new memories), but leave implicit memory intact (e.g., the ability to learn new motor skills). Strokes can impair language abilities without influencing other cognitive functions. Because the adaptive unconscious is a collection of many independent abilities, some of the properties of the adaptive unconscious I describe may apply to some modules more than to others.

Consciousness, on the other hand, seems to be a single entity. Exactly how to define it, and exactly how it is related to brain functioning, are not known. It is relatively clear, however, that it is a solitary mental system, not a collection of different modules. There may be special cases in which consciousness can split into two or more independent systems, such as multiple personalities (although the exact nature and frequency of multiple-personality syndrome is the topic of much current debate). Most people, however, do not possess more than one conscious self. There is only one president, even if that entity does not have as much power or control as it thinks.

PATTERN DETECTOR VERSUS FACT CHECKER

A number of psychologists have argued that the job of the adaptive unconscious is to detect patterns in the environment as quickly as possible and to signal the person as to whether they are good or bad. Such a system has obvious advantages, but it also comes with a cost: the quicker the analysis, the more error-prone it is likely to be. It would be advantageous to have another, slower system that can provide a more detailed analysis of the environment, catching errors made by the initial, quick analysis. This is the job of conscious processing.

Joseph LeDoux, for example, suggests that humans have a nonconscious "danger detector" that sizes up incoming information before it reaches conscious awareness. If it determines that the information is threatening, it triggers a fear response. Because this nonconscious analysis is very fast it is fairly crude and will sometimes make mistakes. Thus it is good to have a secondary, detailed processing system that can correct these mistakes. Suppose that you are on a hike and suddenly see a long, skinny, brown object in the middle of the path. Your first thought is "snake!" and you stop quickly with a sharp intake of breath. Upon closer analysis, however, you realize that the object is a branch from a small tree, and you go on your way. According to LeDoux, you performed an initial, crude analysis of the stick nonconsciously, followed by a more detailed, conscious analysis. All in all, not a bad combination of systems to have.[8]

THE HERE-AND-NOW VERSUS THE LONG VIEW

Useful though the nonconscious pattern detector is, it is tied to the here-and-now. It reacts quickly to our current environment, skillfully detects patterns, alerts us to any dangers, and sets in motion goal-directed behaviors. What it cannot do is anticipate what will happen tomorrow, next week, or next year, and plan accordingly. Nor can the adaptive unconscious muse about the past and integrate it into a coherent self-narrative. Among the major functions of consciousness are the abilities to anticipate, mentally simulate, and plan.

An organism that has a concept of the future and past, and is able to reflect on these time periods at will, is in a better position to make effective long-term plans than one that does not—providing a tremendous survival advantage. In some lower organisms, planning for the future is innate: squirrels "know" to store nuts for the winter, and migratory birds "know" when to fly south to warmer weather. Imagine the advantage of having a more flexible mental system that can muse, reflect, ponder, and contemplate alternative futures and connect these scenarios to the past. The practice of agriculture, for example, requires knowledge of the past and thinking about the future; why bother putting seeds in the ground now if we cannot envision what will happen to them over the next few weeks?

The idea that consciousness plans for the future probably does not come as much of a surprise. Those who endorse the consciousness-as-chief-executive model would agree that a major function of consciousness is to engage in long-term planning. A good CEO leaves the little stuff to underlings and spends his or her time on the big questions, such as what the long-term goals should be and how to implement them.

Our consciousness-as–Ronald Reagan model, however, portrays long-term planning a little differently. The federal government (the mind) is a vast, interrelated system that operates quite well on a day-to-day basis. The chief executive can look into the future and try to set long-term goals, but might find it difficult to make major changes in policy. Often the best he or she can do is to nudge the vast bureaucracy onto a slightly different course. In fact there is a danger to making major policy changes for which the rest of the mind is unsuited.

Consider Herman, who believes that he is a loner who is happiest when by himself doing his own thing, when in fact he has a strong, nonconscious need for affiliation with other people. Because it is his conscious self-view that plans his future and determines his behavior, Herman avoids large gatherings and parties and chooses a career as a computer consultant so that he can work out of his home. His nonconscious need for affiliation is unfulfilled by these choices, however, leading to unhappiness. Perhaps the best use of consciousness is to put ourselves in situations in which our adaptive unconscious can work smoothly. This is best achieved by recognizing what our nonconscious needs and traits are and planning accordingly.[9]

But how do we recognize what our nonconscious needs and motives are? That is the million-dollar question. For now, I note simply that the ability to think about and plan for the future endows humans with a tremendous advantage, but can be a two-edged sword. Following our conscious wishes can be problematic if they conflict with the desires of the adaptive unconscious.

AUTOMATIC VERSUS CONTROLLED PROCESSING

It is well known that people can perform many behaviors (e.g., riding a bicycle, driving a car, playing the piano) quickly, effortlessly, and with little conscious attention. Once we have learned such complex motor behaviors, we can perform them better when we are on automatic pilot and are not consciously thinking about what we are doing. The moment I begin to think about what my pinkie and index fingers are doing as I type these words, typos result. There is a term for this in athletics: when a player is "unconscious," she is performing at an optimal level without any awareness of exactly *what* she is doing. She is in the zone.

Although we do not often conceive of thinking in the same way, it, too, can happen automatically. Just as playing the piano can become automatic, so can habitual ways of processing information about the physical and social world. Indeed, a defining feature of the adaptive unconscious is its ability to operate on automatic pilot. Automatic thinking has five defining features: it is nonconscious, fast, unintentional, uncontrollable, and effortless. As noted by the social psychologist John Bargh, different kinds of automatic thinking meet these criteria to varying degrees; for our purposes we can define automaticity as thinking that satisfies all or most of these criteria.

We have already encountered examples of this type of thinking in Chapter 2—namely, the way in which the adaptive unconscious selects, interprets, and evaluates incoming information. Consider the cocktail-party phenomenon, in which the adaptive unconscious blocks out all the conversations except the one we are in, but at the same time monitors what other people are saying (and alerts us if they say something important, such as our name). This process meets all five of the criteria of automaticity: it occurs quickly, nonconsciously, and without intention, in the sense that our nonconscious filter operates even when we have no intention that it do so. It is uncontrollable, in the sense that we have little say over the operation of the nonconscious filter and could not stop it if we tried. Finally, it operates effortlessly, in the sense that the nonconscious filter takes up little mental energy or resources.

Another example of automatic thinking is the tendency to categorize and stereotype other people. When we meet somebody for the first time, we pigeonhole them according to their race or gender or age very quickly, without even knowing we are doing so. This process of automatic stereotyping is probably innate; we are prewired to fit people into categories. The nature of the pigeonholes, however—the content of our stereotypes—is certainly not innate. No one is born with a specific stereotype about another group, but once we learn these stereotypes, usually from our immediate culture, we are inclined to apply them nonconsciously, unintentionally, uncontrollably, and effortlessly. In contrast, conscious thinking occurs more slowly, with intention (we typically think what we want to think), control (we are better able to influence what we think about), and effort (it is hard to keep our conscious minds on something when we are distracted or preoccupied).[10]

THE RIGIDITY OF THE ADAPTIVE UNCONSCIOUS

A disadvantage of a system that processes information quickly and efficiently is that it is slow to respond to new, contradictory information. In fact we often unconsciously bend new information to fit our preconceptions, making it next to impossible to realize that our preconceptions are wrong. An example is my assumption that Phil, the man I met at a PTO meeting, was the pushy, rude fellow I had heard about, when in fact he was not.

What happens when the nonconscious system quickly detects a violation of a pattern? Does it recognize that the old way of seeing things no longer applies? Suppose, for example, that a business manager notices (at a nonconscious level) that the last two employees she had to fire had degrees from small, liberal-arts colleges and that the last three people she promoted had degrees from large, state universities. It is now job-performance time, and the manager is evaluating a new batch of employees, some of whom went to small, liberal-arts colleges and some of whom went to state universities. On average, the two groups have performed at the same level, although each did better on some tasks than on others. How will the manager evaluate these employees?

A smart, flexible system would recognize that the previously learned correlation, from a very small sample, does not generalize to this larger sample of employees. And yet once a correlation is learned, the nonconscious system tends to see it where it does not exist, thereby becoming more convinced that the correlation is true. When evaluating the employees who went to small colleges, the manager may focus on and remember the times they did poorly. When evaluating the employees who went to large universities, she is likely to focus on and remember the times they did well, thereby strengthening her belief that the size of a person's alma mater is predictive of job performance—even though it is not.

Even worse, people can unknowingly behave in ways that make their expectations come true, as in Robert Rosenthal and Lenore Jacobson's classic research on the self-fulfilling prophecy. They found that teachers not only view their students in the ways that they expect them to be, but act in ways that make these expectations come true. At the beginning of the school year, they administered a test to all the students in an elementary school and told the teachers that some of the students had scored so well that they were sure to "bloom" academically. In fact this was not necessarily true: the students identified as "bloomers" had been chosen randomly by the researchers. Neither the students nor their parents were told anything about the results of the test. The "bloomers" differed from their peers only in the minds of the teachers.

When researchers tested all the children again at the end of the year with an actual I.Q. test, the students who had been labeled as bloomers showed significantly higher gains in their I.Q. scores than the other students did. The teachers had treated the bloomers differently, in such a way that made their expectations come true.

The teachers' expectations about their students were conscious, but the way in which they made their expectations come true was not. When the teachers expected their students to do well, they unknowingly gave them more personal attention, challenged them more, and gave them better feedback on their work. Myra and David Sadker suggest that a similar self-fulfilling prophecy, operating at a nonconscious level, influences the relative performance of boys and girls in American classrooms. At a conscious level, most teachers believe that girls and boys are receiving equal treatment. In one study, the Sadkers showed teachers a film of a classroom discussion and asked who was contributing more to that discussion—boys or girls. The teachers said that the girls had participated more than the boys. Only when the Sadkers asked the teachers to watch the film and count the number of times boys and girls talked did the teachers realize that the boys had outtalked the girls by a factor of three to one.

At a nonconscious level, argue the Sadkers, teachers often treat boys in more favorable ways than girls, thereby causing boys to do better in their classes. The nonconscious mind can jump to conclusions quite quickly ("the boys in my math class are smarter"), leading teachers to treat boys in preferential ways—even when they believe, consciously, that they are treating everyone the same.[11]

It is fair to say that the tendency for the adaptive unconscious to jump to conclusions, and to fail to change its mind in the face of contrary evidence, is responsible for some of society's most troubling problems, such as the pervasiveness of racial prejudice (discussed in Chapter 9). Why would an *adaptive* unconscious lead to such erroneous inferences? Again, the fact that mental processes have conferred a survival advantage does not mean that they are error free; in fact the advantages they bring (e.g., quick appraisals and categorizations) often have unfortunate by-products.

DOING BEFORE KNOWING

Children are especially likely to act on automatic pilot, with their adaptive unconscious guiding their behavior in sophisticated ways before they are aware of what they are doing or why they are doing it. Nonconscious skills such as implicit learning and implicit memory appear early, before children have the ability to reason consciously at a very sophisticated level. Infants have the ability to remember things implicitly (nonconsciously) at birth or even before (in utero), whereas the ability to remember things explicitly (consciously) does not begin to develop until the end of the first year of life. Further, the parts of the brain that appear to be involved in explicit memory develop later in childhood than the parts of the brain that are involved in implicit memory.[12]

Adults are often in the same quandary: they have no access to their nonconscious minds and have to rely on their conscious interpreters to figure out what is going on inside their own heads. Adults, at least, have a sophisticated, clever interpreter that often constructs an accurate narrative. Children are especially likely to be in the dark, because their conscious interpreter develops more slowly and does not yet have the sophistication to guess what the nonconscious mind is doing.

This predicament creates a dilemma for psychologists interested in the development of the mind. One of the easiest ways of assessing what people are thinking is to ask them, and many studies of cognitive development rely on children's self-reports. Because the conscious system develops more slowly than the nonconscious one, relying solely on these reports can yield a misleading answer about the age at which a specific skill or trait develops. This error has been made in some well-known areas of developmental research.

When do children learn the discounting principle? Both Suzie and Rosemary practiced the piano for half an hour. Suzie's mother gave her an ice cream cone for practicing the piano, whereas Rosemary practiced without receiving an ice cream cone. Who liked playing the piano more? Most adults say that Rosemary did, assuming that Suzie might have been motivated in part by the reward. Because Rosemary practiced without receiving any reward, she probably was motivated more by the intrinsic joy of playing. This is known as the *discounting principle,* the tendency to lower our estimate of the causal role of one factor (intrinsic interest in piano playing) to the extent that other plausible causes are present (the ice cream cone).

Developmental psychologists have been interested in the age at which children begin to use the discounting principle. In the typical study, children listen to stories like the one about Suzie and Rosemary and report who liked the activity more. Before the age of eight or nine, children seem to use an additivity principle, whereby they think that people who performed activities for a reward like it more (assuming that intrinsic interest + a reward = greater intrinsic interest). By the age of eight or nine, children begin to use the discounting principle, assuming that people who do things for rewards like them less than people who do not (e.g., intrinsic interest + a reward = less intrinsic interest).

But studies that rely on what children do instead of what they say show that children can use the discounting principle at a much earlier age than eight or nine. In these studies, children are given a reward for performing an attractive activity themselves, and their subsequent interest in the activity is measured by observing how much they choose to engage in it. For example, Mark Lepper, David Greene, and Richard Nisbett asked three- to five-year-old preschool children to draw with felt-tip pens, which at the time was a novel, fun activity for young children. Some of the kids were rewarded with a "Good Player Certificate" for drawing with the pens and some were not.

Later the researchers put the pens in the classroom during a free-play period and measured how much time each child spent playing with them. As predicted, the children who had been rewarded earlier played with the pens significantly less than those who had not been rewarded. They seemed to have applied the discounting principle to their own behavior, concluding—not necessarily consciously—that if they played with the pens in order to get the Good Player Certificate, they must not have liked the pens very much.[13]

Why don't children use this same discounting principle when explaining other people's behavior until the age of eight or nine? Perhaps the adaptive unconscious learns the discounting principle earlier than the conscious interpreter. Young children act according to the discounting principle because their nonconscious inference system is driving their behavior (e.g., whether they play with the pens in the classroom). Interpreting behavior consciously and verbally reporting why it occurred, however, is the job of the conscious system, which takes longer to learn and apply the discounting principle.

This schism between what people do and what they say persists into adulthood. On the basis of what they do, adults often seem to have discounted their interest in a rewarded activity. During unconstrained, free-time periods, those who have been rewarded for engaging in the activity (such as playing with puzzles) spend less time with the activity than do people who have not been rewarded for engaging in the activity. Given what people reported, however, they did not seem to have discounted their interest in the activity: they said they liked the activity as much as people who had not been rewarded.

If there really are two systems implicated in these studies, a nonconscious one that determines what people do and a conscious one that determines what people say, are there ways of getting them more in synch? How can the conscious system do a better job of inferring what the nonconscious system already knows? Given that consciousness appears to take longer to learn the discounting principle, maybe it needs a little more of a nudge to apply it. That is, whereas the nonconscious system discounts intrinsic interest in the presence of rewards quite readily, maybe the conscious system has to think about it a little more carefully. I tested this hypothesis with Jay Hull and Jim Johnson in a study in which college students were given a reward to play with an interesting puzzle. As in many studies of this type, the students' behavior indicated that the reward reduced their interest in the puzzle: they played with the puzzle less in a subsequent, free-time period than did unrewarded students.

As is also common, however, the students did not report, on a questionnaire, that they disliked the puzzle—unless they had first been asked to think about the reasons for their actions. Whereas putting people in this reflective mode did not, for the most part, influence their behavior—they still engaged less in an activity if they had been rewarded for it—it did influence their reported liking for the activity. When in the reflective mode, people who were rewarded for doing the activity now reported that they liked it less. These results suggest that when people think about it carefully, they can apply the discounting principle, deducing that they must like an activity less if they were rewarded for doing it. If they are not thinking carefully about it, however, their conscious system fails to apply the discounting principle (which, after all, was learned rather late in development)—even though the adaptive unconscious already has.[14]

When do children acquire a theory of mind? At some point, people come to realize that they are not the only ones with a mind—other people have them, too. Because we cannot tell this directly by looking inside another person's head, we develop what psychologists call a *theory of mind*—the inference that other people have thoughts, beliefs, and feelings, just as we do. We believe that humans and inanimate objects are quite different (humans have minds, rocks do not), we often look where other people are looking (we want to learn what they are thinking that we are not), we can pretend to be someone else (by simulating their thoughts and feelings), and we often try to deceive other people (by encouraging them to develop false beliefs). All these are signs that we have a theory of mind.

We rarely pretend to be a rock or try to deceive a tree, precisely because we presume that they do not have minds that contain beliefs, thoughts, and feelings.

The prevailing wisdom is that a theory of mind develops around the age of four, as shown by children's performance in what is called the false-belief paradigm. In a typical study, children watch an actor place something in a hidden location. They might see Matt, for example, hide a piece of candy in a box and leave the room. Sally then enters the room, finds the piece of candy, and puts it in a basket a few feet away. When Sally leaves and Matt returns, the stage is set. Where will Matt look for the candy: in the box where he put it, or in the basket where Sally hid it? Most four-year-olds reply to this question by saying, "the box where he hid it." They recognize the seemingly obvious point that Matt still believes the candy is in the box because he did not see Sally put it in the basket. Most three-year-olds, however, say that Matt will look in the basket where Sally hid the candy. They seem unable to separate their own knowledge from another person's, assuming that because they know that the candy is in the basket, Matt knows this too. They do not yet have a well-developed theory of mind that tells them that other people can have different beliefs from their own.

Or do they? Wendy Clements and Josef Perner performed an intriguing variation on the false-belief task that suggests that even three-year-olds have a theory of mind, at least at an implicit or nonconscious level. Their study was very much like the one described above, except that in addition to asking the children where Matt would search for the candy, they also observed where the children looked when Matt returned to the room: Did they look in the location in which Matt had hidden it, or in the location where it had been moved by someone else? The researchers assumed that children would look first to the location in which they anticipated Matt would search for the candy. If they had a correct theory of mind, they should look where Matt thought the candy was, not where they knew it was. If they did not have a correct theory of mind, they should look where they knew it was, not where Matt thought it was.

On the standard measure of where children say Matt will look, the researchers found the same thing as previous studies: almost none of the very young children (those between the age of two years five months and two years ten months) got the question "right"; that is, almost all of them said that Matt would look for the candy in the basket, where they knew it to be—suggesting that they did not yet have a theory of mind. In the older groups, the percentage of children who gave the right answer steadily increased, such that by the age of four, most of the children gave the right answer.

As for where children looked when Matt reentered the room, the youngest children's gaze was consistent with their verbal reports: they looked at the basket where they knew the candy was and said that this was where Matt would look. That is, both measures indicated that these children did not have a theory of mind. However, the two measures diverged dramatically in children right around three years of age. They looked in the correct location, even though they gave a different answer when asked where Matt would search for the candy. Judging by what these children did, they had developed a theory of mind earlier than revealed by what they said. The children who were three years eight months and older looked in the correct location and gave the correct answer when asked.[15]

The best explanation of this and subsequent studies is that the looking and verbal measures reflect different kinds of knowledge that develop at different rates. The looking measure may have tapped a nonconscious, implicit type of knowledge—in my terms, knowledge acquired by the adaptive unconscious—whereas the verbal measure tapped a conscious understanding of the theory of mind that takes longer to develop.

There is even evidence that nonhuman primates have a rudimentary theory of mind, judging by where they look during a false-belief task like the one described above. Thus, very young children, and possibly even nonhuman primates, may possess a nonconscious theory of mind that guides their behavior. This view is quite compatible with the developmental literature on children's understanding of the discounting principle. Developmental psychologists who rely too heavily on verbal measures may not be giving children their due. They are studying children's verbal, conscious system, which may develop more slowly than the adaptive unconscious.[16]

Does the conscious system ever catch up? Perhaps people's conscious abilities are especially limited early in life, but when they reach adulthood they acquire a full-blown, conscious self and achieve greater insight into their adaptive unconscious. Although people's conscious theories and insights surely become more sophisticated as they age, there is reason to believe that people do not gain perfect insight.

One example is people's ability to detect complex patterns in the environment. As we have seen, the nonconscious system is skilled at quick, accurate pattern detection. Recall the study by Pawel Lewicki, Thomas Hill, and Elizabeth Bizot mentioned in Chapter 2, in which people learned a very complex rule that predicted where the letter X would appear on a computer screen, as indicated by the fact that their performance improved over time and deteriorated when the rule was changed. None of the participants ever learned the rule consciously; the adaptive unconscious clearly outperformed the conscious system in this case.

Numerous studies on covariation detection show that the conscious system is notoriously bad at detecting correlations between two variables (e.g., whether there is a relationship between people's hair color and their personalities). In order to detect such relationships, the correlation has to be very strong, and people must not have a prior theory that misleads them about this correlation. For example, many people persist in believing that they are more likely to catch a cold when they go outside without a coat on a winter day, even though there is no evidence that exposure to cold weather is related to catching a cold. Most people are unaware of the relationship between touching their noses and eyes with their fingers and catching a cold, even though there is good evidence that this is the main way in which rhinoviruses enter our bodies. The adaptive unconscious is not perfect and may not have recognized this covariation either. Or maybe it has, preventing us from touching our eyes even more than we do![17]

IS THE ADAPTIVE UNCONSCIOUS MORE SENSITIVE
TO NEGATIVE INFORMATION?

Now we come to the most speculative point about differences between nonconscious and conscious processing: there may be a division of labor in the brain, in which the unconscious is more sensitive to negative information than the conscious self.

As mentioned earlier, Joseph LeDoux has shown that animals and people possess preconscious danger detectors that size up their environments very quickly. The sensory thalamus evaluates incoming information before it reaches conscious awareness. If it determines that the information is threatening, it triggers a fear response. In evolutionary terms, it can be seen how adaptive it is for the brain to trigger a fear reaction to a dangerous (i.e., negative) stimulus as soon as possible.

Recall also the experiment by Antoine Bechara and his colleagues, in which people developed gut responses signaling them which decks of cards had the better monetary payoffs—before they knew consciously which decks were the best. The cards in decks A and B resulted in large gains or losses of money, adding up to a net loss if played consistently. The cards in decks C and D resulted in small gains or losses of money, adding up to a net gain if played consistently. People quickly developed gut reactions (as indicated by their skin conductance responses) warning them that decks A and B were to be avoided.

But how did their adaptive unconscious figure this out? One possibility is that it kept a mental tally of the different cards and figured out that on balance, decks A and B resulted in a net loss. It is also possible, however, that it had a simpler strategy: avoid big losses. If the nonconscious system is especially sensitive to negative information, it should focus on the large losses that sometimes came up in deck A. An intriguing implication of this finding is that the nonconscious system will not always make the correct choice. For example, if on balance decks A and B resulted in a higher payoff despite its occasional big losses, then the adaptive unconscious would shy away from the decks that would make the most money.[18]

There is increasing evidence that positive and negative information is processed in different parts of the brain, though the extent to which these different brain regions map onto conscious versus nonconscious processing is unclear. There is at least the possibility that the adaptive unconscious has evolved to be a sentry for negative events in our environments.[19]

Is the Adaptive Unconscious Smart or Dumb?

So which part of the mind is smarter, anyway? This question has been posed by several researchers, notably the social psychologist Anthony Greenwald. Greenwald concluded that unconscious cognition is a rather primitive system that can analyze information in only limited ways. He suggested that modern research has revealed a very different kind of unconscious from the Freudian unconscious, one that is considerably less clever.

Greenwald focused mostly on research that presents words to people at speeds too fast to be perceived consciously. Several studies have found that such subliminally presented words can influence people's responses to some extent. For example, Draine and Greenwald presented people with words on a computer (e.g., "evil," "peace") and asked them to make very quick judgments of whether they were good or bad in meaning. Unbeknownst to participants, these words were preceded by very fast presentations of "priming" words that were also good or bad in meaning. The prime words were flashed so quickly that people did not see them consciously. Nonetheless, they influenced people's responses to the second, target words. When the prime word was opposite in valence to the target word—for example, when "peace" was preceded by a subliminal presentation of "murder"—people were more likely to make a mistake and judge "peace" as bad. When the prime word was the same valence as the target—for example, when "peace" was preceded by a subliminal presentation of "sunset"—people made very few mistakes in judging "peace" as good. Most psychologists view this as evidence that people unconsciously saw the subliminal word and processed its meaning, which either interfered with or helped their judgment of the second word.[20]

Greenwald notes, however, that the unconscious mind's ability to recognize and process subliminally presented words is limited. There is no evidence, for example, that it can perceive the meaning of a two-word sequence that is different from the meaning of each individual word. Consider the words "enemy loses," which have a positive meaning when read as a unit, but a negative meaning when each word is considered individually. When two-word sequences such as this are flashed subliminally, people extract the meaning of the individual words (negative, in the example above), not the meaning of the unit. Hence, the unconscious mind may have limited cognitive abilities.

This conclusion is at odds, however, with much of what we have just reviewed—for example, research showing that the nonconscious mind is superior to the conscious mind in detecting covariations in the environment. It is no surprise, perhaps, that our minds can make limited judgments of information that it saw for only a few hundredths of a second. What is more surprising is that it can detect any meaning from a word that is flashed so quickly. In fact, a point that is often overlooked is that the unconscious mind is doing a superior job to the conscious mind on these tasks. Even if it is making only rudimentary judgments of subliminally flashed words, it is still doing better than the conscious mind, which has no idea that it saw anything at all. On these tasks, the unconscious mind is a lot smarter than the conscious interpreter.

What about when people have more time to examine and process incoming information? As we have seen, the nonconscious mind still outperforms the conscious self on at least some tasks, such as covariation detection. One study found, for example, that people could learn a complicated rule in which the presentation of a stimulus on one trial depended on what had been presented seven trials earlier, even though they could not consciously remember what had been presented that long ago.[21]

To be sure, the adaptive unconscious can be rigid and inflexible, clinging to preconceptions and stereotypes even when they are disconfirmed, in contrast to the more flexible conscious mind. There is no single answer to the question of how smart or dumb each system is—it depends on what you ask them to do. The adaptive unconscious is smarter than the conscious mind in some ways (e.g., detecting covariation), but less smart in other ways. The bottom line is that it is different, and whether we assign the labels "smart" or "dumb" to these differences is arbitrary. A more useful approach is to map out the differences and try to understand the functions of the two systems. The adaptive unconscious is an older system designed to scan the environment quickly and detect patterns, especially ones that might pose a danger to the organism. It learns patterns easily but does not unlearn them very well; it is a fairly rigid, inflexible inferencemaker. It develops early and continues to guide behavior into adulthood.

Rather than playing the role of CEO, the conscious self develops more slowly and never catches up in some respects, such as in the area of pattern detection. But it provides a check-and-balance to the speed and efficiency of nonconscious learning, allowing people to think about and plan more thoughtfully about the future.

It is tempting to view the tandem of nonconscious and conscious thinking as an extremely well-designed system that operates optimally. But this would be a mistake. First, there was no grand design. In real engineering, old designs can be completely thrown out and new ones started from scratch. The Wright brothers, for example, did not take a horse buggy and stick some wings on it to make a flying machine; they were able to begin afresh and build every part of their plane with the final goal (to fly) in mind. By contrast, natural selection operates on the current state of an organism, such that new systems evolve out of old ones. It is not as if someone sat down in advance and drew up the blueprints for the grand design of the human mind. Evolution works with what it has.

The human mind *is* an incredible achievement, perhaps the most amazing in the history of the Earth. This does not mean, however, that it is an optimal or perfectly designed system. Our conscious knowledge of ourselves can be quite limited, to our peril.

4

Knowing Who We Are

Our greatest illusion is to believe that we are what we think
ourselves to be.
—*H. F. Amiel, The Private Journal of Henri Frédéric Amiel (1889)*

We tell ourselves stories in order to live ... We live entirely, especially
if we are writers, by the imposition of a narrative line upon disparate
images, by the "ideas" which we have learned to freeze the shifting
phantasmagoria which is our actual experience.
—*Joan Didion, The White Album (1979)*

In the play *Pygmalion*, Henry Higgins succeeds in transforming Eliza from a crude flower girl into a refined and
lovely lady—while failing to do anything about his own
unsavory personality. Higgins is convinced that he is a gracious, fair-minded, cultured English gentleman with the
most honorable of intentions, failing to see that he is
coarse, misogynous, controlling, and fussy. After his housekeeper, Mrs. Pearce, chastises him for swearing, using his
dressing gown as a napkin, and putting a saucepan of por-
ridge on the clean tablecloth, Higgins is genuinely per-
plexed. He remarks to his friend Colonel Pickering: "You
know, Pickering, that woman has the most extraordinary
ideas about me. Here I am, a shy, diffident sort of man. I've
never been able to feel really grown-up and tremendous,

67

like other chaps. And yet she's firmly persuaded that I'm an arbitrary overbearing bossy kind of person. I can't account for it."[1]

How can Higgins be so blind to the nature of his own personality? Freudian repression might be the culprit; viewing himself as a refined English gentleman, instead of looking in the mirror and seeing himself as he really is, might allow him to avoid considerable psychic pain.

There may, however, be a simpler explanation. Many of people's chronic dispositions, traits, and temperaments are part of the adaptive unconscious, to which they have no direct access. Consequently, people are forced to construct theories about their own personalities from other sources, such as what they learn from their parents, their culture, and yes, ideas about who they prefer to be. These constructions may be driven less by repression and the desire to avoid anxiety than by the simple need to construct a coherent narrative about ourselves, in the absence of any direct access to our nonconscious personalities. Like Henry Higgins, people often construct narratives that correspond poorly to their nonconscious dispositions and abilities.

This is surprising because one of the main things people want to know about themselves is the core of their personality. "Am I a truly honest person?" "Do I have what it takes to be a successful teacher?" "Am I capable of being a good parent?" This is the self that people want to uncover when they ask, "Who am I?" It is the self that the Greek oracle at Delphi advised people to know and the self to which, according to Shakespeare, we should all be true.

But it makes little sense to talk about a single "self" when we consider that both the adaptive unconscious and the conscious self have regular patterns of responding to the social world. This distinction has largely been overlooked by psychological theories of personality.

The Current State of Personality Psychology

Gordon Allport defined personality as the psychological processes that determine a person's "characteristic behavior and thought"—a definition that is as good today as it was when Allport proposed it.[2] Few issues are so fundamental or have received as much attention as those concerning the nature of human personality—and few have been as controversial. The field of personality psychology is made up of a fragmented collection of conflicting approaches that disagree on such basic questions as, is there a single, core self that determines people's behavior? If so, what is it, and how can it be measured?

Consider these brief sketches of the major approaches to human personality. Classic psychoanalytic theory argues that the defining feature of personality is how people deal with their repressed drives, such as sexual and aggressive impulses. The battles, compromises, and truces among the id, ego, and superego define who we are. This is the only major approach to personality that stresses the importance of unconscious forces in shaping who the person is. At the opposite end of the mentalism continuum is behaviorism, which asks why we should look inward at the person when it is behavior we want to predict. Though dwindling in number, there are still behaviorists who focus solely on the external contingencies that determine behavior, rather than internal, psychological constructs.

Midway on the mentalism continuum is the phenomenological approach, which argues that to understand why people do what they do, we must view the world through their eyes, examining each person's unique construals of herself and the meaning she finds in her social world. Many social psychologists have adopted this approach by studying the self-concept, which consists of people's beliefs about who they are. For the most part, researchers have assumed that people are aware of their construals, although this approach has typically skirted questions about consciousness.

In recent years the dominant area of personality research has been the trait approach, which attempts to isolate a small number of basic personality traits that are common to all people. This approach is less concerned with theories about the origins of traits and more with quantitative analyses of the results of personality tests, on which people rate their own or others' personalities. Sophisticated analyses have uncovered five basic traits: extraversion, emotional stability, agreeableness, conscientiousness, and openness to experience. These traits are viewed as the fundamental building blocks of personality that everyone possesses to some degree; the particular constellation of people's standing on these traits defines their core or "true" self. The trait approach has been adopted by behavior geneticists, who study the extent to which human personality traits are heritable (largely by comparing the personalities of identical twins reared in different families). Typically, genetic factors have been found to account for 20–50 percent of the variance in personality traits.[3]

In contrast to all these approaches, postmodernists argue that there is no single, coherent personality or self. In today's complex world, the argument goes, people are subjected to a multitude of conflicting influences, making it very difficult to have a single, unified sense of "me." The self may be fluid, changing as our culture, roles, and context change, and attempts to measure and define a core set of traits that people carry with them is meaningless.[4]

MISCHEL AND THE EMPEROR'S CLOTHES

These major approaches have little in common and make fundamentally different assumptions about the nature of personality. Further, in a review of personality research published in 1968, Walter Mischel found that none of the approaches met the gold standard of personality research very well, namely Allport's criterion of predicting with any certainty what people actually do. An extravert should make friends more easily than an introvert, whereas a conscientious person should meet more deadlines than a person who is not conscientious. Mischel found, however, that the typical correlation between personality traits and behavior was quite modest. This news shook up the field, because it essentially said that the traits personality psychologists were measuring were just slightly better than astrological signs at predicting behavior.

Mischel did not simply point out the problem; he diagnosed the reasons for it. First, he argued that personality researchers had underestimated the extent to which the social situation shapes people's behavior, independently of their personality. To predict whether a person will meet a deadline, for example, knowing something about the situation—the consequences of not meeting it, how much time the person has, how much work remains to be done—may be more useful than knowing the person's score on a measure of conscientiousness. Situational influences can be very powerful, sometimes overwhelming individual differences in personality.[5]

This argument set off a turf war between personality psychologists, who place their bets on individual differences as the best predictors of behavior, and social psychologists, who place their bets on the nature of the social situation and how people interpret it. This war has often been waged in silly ways, with researchers in the two camps waving correlation coefficients and effect sizes at each other like sticks, arguing that theirs is bigger than the other camp's. Nonetheless, this battle was useful in revealing some important lessons. Personality variables, as traditionally conceived, are not all we need to know to predict human behavior.[6]

By criticizing trait research and pointing to the importance of the social situation, Mischel has often been portrayed as the Antichrist of personality theory. His second explanation of the low correlations between traits and behavior, however, is sometimes overlooked: personality *is* a good predictor of people's behavior; it's just that it has been conceptualized poorly. Ironically, it is Mischel and his colleagues who have demonstrated how individual differences can be conceptualized and measured in such a way that they account for impressive amounts of variance of behavior.

Rather than a collection of static traits that we can use to classify people, Mischel argued, personality is better conceived as a set of unique cognitive and affective variables that determine how people construe the situation. People have chronic ways of interpreting and evaluating different situations, and it is these interpretations that influence their behavior. Barbara's cognitive and affective personality system causes her to feel threatened when she suffers academic setbacks, and it is then that she is most likely to act aggressively. Sam's cognitive and affective personality system causes him to feel threatened when he perceives that he is being ignored by significant others, and that is when he is most likely to act aggressively. According to this view it makes little sense to try to classify how aggressive Barbara and Tom are on a single trait dimension; instead, we must understand how each person interprets and understands a social situation and acts accordingly.

It has not been entirely clear how aware people are of the operation of their cognitive and affective systems. In fact very few personality theories, with the exception of psychoanalysis, have said much about the role of conscious versus nonconscious processing. A recent collection of scholarly, cutting-edge articles on personality psychology takes up a full 967 pages and is touted by its publisher as "the most comprehensive single volume ever published on the subject." However, the index contains only two page references to consciousness and only six to unconsciousness. There are several more entries on psychoanalysis, but none on the modern, adaptive unconscious (or its synonyms).[7]

A lot of the confusion about personality and its relation to behavior has resulted from a failure to distinguish between the conscious and nonconscious systems. I believe that Mischel's cognitive and affective personality system is best thought of as part of the adaptive unconscious, whereas other personality theories have focused more on people's conscious construals of themselves.

TWO PERSONALITIES: THE ADAPTIVE UNCONSCIOUS AND THE CONSCIOUS SELF

My central thesis is that human personality resides in two places: in the adaptive unconscious and in conscious construals of the self. The adaptive unconscious meets Allport's definition of personality. It has distinctive, characteristic ways of interpreting the social environment and stable motives that guide people's behavior. These dispositions and motives are measurable with indirect techniques (i.e., not by self-report questionnaires). They are rooted in early childhood, are in part genetically determined, and are not easily changed.

But the conscious self also meets Allport's definition. Because people have no direct access to their nonconscious dispositions and motives, they must construct a conscious self from other sources. The constructed self consists of life stories, possible selves, explicit motives, self-theories, and beliefs about the reasons for one's feelings and behaviors. As Joan Didion says, "We tell ourselves stories in order to live."

Oddly, these two selves appear to be relatively independent. There is increasing evidence that people's constructed self bears little correspondence to their nonconscious self. One consequence of this fact is that the two personalities predict different kinds of behavior. The adaptive unconscious is more likely to influence people's uncontrolled, implicit responses, whereas the constructed self is more likely to influence people's deliberative, explicit responses. For example, the quick, spontaneous decision of whether to argue with a coworker is likely to be under the control of one's nonconscious needs for power and affiliation. A more thoughtful decision about whether to invite a coworker over for dinner is more likely to be under the control of one's conscious, self-attributed motives.

Because people cannot directly observe their nonconscious dispositions, they must try to infer them indirectly, by, for example, being good observers of their own behavior (e.g., how often they argue with their coworkers). How important is this kind of insight? It doesn't have to be perfect, because some positive illusions are beneficial. However, it is to people's benefit to make generally accurate inferences about the nature of their adaptive unconscious.

The Personality of the Adaptive Unconscious

There is considerable evidence that the adaptive unconscious has a stable, characteristic way of responding to the environment, thereby meeting Allport's definition of personality.[8] In Jonathan Miller's words, "Human beings owe a surprisingly large proportion of their cognitive and behavioral capacities to the existence of an 'automatic self' of which they have no conscious knowledge and over which they have little voluntary control."[9]

NONCONSCIOUS "IF-THEN" JUDGMENTS

As we have seen, Walter Mischel and his colleagues argued that people possess a unique set of cognitive and affective variables that determine how they react to the social world. They describe five components of this "personality mediating system" that guide people's behavior: encodings (people's construals of themselves, others, and situations); expectancies about themselves and the social world; affect and emotions; goals and values; and competencies and self-regulatory plans. In short, they argue, people have distinctive "if-then" rules that determine how they respond in a particular situation; for example, "If I feel that I'm being ignored, I then get angry and aggressive."

Each of the five components of Mischel's cognitive-affective system are signatures of the adaptive unconscious, such as chronic encodings of a situation. Consider, for example, how these encodings might be measured. One way would be simply to ask people to report their construals. To measure the distinctive ways in which people respond when they perceive that someone is not paying attention to them, we could construct a questionnaire that asked questions like this:

> Suppose you notice that your boss has not paid much attention to you over the past couple of weeks. Which of the following best reflects how you would interpret this lack of attention?
>
> (a) He/she has great confidence in my abilities.
> (b) He/she has lost faith in my abilities.
> (c) He/she has been quite busy—it has nothing to do with me.

People's answers to questions like this might well reveal interesting things about their conscious belief system. Their answers might say little, however, about how their adaptive unconscious would interpret actual situations in which they think they are being ignored. Recall that a fundamental property of the adaptive unconscious is that people have no access to the ways in which it selects, interprets, and evaluates information. Thus, asking people to report their nonconscious reactions is fruitless; people may not know how they are likely to react.

Alternatively, we could observe people's behavior very closely and try to deduce the "if-then" patterns of their adaptive unconscious. Though by no means easy, this approach bypasses the conscious explanatory system and may get directly at nonconscious encodings. This is the approach that Mischel and his colleagues have adopted. In one study, they systematically observed children in a residential camp for many hours, carefully noting the ways in which they behaved in a variety of situations. They were able to find "distinctive behavioral signatures" that permitted them to infer the children's "if-then" patterns of construal. For example, they observed how verbally aggressive the children were in five situations: when approached by a peer, when teased by a peer, when praised by an adult, when warned by an adult, and when punished by an adult. Some children were found to be very aggressive when warned by an adult, but relatively unaggressive in the other situations. Others were found to be very aggressive when a peer approached them, but relatively unaggressive in the other situations. Each of these children's "behavioral signatures" was stable over time; they seemed to reflect characteristic ways in which they interpreted the different situations.[10]

Although this result might seem pretty straightforward—even obvious—it contrasts strongly with the way in which most personality psychologists study individual differences. Trait theorists would give the boys a standardized questionnaire and classify each on the trait of aggressiveness. The assumption would be that each boy possesses a certain level of aggressiveness that would allow predictions of their behavior, regardless of the nature of the situation. But clearly the trait approach would not be very useful here, because it does not take into account the fact that (1) the boys' aggressiveness would depend on how they interpret the situation (e.g., how threatening they found it); (2) not everyone interprets a situation in the same way; (3) their interpretations are stable over time; and (4) the interpretations are made by the adaptive unconscious. By taking each of these points into account we can predict the boys' behavior pretty well—better than if we had given them a questionnaire and assigned them a value on a single trait dimension.

SCANNING PATTERNS: CHRONIC ACCESSIBILITY

One rule the adaptive unconscious uses to judge information is accessibility, or how "energized" a category or construct is. Consider two people, Charlotte and Simon. For Charlotte, the category of "intelligence" is more accessible than the category of "friendliness," whereas for Simon it is the reverse. This means that when Simon and Charlotte meet a new coworker, Marsha, Simon is more likely to notice and remember how friendly she was, whereas Charlotte is more likely to notice and remember how intelligent she was. George Kelly referred to these accessible categories as "scanning patterns" that guide our construals of our social environments.[11]

A number of experiments have shown that these scanning patterns allow people to pick up information from their social environments quickly and efficiently. In one study, people were presented with twenty-four sentences about another person very rapidly—one sentence every two seconds. Imagine you were a participant; just as you read one sentence about the person, such as "admitted his blunder," another one appears on the screen, such as "stole from his friend's wallet." You might well experience information overload, finding it difficult to keep track of all the information and figuring out what the person is like.

Unless, that is, you have a nonconscious scanning pattern that helps you organize the information. On an earlier test, some of the participants were found to have a chronically accessible category of "honesty." That is, honesty was one of the first traits on which they judged other people. For the remainder of the participants, honesty was not chronically accessible; it was not a trait that they used regularly to judge other people. In the experiment, the people for whom honesty was chronically accessible found it easiest to read the sentences and form an impression of the person, because many of the sentences had to do with honesty and these people were more prepared to process the sentences. In contrast, the people for whom honesty was not chronically accessible were more likely to experience information overload, finding it difficult to form an impression and showing poorer recall of the sentences. It is as if we have our antennae up for certain kinds of information about other people, depending on which categories are accessible to us. And this happens quickly, with no conscious awareness.[12]

But how does a category (such as honesty) become chronically accessible to someone in the first place? George Kelly noted that people develop constructs to make sense out of and predict their environments. As a result of their background and learning history, people develop regular, idiosyncratic ways of construing the world. The construct of honesty might be useful for one person, and the construct of friendliness more useful to another. A specific type of construct—our stored representations of significant others—is especially likely to become chronically accessible and applied when we meet new people.

TRANSFERENCE: SEEING THE OLD IN THE NEW

In Janet Malcolm's book *Psychoanalysis: The Impossible Profession*, one analyst poses the following question to another: "What would you call an interpersonal relationship where . . . the persons within that relationship don't see each other for what they objectively are but, rather, view each other in terms of their infantile needs and their infantile conflicts?" The analyst replies, "I'd call that life."[13]

Freud's discovery of transference—the way in which we superimpose infantile feelings toward our parents onto new relationships—has been called his "most original and radical discovery."[14] Freud focused primarily on the way in which unconscious sexual and aggressive drives, such as the Oedipus conflict, are played out in a person's relationship with the analyst. Harry Stack Sullivan and Melanie Klein took a broader view of transference, discussing how past relationship can influence people's perceptions of any new person they meet.

The social/personality psychologist Susan Andersen argues that transference is best understood not in psychoanalytic terms, but as part of the nonconscious, social information-processing system—namely, the adaptive unconscious. Much as in our discussion in Chapter 1 of why the unconscious exists, Andersen suggests that there is no need to assume that transference is rooted in unconscious motivation, whereby people seek to cover up anxiety-provoking thoughts and feelings (e.g., "I love him because he is like my father"). Instead, transference may be part of the normal functioning of everyday life that is best understood in terms of modern research on social cognition. She argues that our mental representations of other people are stored in memory like any other chronic category. Because representations of relationships with significant others are self-relevant and frequently brought to mind, they become chronically accessible and are often used to interpret and evaluate new people we meet. In short, just as the construct of "honesty" or "kindness" can be activated and applied to a new person, so can the construct of a specific person such as "my mother" or "Uncle Henry."

In a typical study, Andersen first asks people to name a significant other and to answer questions about what this person is like. Then, in what is ostensibly a different study, people receive descriptions of people they have never met. Andersen rigs it so that one of these new people shares characteristics of participants' significant others. For example, if you were in this study, you would be given information about several people, one of whom turns out to share some characteristics of an important person in your life (e.g., your mother).

Andersen and her colleagues have found that people react quite differently to the new acquaintance who is like their significant other. They are more likely to remember things about this person and to evaluate them similarly to their significant other. For example, if you have fond feelings for your mother, you would have a positive reaction to the new acquaintance who is like her. If you have negative feelings toward your mother, you would dislike the new acquaintance.

To what extent are people aware of this process? Andersen suggests that it occurs quickly and nonconsciously. It is not as if people say, "Hm, Sue is a lot like my mother, so I guess she is a warm, nurturing person." Instead, the adaptive unconscious selects, interprets, and evaluates new information very quickly and does so in terms of categories that are accessible—in this case, accessible representations of important people in our lives. In support of this interpretation, the transference process occurred in one study when the information indicating that a target person was like a significant other was presented subliminally. Even though people were unaware that the target person shared some characteristics with their significant other, they still "transferred" their feelings about their significant other onto the target person. This transference process, which occurs outside of awareness, appears to be an important source of individual differences in how people react to new acquaintances.[15]

To the psychoanalytically inclined, Andersen's research is likely to seem quite consistent with what is already known about transference and object relations; and indeed, in some ways it is. To the more empirically inclined student of the adaptive unconscious, however, Andersen's work is novel in two respects. First, she has developed a new method to study transference systematically in controlled experiments. Second, she has shown that transference can be explained easily by modern theories of social cognition (e.g., ideas about how chronically accessibility constructs of all sorts, including those about significant others, influence people's judgments and behavior), with no need to introduce additional theoretical constructs such as repression, resistance, or the management of anxiety. It is part of the normal functioning of an adaptive unconscious, and not necessarily part of the emotional hijinks of a dynamic unconscious.

WORKING MODELS OF ATTACHMENT

Further evidence for the nonconscious influence of past relationships comes from research on attachment relationships. Initially this work focused on the internal working models of attachment that infants formed about their parents, which are measured by observing how an infant interacts with his or her parent and a stranger in a laboratory setting (in a procedure known as the Strange Situation). The parent is asked to leave the room and then return several times, and the infant's reactions to these separations and reunions are observed. On the basis of these reactions, the infant is classified as having a secure, avoidant, or anxious/ambivalent working model of attachment. Infants with secure attachment models are distressed when their parent leaves but seek comfort when he or she returns. They have parents who are sensitive to and responsive to their needs. Infants with avoidant attachment models typically have parents who have rebuffed their attempts to be intimate. In the laboratory session they typically show little distress when their parent leaves and they do not seek comfort from their parent when he or she returns. Infants with anxious/ambivalent attachment models typically have parents who alternate between unresponsiveness and excessive affection. They fear that others will not reciprocate their desire for intimacy and are preoccupied with their parent's availability in the laboratory session. A fourth attachment style has recently been identified called "disorganized." Infants with this style show contradictory reactions, such as crying when they are separated from their parent but ignoring their parent when he or she returns. Some researchers suggest that infants with this attachment style are more likely to have parents who are depressed or neglectful.

These attachment styles are hypothesized to become internalized and to guide how people react to others, even outside the parent-child relationship. One study, for example, measured infants' attachment styles in their second year of life and then observed their behavior in a summer camp at ages ten and eleven. Compared to children with avoidant or anxious/ambivalent models of attachment, children with secure attachment styles as infants spent more time with peers at the summer camp, were more likely to develop friendships, and were more likely to evaluate other children in a positive light.[16]

In recent years, researchers have looked at working models of attachment in adults. They assume that people's chronic way of viewing important past relationships (i.e., with their parents) colors their perception of behavior in current relationships, particularly with romantic partners. One way of measuring adult attachment models is to ask people to report their feelings about their romantic relationships, with the assumption that they can easily access and report these feelings. In one version, people are given descriptions of three adult attachment relationships and asked to choose the one that best applies to them. For example, if you chose the following statement, your adult romantic relationships would be classified as anxious/ambivalent: "I find that others are reluctant to get as close as I would like. I often worry that my partner doesn't really love me or won't stay with me, I want to merge completely with another person, and this desire sometimes scares people away."[17]

A second method of measuring adult attachment is the Adult Attachment Interview (AAI), which involves a lengthy interview in which people are asked questions about their relationship with their parents. The interviewer pays attention not only to what people say but to how they say it and to their nonverbal reactions. Researchers who use this method assume that people are not fully aware of their working models of attachment; hence the need to infer what these models are from people's behavior during the interview. The AAI appears to be a valid measure of adult attachment, in that it also predicts interesting things, such as problem behaviors in adolescence (e.g., delinquency, drug use, school dropout, and teenage pregnancy) and the bonds people establish with their own children.

So far the story is pretty straightforward: there are two ways of measuring adult models of attachment (self-report questionnaires and the AAI), and both seem to do a pretty good job, in that they predict interesting social behaviors. But here's the rub: the two measures do not correlate very well. If you came out as securely attached on one measure, you are likely to be classified as securely attached on the other at a level only slightly better than chance.[18]

One explanation for this lack of correspondence might be that the techniques are simply measuring different kinds of attachment. The AAI focuses on people's memories of their relationship to their parents, for example, whereas the self-report measures focus on people's conceptions of their current romantic relationships. Most researchers in this area, however, assume that memories of parental relationships and views of romantic relationships are influenced by the same internal models of attachment and thus should be related.

Perhaps the AAI taps people's chronic level of attachment that has become the signature of the adaptive unconscious, whereas self-report questionnaires tap people's conscious beliefs about their attachment relationships. But how can this be? Can we really have such disconnected systems that disagree on something as basic as an internal model of attachment relationships? The answer may be that we can, not only in the area of attachment but in other basic areas of personality as well.

DUAL MOTIVES AND GOALS

If we were to make a list of the goals that are most important in life, surely the desire for close relationships, success in life (e.g., a career), and power would make most people's short list. There is a long tradition in personality psychology of studying these three motives; indeed, psychologists such as H. A. Murray and David McClelland have argued that people's level of needs for affiliation, achievement, and power are major components of human personality.

There is growing evidence that these motives are an important part of the personality of the adaptive unconscious. Murray and McClelland assumed that these basic motives are not necessarily conscious and must therefore be measured indirectly. They advocated the use of the Thematic Apperception Test (TAT), in which people make up stories about a set of standard pictures, and these stories are then coded for how much of a need for affiliation, power, or achievement people expressed.

Other researchers have developed explicit, self-report questionnaires of motives, with the assumption that people are aware of their motives and can freely report them. A controversy has ensued over which measure of motivation is the most valid: the TAT or self-report questionnaires. The answer, I suggest, is that both are valid measures but tap different levels of motivation, one that resides in the adaptive unconscious and the other that is part of people's conscious explanatory system.

David McClelland and his colleagues made this argument in an influential review of the literature. First, they noted that the self-report questionnaires and the TAT do not correlate with each other. If Sarah reports on a questionnaire that she has a high need for affiliation, we know virtually nothing about the level of this need that she will express, nonconsciously, on the TAT. Second, they argued that both techniques are valid measures of motivation, but of different types. The TAT assesses *implicit motives*, whereas explicit, self-report measures assess *self-attributed motives*.

Implicit motives are needs that people acquire in childhood that have become automatic and nonconscious. Self-attributed motives are people's conscious theories about their needs that may often differ from their nonconscious needs. McClelland reports a study, for example, that measured people's need for affiliation with both the TAT and a self-report questionnaire. People's affiliation needs, as assessed by the TAT, predicted whether they were talking with another person when they were beeped at random intervals over several days, whereas a self-report measure of affiliation did not. Affiliation needs as assessed with the self-report measure were a better predictor of more deliberative behavioral responses, such as people's choices of which types of behaviors they would prefer to do alone or with others (e.g., visit a museum). The picture McClelland paints is of two independent systems that operate in parallel and influence different types of behaviors. In our terms, the adaptive unconscious and the conscious explanatory system each has its own set of needs and motives that influence different types of behaviors.

This separation between nonconscious and conscious motives may be very similar to the separation we encountered between nonconscious and conscious attachment styles. It is also characteristic of several other kinds of motives, such as dependency needs (people's desire to associate and interact with other people). A number of tests of dependency have been developed, some of which are explicit, self-report questionnaires and some of which are implicit, projective instruments. The two types of instruments are only moderately correlated and tend to predict different kinds of behavior. Further, women reliably score higher on explicit, conscious measures of dependency, whereas men tend to score higher on nonconscious measures. Indirect measures of dependency appear to tap nonconscious motives, whereas self-report questionnaires tap conscious, self-attributed motives.[19]

DO WE SEE OURSELVES AS OTHERS SEE US?

If there are two sides to people's personality—a nonconscious and a conscious one, each producing unique behavior—then it is interesting to consider how other people get to know us. People could form impressions from our automatic, uncontrolled actions that reflect our implicit motives and traits (e.g., our implicit need for affiliation), or they could form impressions from our controlled, deliberative actions that reflect our explicit motives. It seems likely that people attend at least in part to behaviors that emanate from the adaptive unconscious (e.g., "Jim says that he's shy, but he's often the life of the party"). If so, other people might know us better than we know ourselves. As a character in Richard Russo's novel *Straight Man* said, "The truth is, we never know for sure about ourselves . . . only after we've done a thing do we know what we'll do . . . Which is why we have spouses and children and parents and colleagues and friends, because someone has to know us better than we know ourselves."[20]

There is some evidence that supports this startling conclusion. First, the correspondence between people's ratings of their own personality and other people's ratings of their personality is not very high. It depends somewhat on the trait; for example, people tend to agree with others about how extraverted they are, but on most other personality traits the level of agreement is modest (correlations in the range of .40). Thus, Suzie's judgment of how agreeable and conscientious she is correlates only modestly with how agreeable and conscientious her friends think she is.

Furthermore, other people agree more among themselves about what another person is like than they agree with that person's own ratings. Jane, Bob, Sam, and Denisha are likely to agree more with each other about how agreeable and conscientious Suzie is than they are to agree with Suzie.

But who is more "right"? Does Suzie know best how agreeable she is, or do her friends know her better than she knows herself? To try to answer this question, some researchers have looked at who can better predict what a person actually does: the person's ratings of his or her own personality or other people's ratings of his or her personality. If we wanted to predict how nervous Suzie will be when she meets someone new, for example, would we be better off going by her own report of how extraverted and agreeable she is or by her friends' reports? There is some evidence that peer reports (Suzie's friends' ratings) predict people's behavior better than their self-reports (Suzie's own ratings). In one study, for example, college students were worse at predicting how nervous and talkative they would be when chatting with a new acquaintance than were peers who had just met them for the first time.[21]

Other studies have found that people are worse at making specific predictions about how they will behave than they are at predicting how other people will behave. When asked whether they would purchase a flower as part of a campus charity drive in the upcoming weeks, students made overly rosy predictions; 83 percent said they would, whereas in fact only 43 percent actually did. When asked how likely it was that other students would purchase a flower, people were more accurate; they predicted that 56 percent would, which was closer to the 43 percent figure. In another study, people predicted that they would donate an average of $2.44 of their earnings in an experiment to charity, whereas other people would donate only $1.83. Once again they were more accurate in their predictions about other people; the actual figure donated was $1.53.

One reason people fail to predict their own behavior very accurately is that they believe that they are "holier than thou" and would be more likely than the average person to perform moral acts of kindness. Another is that people use different kinds of information when predicting their own versus other people's behavior. When predicting other people's actions, we rely mostly on our cumulative experience of how the average person would act, including our hunches about the kinds of situational constraints people will face ("Probably many people who intended to buy a flower will never walk past one of the people selling them"). When predicting our own actions, we rely more on our "inside information" about our own personalities ("I am a kind person who wants to help others"). This can be a problem for two reasons: relying only on inside information causes people to overlook situational constraints on their actions, such as the possibility that they, too, will fail to pass by someone selling the flowers; second, as we have seen, people's inside information is not the full story about their personalities and might not be completely accurate.[22]

When it comes to asking who makes better judgments about our personality, however—we ourselves or other people—it might not make much sense to ask who is more accurate. Suzie and her friends might have different views of her personality, but both may be "right" in some sense. Her friends might be keying in more on her adaptive unconscious, as revealed in her behavior—particularly behaviors she is not monitoring and controlling consciously, such as how much Suzie fidgets and plays with her hair when she meets a new acquaintance. Suzie, on the other hand, might be basing her estimate on her general theory about how nervous she is in novel social settings.

Suzie's friends might be more accurate at predicting her future behaviors that are spontaneous and unmonitored, such as how nervous she will appear to be on a first date. Suzie's self-view, however, might be more accurate at predicting her more controlled, deliberate actions, such as whether she decides to accept a blind date. Suzie has a *constructed self* that may be at odds with her adaptive unconscious but still predicts behaviors that she consciously monitors and controls.

The Constructed Self

What is the nature of the conscious self that exists independently of the personality of the adaptive unconscious? There has been a great deal of research on the self-concept, including how it helps people organize information about themselves, interprets ambiguous information, and guides behavior. This research also examines different functions of the self, its affective implications, and how the self-concept differs across cultures.[23]

Self theorists have been reticent, however, about discussing the extent to which the self-concept is conscious or nonconscious. It is important to focus on this question, I believe, in order to clarify a number of confusing findings (such as those reviewed already, in which implicit and explicit measures of personality predict different kinds of behavior). We need to distinguish between those aspects of the self-concept that reside in the adaptive unconscious and those that consist of conscious beliefs about the self.[24]

Dan McAdams has studied an important part of the conscious self-concept, namely the life stories that people construct about themselves, which he describes as a continuing narrative that people tell about their past, present, and future. The major function of these stories, McAdams argues, is to integrate the many aspects of oneself into a coherent identity that is stable over time but also subject to revision. McAdams' work suggests that an important role of this deliberative system is to link together the many disparate parts of the self into a coherent story.

McAdams argues that life stories do not (and need not) correspond perfectly with external reality. They are people's construals of their lives rather than the fact-based reporting of an objective historian. However, a life story should not be a complete fabrication; people whose life stories bear no relation to their actual lives often end up in mental hospitals. One of McAdams' criteria for what makes a good story is that it be at least somewhat reality-based.[25]

Although life stories constitute a compelling approach to personality, others have questioned the extent to which such stories are important determinants of people's behavior, versus epiphenomenal, after-the-fact accounts of one's actions. The personality psychologist Robert McCrae phrased this question well: "I do not yet know quite what to make of them. Are life stories the unifying themes that guide our life, as the jet stream guides weather systems, or are they mere epiphenomena, more-or-less adequate rationalizations and secondary elaborations that convey the gist of our life history in a form suitable for the occasion?"[26]

McCrae's question gets to the heart of issues we discussed in Chapter 3 concerning the role of consciousness, such as whether it is similar to the child at a video arcade who turns the steering wheel on a racing-car game without putting any money into it, unaware that she is viewing a demonstration program, which is not at all influenced by her conscious intentions and goals—an agent that thinks she is in control of the action but really isn't.

But surely this position is too extreme. Consistent with the consciousness-as–Ronald Reagan analogy, it is clear that people's conscious beliefs about their traits and motives play a causal role (albeit not as much as they might think). The conscious self system is not completely epiphenomenal; as we have seen, explicit beliefs about attachment and motivation influence some important social behaviors.

A number of theorists, for example, have pointed to the importance of people's conscious constructions of the kind of person they ought to be or might become. In psychoanalytic theory, children are said to develop ego ideals as part of the superego, based on their conceptions of their parents' moral stance, and these ego ideals play an important role in the kinds of decisions people make when faced with moral dilemmas and the kinds of emotions they experience. Social psychologists have also discussed the importance of people's constructions of alternative selves. People have mental constructs of the kind of person they would like to become (e.g., a successful lawyer), the kind of person they feel they ought to become (e.g., a parent), and the kind of person they are afraid of becoming (e.g., a bag lady). Possible selves are conscious embodiments of our hopes and fears about ourselves, and these constructions shape our behavior, at least to some extent.[27]

The bottom line is that when people describe their own personalities, they are often reporting their conscious theories and constructions that may or may not correspond to the dispositions and motives of their adaptive unconscious.

Origins of the Nonconscious and Conscious Personalities

If people have two "selves"—a nonconscious and a conscious one that are only loosely related—where do these systems come from? There is evidence that some of the dispositions of the adaptive unconscious, such as temperament, have a genetic basis. It is also clear that culture and experience play a role. A hallmark of the adaptive unconscious is automaticity, whereby information is processed in rapid, nonconscious, involuntary ways. One way a construct can become automatic is through lots of repetition. People are not born with the kinds of "if-then" patterns of construal discussed by Mischel, or the chronically accessible constructs discussed by social psychologists. These constructs, rooted in childhood experiences, become automatic through frequent use.

What kinds of experiences? David McClelland and his colleagues offer the hypothesis that nonconscious motives are rooted in early infancy, whereas conscious, self-attributed motives result from more explicit, parental teachings. To test this idea, McClelland and his colleagues interviewed a sample of adults in their early thirties, measuring both their nonconscious motives (i.e., their responses to TAT pictures) and their conscious, explicit motives (their responses on a self-report questionnaire). The fascinating thing about this study is that the participants' mothers had been interviewed twenty-five years earlier about their childrearing practices, allowing the researchers to test the extent to which people's implicit and explicit motives, as adults, were related to the childrearing practices of their mothers twenty-five years earlier.

There was some evidence that early, prelingual childrearing experiences were correlated with implicit but not explicit motives. For example, the extent to which mothers used scheduled feedings correlated with the implicit but not explicit need for achievement in the adult sample, and the extent to which the mothers were unresponsive to their infants' crying was correlated with the implicit but not explicit need for affiliation. Postlingual childhood experiences were more likely to correlate with explicit than with implicit motives. For example, the extent to which children were taught not to fight back when provoked was correlated with the explicit but not implicit need for affiliation, and the children of parents who set explicit tasks for them to learn were more likely to have an explicit but not implicit need for achievement.[28]

The nonconscious and conscious selves thus seem to be influenced by one's cultural and social environment, but in different ways. The kinds of early affective experiences that shape a child's adaptive unconscious surely have a cultural basis, given that childrearing practices differ markedly from culture to culture. The conscious theories people develop about themselves also are shaped by the cultural and social environment.

Implications for Self-Insight

To understand better our own nonconscious personality dispositions, we cannot simply remove the veil obscuring our view, for there is no direct view. Instead, we are forced to make educated guesses about our nonconscious dispositions.

But why don't people realize, eventually, that their conscious conceptions are at odds with their nonconscious personalities? Doesn't it seem that over time, people would discover that they are not the person they thought themselves to be? Why didn't Henry Higgins eventually realize that he was not the refined, kindhearted gentleman who abhorred profanity? How can people be so out of touch?

One reason is that people are motivated to have an overly positive view of themselves, and avoid looking too closely at their warts and flaws. There is a good deal of evidence that people see themselves through rose-colored glasses and that, within limits, it is healthy to do so. What is the harm in thinking we are a little more popular and extraverted and kind than we really are?

Another reason is that once people develop a conscious theory about themselves—shaped, perhaps, by explicit parental teaching—it can be difficult to disconfirm. We may be more likely to notice the times we act in accord with our conscious theories than the times we do not. Even if inconsistencies are brought to our attention, we can easily dismiss them as exceptions. When Mrs. Pearce points out to Henry Higgins that just that morning he has uttered swear words "to your boots, to the butter, and to the brown bread," Higgins replies, "Oh that! Mere alliteration, Mrs. Pearce, natural to a poet."[29] A crude person who swears is simply not part of his self-narrative, and thus he easily dismisses any evidence to the contrary.

Surely, however, we do not want our conscious conceptions to get too out of whack. There are many times when we would be better off recognizing our limitations, abilities, and prospects. When choosing a career, for example, it would be to people's advantage to know whether their nonconscious personalities were better suited for a life as a lawyer, salesperson, or circus performer.

There is very little research on the consequences of having disparate conscious and nonconscious "selves" that are out of synch. An exception is the work of Joachim Brunstein and Oliver Schultheiss. In several studies, they measured people's nonconscious agentic motives (needs for achievement and power) and communal motives (needs for affiliation and intimacy), using the TAT test. They also included self-report measures of these same motives. As in previous studies, they found little correspondence, on average, between people's nonconscious and conscious motives.

Some individuals, however, did have nonconscious and conscious motives that corresponded, and these people showed greater emotional well-being than people whose goals were out of synch. In one study, students' nonconscious and conscious goals were assessed at the beginning of the semester and their emotional well-being tracked for the next several weeks. The students whose conscious goals matched their nonconscious goals showed an increase in emotional well-being as the semester progressed. The students whose conscious goals did not match their nonconscious goals showed a decrease in emotional well-being over the same period. It appears to be to people's advantage to develop conscious theories that correspond at least somewhat with the personality of their adaptive unconscious.[30]

Before seeing how this might be done, we need to take a look at other aspects of the adaptive unconscious that people typically overlook, besides the nature of their personalities. For example, how good are people at recognizing the causes of their feelings, judgments, and behavior?

5

Knowing Why

In sooth, I know not why I am so sad,
But how I caught it, found it, or came by it,
What stuff 'tis made of, whereof it is born,
I am to learn;
. . . I have much ado to know myself.
—*Shakespeare, The Merchant of Venice, act I, scene 1 (1596)*

You are allowed to think that adult life consists of a constant exercise of
personal will; but it wasn't really like that, Jean thought. You do things,
and only later do you see why you did them, if ever you do.
—*Julian Barnes, Staring at the Sun (1986)*

How well do people know the causes of their judgments,
feelings, and actions? There are cases in the psychological
literature of people who are so ignorant of why they
respond the way they do that they have to invent explanations. Consider Mr. Thompson, a patient of the neurologist
Oliver Sacks who suffered from Korsakoff's syndrome, a
form of organic amnesia whereby people lose their ability
to form memories of new experiences. Tragically, Mr.
Thompson remembered nothing from one moment to the
next. If you were to introduce yourself to him and left the
room, he would have no conscious memory of ever having
seen you before when you came back a few minutes later.

What would it be like to be Mr. Thompson? Imagine that your consciousness is like a film in which scenes from hundreds of movies are spliced together. Every few seconds a scene from a new movie appears that has no connection to what went before or what comes next. Because Mr. Thompson had no memory for prior scenes, each one appeared to be brand-new, with new characters, new settings, new dialogue.

What a terrible, Faustian nightmare, to lose the thread of memory that weaves together our life stories. Except for one thing: Mr. Thompson had little awareness of his plight. Because he had no memory of the prior "scenes," he had no sense of discontinuity. His consciousness was firmly rooted in the present, with no idea of what he had lost. Further, he had great success in imposing meaning on each scene of his ever-renewing world. He invented a plot to explain each of his "new" experiences.

If you walked into the room he might decide that you were a customer entering the delicatessen he used to own and would ask whether you wanted a pastrami or ham sandwich. But then "click," change of scene. He might notice that you were wearing a white coat and would invent a new story—you are the butcher from down the street. "Click," new scene. The butcher always had bloodstains on his coat; so you must be a doctor. Mr. Thompson would see no inconsistencies in his changing stories. He came up with perfectly good explanations for his current circumstances, with no idea that these explanations changed from moment to moment. Sacks describes it this way: "[Mr. Thompson] continually improvised a world around him—an Arabian Nights world, a phantasmagoria, a dream, of ever-changing people, figures, situations—continual, kaleidoscopic mutations and transformations. For Mr. Thompson, however, it was not a tissue of ever-changing, evanescent fancies and illusion, but a wholly normal, stable and factual world. So far as *he* was concerned, there was nothing the matter."[1]

Mr. Thompson's dilemma bears a remarkable similarity to the behavior of people acting on posthypnotic suggestions. A small percentage of the population can be easily hypnotized, and, when given posthypnotic suggestions, they end up doing things with no conscious awareness of why. G. H. Estabrooks notes that when this happens, the person "finds excuses for his actions and, strange to say, while these excuses may be utterly false, the subject tends to believe them." He relates the following example:

The operator hypnotizes a subject and tells him that when the cuckoo clock strikes he will walk up to Mr. White, put a lamp shade on his head, kneel on the floor in front of him and "cuckoo" three times. Mr. White was not the type on whom one played practical jokes, in fact, he was a morose, nonhumorous sort of individual who would fit very badly in such a picture. Yet, when the cuckoo clock struck, the subject carried out the suggestion to the letter.

"What in the world are you doing?" he was asked.

"Well, I'll tell you. It sounds queer but it's just a little experiment in psychology. I've been reading on the psychology of humor and I thought I'd see how you folks reacted to a joke that was in very bad taste. Please pardon me, Mr. White, no offense intended whatsoever," and the subject sat down without the slightest realization of having acted under posthypnotic compulsion.[2]

A final example of confabulation can be found in some of the "split brain" patients studied by Michael Gazzaniga and Joseph LeDoux. The nerve fibers connecting the two hemispheres of the brain (the corpus callosum) were cut in these patients, to reduce severe seizures that did not respond to other treatments. Much of what we know about the differences in left- and right-brain processing comes from studies of such split-brain patients. Psychologists have conducted clever experiments in which they flash pictures and words to the hemispheres separately, to see if the hemispheres process information the same way. This is done by asking the patients to fix their eyes on the center of a screen and then flashing pictures to the left or right of that point. Because of the way the visual system is structured, pictures flashed to the left of the point go exclusively to the right hemisphere, whereas pictures flashed to the right of the point go exclusively to the left hemisphere.

One memorable study was conducted with a fifteen-year-old split-brain patient named P. S. The researchers flashed pictures to one of his hemispheres and then asked him to choose a card, with his right or left hand, that was most related to the picture. For example, they flashed a picture of a snow scene to his right hemisphere, and then he was shown cards of a shovel, screwdriver, can opener, and saw. He could easily pick the shovel with his left hand, because this hand was controlled by his right hemisphere, which saw the snow scene. When asked to pick a card with his right hand he did no better than chance, because this hand, controlled by the left hemisphere, had not observed the snow scene.

Things got especially interesting when the researchers flashed different pictures to the two hemispheres at the same time. For example, on one trial they flashed the snow scene to P. S.'s right hemisphere and a picture of a chicken claw to his left hemisphere. He picked the card with a shovel with his left hand (because that was most related to the snow scene seen by his right hemisphere) and a card with a chicken with his right hand (because that was most related to the chicken claw seen by his left hemisphere).

The researchers then asked P. S. why he had picked the cards he did. Like most people's, P. S.'s speech center was in his left hemisphere, which knew why he had picked the chicken with his right hand (because it had seen the chicken claw) but had no idea why he had picked the shovel with his left hand (because the snow scene was viewed only by the right hemisphere). No problem; the left hemisphere quickly made up an answer: "I saw a claw and picked a chicken, and you have to clean out the chicken shed with a shovel." Perhaps the most striking thing about P. S.'s response is that he seemed perfectly comfortable with his answer and had no idea that it was a confabulation. In Gazzaniga and LeDoux's words, "The left [hemisphere] did not offer its suggestion in a guessing vein but rather as a statement of fact as to why that card had been picked."[3]

There is an intriguing similarity between split-brain patients, people suffering from organic amnesia, and people acting out posthypnotic suggestions. In each case, people easily generate stories to explain their behavior and circumstances, with no realization that their explanations are works of fiction, even for such bizarre acts as garbing dour Mr. White in a lamp shade.

What do these examples say about the rest of us? Fortunately, most of us are not like P. S., Mr. Thompson, or the subject in Estabrooks' hypnosis study. As far as I know, I have an intact corpus callosum that allows a transfer of information between my right and left hemispheres. Although my memory certainly isn't perfect, it is far superior to Mr. Thompson's. And, as far as I know, I have not been hypnotized and given posthypnotic suggestions to do bizarre things.

Because P. S., Mr. Thompson, and hypnotized people are so different from us, it is tempting to dismiss their confabulations as just a few more candidates for inclusion in the annals of bizarre psychological case histories. But Gazzaniga and LeDoux have made the startling suggestion that we all share the tendency to confabulate explanations, arguing that the conscious verbal self often does not know why we do what we do and thus creates an explanation that makes the most sense.

It may seem a substantial leap to conclude, on the basis of a few patients with brain damage or surgical sections, that all humans are blind to the causes of their actions and therefore have a "confabulator" that invents reasons. Yet there are times when the abilities and deficits of brain-damaged people provide a window into what it is like to be human, in addition to showing that some abilities are lost when the brain is damaged. Gazzaniga and LeDoux had the insight that severing the connection between the hemispheres might not have caused the kinds of confabulations they observed in P. S.; rather, it made it easier to see a common human tendency to confabulate.[4]

Knowing Why in Everyday Life

People's behavior is often determined by their implicit motives and nonconscious construals of the world. Because we do not have conscious access to these aspects of our personalities, we are blind to the ways in which they influence our behavior. If we ask someone why he or she feels a certain way about a new acquaintance, the person is unlikely to say, "I found him to be a tad aggressive because aggressiveness is a chronically accessible trait for me" or "I was bothered by his lack of attention to me because I have an anxious/ambivalent attachment relationship with my parents." We are not privy to the personality of our adaptive unconscious.

Personality, however, is not the sole source of behavior. People's feelings, judgments, and behaviors are as often influenced by the nature of the immediate social situation as by their personalities. The distinction between personality and the social environment is artificial, of course, because people's personality often determines how they construe their environment. When a supervisor skips a weekly project meeting, Joe might interpret it as a sign that the supervisor does not value his work, whereas Sarah might interpret it a sign that the supervisor has great confidence in her abilities and does not feel the need to look over her shoulder.

Nonetheless, social situations can be so powerful that virtually everyone construes them in the same way, such that they "overpower" personality differences. Sometimes this is obvious, as when a burglar points a gun at us and says, "Give me all your money." Virtually all of us would comply, regardless of how stingy we happen to be or the nature of our attachment relationship to our parents. Sometimes the power of social influence is less obvious, as in Stanley Milgram's demonstrations of how easy it is to prod people into delivering near-fatal electric shocks to their fellow humans.[5]

The point is that personality is not the only cause of behavior and people might be better at knowing how factors in their immediate social environments influence their feelings, judgment, and behaviors. It might be difficult to discern how the deep-seated facets of our personality have shaped our behavior, but easier to tell that we are angry at John for forgetting our dinner date, sad because we just heard that our grandmother is ill, or nauseous because we just ate an entire bowl of clam dip. Clearly, it is to our advantage to detect how our immediate environment influences us; otherwise, we wouldn't know to go easy on the clam dip at the next party.

Yet we are sometimes tongue-tied when it comes to understanding the roots of our feelings and beliefs. As Shakespeare noted in the opening lines of *The Merchant of Venice,* we have much ado to know ourselves. There is increasing evidence that Gazzaniga and LeDoux were correct in their hunch that our conscious selves often do not know the causes of our responses and thus have to confabulate reasons.

THE BABY NAMING GAME

Let's begin with an everyday example, why parents find a particular name pleasing and thus choose it for their baby. We all know that names for babies come in and out of fashion. The first names of many our grandparents are not in vogue today; my grandmothers, for example, were named Ruth and Marion, names that are rarely seen in today's birth announcements. Depending on your age, your name might already have gone out of fashion or will before long.

The faddishness of names is curious, because when naming their babies, parents often strive for originality and uniqueness—no one wants to imitate what everyone else is doing. People want original-sounding names like Briana and Madison for girls and Tyler and Ryan for boys; yet the same "original" names end up becoming very popular. (All four of the names above are among the top dozen baby names for the year 2000 in the United States.) Why is it that many people end up giving their babies the same name, thinking that it is original and unique?

One reason, I suspect, is that people often do not know why they thought of a name like Madison or Tyler. A name might come to mind for several reasons, such as the fact that people heard it on a television show or precisely because other people are giving babies that name. If parents-to-be recognize that they thought of a name because it is becoming faddish, they are likely to dismiss it ("Oh, honey, everyone is naming their baby Jessica these days.") If people do not recognize that they thought of the name because it is becoming popular, they are likely to find it pleasing and original.

A few years ago, for example, my wife noticed that the name Ashley

Nicole was appearing with surprising frequency in the birth announcements of our local newspaper. Every week there were at least one or two baby girls who had that combination of names. One day, while chatting with the staff in my departmental office, I mentioned the increasing popularity of "Ashley Nicole." One of the secretaries, who happened to be pregnant, looked stricken: "Oh no," she said. "That's the name I had thought of for my baby!" She and her husband eventually named their child something else.

Psychologists are certainly not free from these failures to recognize why they thought of a certain name. My wife and I named our first child Christopher, and although we certainly recognized that this is a fairly common boy's name, it seemed like a pleasing but not-too-faddish choice. Surely, we figured, it was not as popular as Michael or Joseph. We later learned that the most frequent name for male babies born that year was—you guessed it—Christopher. (That's okay; we still like the name!)

Here's a final example from the world of baby-naming: In the late 1980s and early 1990s the name Hilary (or Hillary) was very popular, but suddenly, for babies born in 1992 and after, it became quite rare. In 1992 Bill Clinton was first elected president of the United States, and Hillary is, of course, Mrs. (now Senator) Clinton's first name. Now, you might interpret the sudden drop in the frequency of "Hilary" to the unpopularity of Mrs. Clinton; who wants to name their baby after someone they dislike? The name became infrequent, however, even among supporters and admirers of Mrs. Clinton. I believe that there is another explanation: now that Mrs. Clinton was in the national spotlight, people no longer had the sense that Hilary was a name that they had thought of themselves. People were more likely to recognize that the name was familiar because of Mrs. Clinton, and thus choose to give their baby a more "original" name—like Briana or Madison.

LOVE ON THE BRIDGE
Such lack of insight is by no means limited to how we thought of a name. Imagine that you are single and meet someone you find attractive. You really want to get to know this person better and hope that he or she feels

the same way. Suppose I were to ask you exactly why you felt the way you did about this person. How accurate would your answer be?

Surely you could answer this question with some accuracy, referring to the person's beauty, charisma, or winning smile. But social psychologists have done studies showing that people can be mixed up about why they are attracted to someone. One study was conducted in a park in British Columbia. An attractive female assistant approached males in the park and asked if they would fill out a questionnaire, as part of a class project on the effects of scenic attractions on people's creativity. When people completed the questionnaire the woman thanked them and said she would be happy to explain the study in more detail when she had time. She tore off a corner of the questionnaire, wrote down her phone number, and said to give her a call if they wanted to talk with her some more. As a sign of how attracted the men were to the woman, the researchers kept track of how many of them telephoned her later and asked her out on a date.

The researchers varied where the men were when the woman approached them. Half of them were on a scary footbridge that spanned a deep gorge. To cross this bridge people had to stoop over and grasp flimsy hand rails firmly, as the bridge swayed from side to side in the stiff breeze. The other half of the participants had already crossed the bridge and were resting on a park bench. The question was, which group of men were more attracted to the woman: those who encountered her on the bridge or those who were resting on the bench?

This probably seems like a ridiculous question. After all, it was the same woman in both cases, and it was arbitrary whether she approached the men on the bridge or the bench. Or was it? When the woman gave her phone number to the men on the bridge, their heart was beating rapidly, they were a bit short of breath, and they were perspiring. The researchers predicted that these men would be mixed up about exactly why they were physiologically aroused. Surely they recognized to some extent that these symptoms were the result of standing on the flimsy footbridge. Nonetheless, the researchers reasoned, the men might misattribute some of their arousal to attraction to the woman. This is exactly what seems to have happened. Sixty-five percent of the men approached on the bridge called the woman and asked for a date, whereas only 30 percent of the men approached on the bench called and asked for a date. By failing to recognize why they were aroused, people were more attracted to someone than they would otherwise have been.[6]

Panty Hose, Vacuum Cleaners, and Reasons Why

Maybe these examples of failing to recognize causes of our responses are exceptions rather than the rule. In everyday life, how accurate are people's explanations of why they respond the way they do? And where do these explanations come from?

A number of years ago, Richard Nisbett and I set out to find the answers to these questions with some simple experiments. We placed people in identical situations, save for one or two key features that we varied. We observed how these key features influenced people's judgments or behavior and then asked people to explain why they responded the way they did, to see if they mentioned the features we had varied.

One of our studies was conducted at Meijer's Thrifty Acres, a bargain store just outside Ann Arbor, Michigan. On a busy Saturday morning Nisbett and I placed a sign on a display table that read: "Consumer Evaluation Survey—Which Is the Best Quality?" We then made sure that four pairs of nylon panty hose were arranged neatly on the table and waited for the first passerby to stop and examine them. We were not moonlighting as marketing researchers or working part-time for a panty-hose manufacturer. This was social psychology in action: Would people be able to express accurately all the reasons why they preferred one pair of panty hose to another?

To be able to answer this question, we had to have some idea of what really influenced people's preferences. Here, serendipity was in our favor. In an earlier version of the study, we noticed that people showed a marked preference for items on the right side of the display. We observed this same position effect in the panty-hose study. The panty hose were labeled A, B, C, and D, from left to right. Pair A was preferred by only

12 percent of the participants, pair B by 17 percent, pair C by 31 percent, and pair D by 40 percent, for a statistically significant position effect. We knew that this was a position effect and not that pair D had superior characteristics because in fact all the pairs of panty hose were identical—a fact that went unnoticed by almost all our participants.

After people announced their choice, we asked them to explain why they had chosen the pair that they did. People typically pointed to an attribute of their preferred pair, such as its superior knit, sheerness, or elasticity. No one spontaneously mentioned that the position of the panty hose had anything to do with the preference. When we asked people directly whether they thought that the position of the panty hose had influenced their choice, all participants but one looked at us suspiciously and said of course not. The lone exception said that she was taking three psychology courses, had just learned about order effects, and was probably influenced by the position of the panty hose. However, this woman showed little evidence of the position effect—she had chosen pair B.

Nisbett and I soon found ourselves thinking of other ways to test the hypothesis that people do not know reasons for their feelings, judgments, and actions. One night we met in Dick's office to kick around ideas for a new study. Our progress was slow; we couldn't seem to think of any good ideas. After a while it became apparent why (or so we thought): we were distracted by the noise of a custodial worker vacuuming outside the office. Suddenly, we had an inspiration: we had just sat in Dick's office for several minutes frustrated by our lack of progress, failing to recognize that the noise from the vacuum was distracting us. Maybe this was just the kind of situation we were searching for: one in which people would overlook a stimulus (an annoying background noise) that was influencing their judgments.

We tried to "bottle" this experience in the following study. College students watched a documentary film and rated how enjoyable it was. Dick Nisbett, posing as a construction worker, operated a power saw outside the door to the room, beginning about a minute into the film. The noise continued intermittently until I, the experimenter, went to the door and asked the worker to please stop sawing until the film was over. The participants then rated how much they had enjoyed the film and how much the noise had influenced their enjoyment. To see if the noise really did have an effect, we included a control condition in which participants viewed the film without any distracting noise. We hypothesized that the noise would reduce people's enjoyment of the film, but that most people would not realize that the noise was responsible for their negative evaluation (just as we did not realize, at first, that the vacuum was disrupting our meeting).

As it happened, we were completely wrong. The students who watched the film in the presence of the noise enjoyed the film as much as the students who saw the film without the noise. In fact they enjoyed the film slightly more. When we asked participants how much the noise had influenced their ratings, however, they had the same hypothesis as we did: most people reported that the noise had lowered their enjoyment of the film. Even though our initial hypothesis was wrong, we managed to find a case in which people reported that a stimulus had influenced their judgments, when in fact it had not—more evidence of people's lack of insight into the causes of their everyday responses.

Why Do People Misunderstand the Causes of Their Responses?

On the basis of studies such as these, Dick Nisbett and I published an article arguing that people often make inaccurate reports about the causes of their responses because there is "little or no introspective access to higher order cognitive processes." If you wonder how we could make such a sweeping statement on the basis of the panty hose and power-saw studies, you are not alone. A number of critics responded to our article, arguing that our claims were far too extreme.[7] In our defense, the conclusions were based on more than the demonstration studies we did; we surveyed several large literatures that were consistent with our conclusions about lack of awareness and inaccurate causal reports, including many studies like Dutton and Aron's "love on the bridge" experiment. Nonetheless, our argument did not go unchallenged.

Perhaps the most controversial part of our article was the claim that people have limited introspective access to their mental processes. Any sentient human being knows that an extreme version of this argument is false. The fact that people make errors about the causes of their responses does not mean that their inner worlds are a black box. I can bring to mind a great deal of information that is inaccessible to anyone but me. Unless you can read my mind, there is no way you could know that a specific memory just came to mind, namely an incident in high school in which I dropped my bag lunch out a third-floor window, narrowly missing a gym teacher who happened to walk around a corner at just the wrong time. Isn't this a case of my having privileged, "introspective access to higher order cognitive processes"?

Ah, Nisbett and I argued, it is true that people have privileged access to a great deal of information about themselves, such as the content of their current thoughts and memories and the object of their attention. But these are mental *contents*, not mental *processes*. The real action in the mind is mental processing that produces feelings, judgments, and behaviors. Although we often have access to the results of these processes— such as my memory of the lunch-dropping incident—we do not have access to the mental processes that produced them. I don't really know, for example, why that particular memory came to mind, just as the participants in the panty-hose study did not know exactly why they preferred pair D over A. Maybe I just saw someone who looked like the gym teacher, heard a song that was popular at the time, or saw something fly by my office window that looked suspiciously like a peanut butter and jelly sandwich. Who knows.

As some of our critics pointed out, however, the distinction between mental content and process is not very tenable. Suppose I heard a song on the radio, which reminded me of the lunch-dropping incident, which reminded me that the teacher I almost hit was also the wrestling coach, which reminded me of professional wrestler Hulk Hogan, which reminded me of Minnesota governor Jesse Ventura. Is each step in this chain of associations a mental content, or is the entire chain a mental process that led from hearing the song to the image of Jesse Ventura?

A better distinction, I believe, is the by now familiar one between the adaptive unconscious and the conscious self. The Nisbett and Wilson argument can be reworked as follows:

- Many human judgments, emotions, thoughts, and behaviors are produced by the adaptive unconscious.
- Because people do not have conscious access to the adaptive unconscious, their conscious selves confabulate reasons for why they responded the way they did, just as P. S., Mr. Thompson, and Estabrooks' hypnotized subject did.

In other words, to the extent that people's responses are caused by the adaptive unconscious, they do not have privileged access to the causes and must infer them, just as Nisbett and I argued. But to the extent that people's responses are caused by the conscious self, they have privileged access to the actual causes of these responses; in short, the Nisbett and Wilson argument was wrong about such cases.

THE CONSCIOUS CAUSALITY QUESTION

But to what extent are human responses the products of the adaptive unconscious versus conscious thoughts? It is clear that the adaptive unconscious is responsible for a good deal of our behavior, and in these instances the reasons for our responses are impossible to access directly. But people also possess a conscious self that directs behavior, at least at times.

Suppose, for example, we observe a customer in a fast-food restaurant ask for a chicken sandwich, and we ask her why she ordered what she did. She would probably say something like, "Well, I usually order the burger, fries, and shake, but I felt more like a chicken sandwich and unsweetened iced tea today. They taste good and are a little healthier." These are precisely the thoughts she was thinking before she asked for the sandwich and thus were responsible for what she ordered—a clear case of conscious causality.

Or is it? Suppose that earlier in the day the fast-food customer encountered someone who was quite obese, which primed issues of weight and self-image, which made her more likely to order food with less fat and calories than the burgers, fries, and shake. The customer was aware of part of the reason she ordered what she did—her conscious thoughts preceding her action—but unaware of what triggered these thoughts. This example illustrates that the question of conscious causality is a very difficult one to answer. There may be relatively few cases in which a response is the pure product of only the adaptive unconscious or only conscious thoughts.

Here's another complication: in examples like this one, it is not even clear that the conscious thoughts preceding the action played any causal role at all. As noted in Chapter 3, Daniel Wegner and Thalia Wheatley argue that the experience of conscious will is often an illusion akin to the "third variable" problem with correlational data. We experience a thought followed by an action and assume that it was the conscious thought that caused that action. In fact a third variable—a nonconscious intention—might have produced both the conscious thought and the action. Seeing the obese person, for example, might have been the cause of thoughts about healthy food and the ordering of the chicken sand-wich. The conscious thoughts may not have caused the behavior, despite the illusion that they did so.

Wegner and Wheatley's provocative theory illustrates that a sense of conscious will cannot be taken as evidence that conscious thoughts really did cause our behavior. The causal role of conscious thought has been vastly overrated; instead, it is often a post-hoc explanation of responses that emanated from the adaptive unconscious.

DO STRANGERS KNOW THE REASONS FOR YOUR RESPONSES
AS WELL AS YOU DO?

Where do people's confabulations come from? Suppose that someone asked you to describe the major influences on your daily mood. To the extent that your adaptive unconscious influences your mood, you will not be able to examine these influences directly. Instead, there are four general types of information you can use to create an explanation:

- *Shared causal theories.* There are many cultural theories about why people respond the way they do, such as "absence makes the heart grow fonder" and "people are in bad moods on Mondays." If people do not have a ready-made theory to explain a particular response, they can often generate one based on their storehouse of cultural knowledge about what makes people tick. ("Why did Jane break up with Tom? The fact that he kept calling her by his ex-girlfriend's name probably had something to do with it.")

- *Observations of covariation between one's responses and prior conditions.* People can observe their own responses and infer what is causing them. People discover what they are allergic to, for example, not by directly examining their digestive processes but by observing the covariation between eating certain foods (e.g., pecans) and allergic reactions (e.g., breaking out into hives). In the same way, people might deduce that they like movies starring Robert DeNiro, are in bad moods when they get less than seven hours of sleep, and catch colds when they forget to wear a jacket in freezing weather.

- *Idiosyncratic theories.* People have idiosyncratic theories about the causes of their responses that are not shared by the culture at large, such as the theory that going to large parties often makes them depressed. These theories might result from observations of covariation; for example, Jim might observe that he was depressed after the last few parties he attended. People can also learn idiosyncratic theories from others. A person's spouse, for example, might say, "Honey, I noticed that you were down in the dumps at the Jones's lawn party, the Greenbergs' anniversary party, and Sam's birthday party. What's up with you and large parties?"

- *Private knowledge (thoughts, feelings, and memories).* Although access to one's own mind is not perfect, people have a wealth of privileged knowledge about their own conscious thoughts, feelings, and memories that they can use to deduce what is causing them to respond the way they do. If Jim is feeling sad and knows that he has been thinking a lot about the time his cat ate his favorite goldfish, he might deduce that it is the memories of Goldie's demise that are making him sad.

Perhaps the most radical part of Nisbett and Wilson's argument is that despite the vast amount of information people have, their explanations about the causes of their responses are no more accurate than the explanations of a complete stranger who lives in the same culture.[8] How can this possibly be true? Can it really be the case that a complete stranger, chosen randomly out of the phone book, will know as much as we do about why we respond the way we do? Surely the vast amount of "inside information" we have about ourselves gives us an advantage. Suppose that we are avid baseball fans and that during baseball season our mood fluctuates with the fortunes of our favorite team. Because a stranger doesn't know whether we are baseball fans, political junkies who watch *Crossfire* every night, or frequent bidders at auctions on the eBay website, how could this person possibly know as accurately as we do what influences our moods?

True enough, we do have a lot more information about ourselves than a stranger does. However, this information may not always lead to accurate inferences about the causes of our responses. Of the four kinds of information listed above, the stranger has only the first—shared cultural theories. The fact that we also have covariation information, idiosyncratic theories, and private knowledge, however, can be a hindrance as well as an advantage.

For one thing, some of this privileged knowledge isn't as accurate as it might seem. There is considerable evidence that people are not very skilled at consciously observing the covariation between their responses and its antecedents. Sometimes a covariation is so striking that we can't help but notice it, such as the fact that we broke out in hives immediately after eating pecans for the first time. More commonly there are many antecedents of our responses, and it is difficult to tease apart which ones are the causes. Because of this difficulty, people's beliefs about covariation are often a function of their shared cultural theories, rather than deductions based on accurate observations of their own behavior. There is no evidence, for example, that going outside without a jacket increases the likelihood that people will catch colds, despite the cultural theories to this effect.[9]

In addition, the vast amount of privileged information people have might make it harder to recognize causes of their behavior that a stranger, relying on cultural theories, would see. Suppose, for example, that a medical student who has just learned about diabetes stands up quickly and gets dizzy. The student might think, "Uh oh, I better have my blood sugar checked; I could be in the early stages of diabetes, which is impeding my blood circulation." A stranger, who knows nothing about what the student has been studying or thinking about, is likely to say, "She got dizzy because she stood up too quickly." The stranger may be right in this case, which would be an example of a person's inside information (the student's knowledge of diabetes) leading to inaccurate causal reports.

HOW WELL DO PEOPLE KNOW WHAT PREDICTS THEIR MOOD?

The diabetes case might seem an exception to a more general rule, namely that people's inside knowledge usually helps them understand the causes of their responses. To find out, I conducted a study with Patricia Laser and Julie Stone to see how well people understand what predicts a common response, namely their daily moods, and how this understanding compares with guesses made by complete strangers. We asked college students to keep track of their moods every day for five weeks. The students also made daily ratings of several variables that might predict their moods, such as the weather, the quality of their relationships with friends, and how long they had slept the night before. For each participant we computed the correlations between the predictor variables (e.g., length of sleep) and his or her daily mood. At the end of the five weeks people judged what they thought the relationships were—for example, how much they thought their daily moods were related to the amount of sleep they got. By comparing the actual relationships with people's estimates of the relationships, we could see how accurate people were at knowing the predictors of their moods.

People were right about some of the predictors, such as the quality of their relationships. Most people correctly believed that this factor was correlated with their moods. Overall, however, people achieved only a modest level of accuracy. Most people believed that the amount of sleep they got was correlated with their mood the next day, for example, when in fact this wasn't true: amount of sleep was unrelated to virtually all the participants' moods.

The next step was to see how people's level of accuracy about the predictors of their mood compared with the accuracy of complete strangers' reports. We asked a separate group of students to judge the relationship between the predictor variables and daily moods of the "typical undergraduate" at their university. These students were not told anything about the individual participants and thus knew nothing about their particular habits, idiosyncrasies, or private thoughts. All they had to go on was their theories.

Remarkably, the guesses of these "observer" subjects were as accurate as the participants' own guesses about what predicted their mood. Like the participants themselves, the strangers guessed that relationships with others were an important predictor of mood, and they were right. Like the participants themselves, they guessed that amount of sleep was also a predictor of mood, and they were wrong. The tremendous amount of information the participants had about themselves—their idiosyncratic theories, their observations of covariation between their moods and its antecedents, and their private knowledge—did not make them any more accurate than complete strangers.

One reason for this result might be that the participants and the strangers were using the same information, namely shared cultural theories. That is, perhaps the participants neglected to use the extra information they had, such as their private thoughts and feelings. There was evidence, however, that the participants did use private information. For example, the extremely high agreement among the strangers about the predictors of mood suggests that they were using the same, shared base of knowledge—namely, shared cultural theories. The much lower agreement among the participants about the predictors of their mood suggests that they were relying more on idiosyncratic knowledge.

An obvious conclusion from this study (and others like it) is that when people make inferences about the causes and predictors of their responses, such as their mood, they use information that strangers do not have access to, such as their private thoughts and feelings. A less obvious conclusion is that private information both helps and hurts. It can make people more accurate than observers; I might well be right that my mood is dependent on the fortunes of a certain professional baseball team. However, I might be misled by my inside knowledge. It may seem as though my mood fluctuates more with the fortunes of my favorite team than it in fact does. A stranger who does not know that I am a baseball fan might be more accurate in using shared cultural theories about the determinants of mood. Averaging across several studies, there seems to be no net advantage to having privileged information about ourselves: the amount of accuracy obtained by people about the causes of their responses is nearly identical with the amount of accuracy obtained by strangers.[10]

If you find this argument hard to swallow—that on balance, a stranger knows as much as you do about the causes of your feelings, judgments, and actions—I confess that I do too. Think of the implications of this argument: if you are wondering about the determinants of your mood (perhaps with the aim of improving it), you might just as well ask a complete stranger as rely on the vast amount of knowledge you have about yourself and your history.

The amount of research in this area is not huge, and, as in any area, the individual studies are open to criticisms. Perhaps Wilson, Laser, and Stone's measures of mood were inadequate, for example, or perhaps they failed to ask people about some key predictors of mood, about which they would have been more accurate than the strangers. Further, there is no way of telling how representative the kinds of responses and influences are of the ones people care about in everyday life. If a broader range of responses were studied, strangers' causal reports might not prove as accurate as people's own reports.

It is remarkable, though, that a personal advantage over strangers' reports has been difficult to find. Further, as seen in Chapter 4, there is evidence that when it comes to judging our personalities (as opposed to judging the causes of a specific response), other people may sometimes be *more* accurate than we are ourselves. Although I would not yet recommend dialing a random person in the phone book to find out why you feel the way you do, we all might want to be more humble about the accuracy of our causal judgments.

The Illusion of Authenticity

There is a final puzzle about people's explanations of their own responses. Why don't we realize that our explanations are confabulations, no more accurate than the causal reports of strangers? One of the major points of this chapter is that people's reasons about their own responses are as much conjectures as their reasons for other people's responses. Why, then, don't they feel this way?

One explanation is that it is important for people to feel that they are the well-informed captains of their own ship and know why they are doing what they are. Recognizing that we are no more informed about the causes of our responses than a complete stranger is likely to make people feel less in control of their lives, a feeling that has been shown to be associated with depression.

Another key, I suggest, is that the amount of inside information we have produces a misleading feeling of confidence, namely the sense that with so much information we must be accurate about the causes of our responses, even when we are not. Suppose you are thinking of investing in two Internet stocks, both of which you think have the same potential to increase in value. Your faith in Alpha.com is based on a visit to the company and an extended conversation with its president. Your faith in Beta.com is based on an article you read in the newspaper. Surely you will be more confident in your judgment of Alpha.com, given that your judgment is based on a great deal of firsthand knowledge. But there is no guarantee that this firsthand knowledge will lead to a more accurate judgment; in fact you may have been misled by the president's enthusiasm and exaggerated claims. Similarly, the vast amount of inside knowledge we have about ourselves increases confidence in our self-knowledge, but does not always lead to greater accuracy.

If so, then this illusion of authenticity should be reduced by equalizing the amount of inside information people have about themselves and another person. Suppose you have an extended conversation with your best friend about her experiences on beach vacations over the years, and I now ask you why she feels the way she does about vacations at the beach. You can use a good deal of specific information about your friend other than your general theories about why people like or dislike the beach—the fact that your friend met her husband at the beach, loves saltwater taffy and wind-swept hair, and is an avid surfer. You are likely to be very confident in your reasons for why she loves the beach. Perhaps you are not quite as confident as you are in your own reasons, given that we never have as much information about someone else as we have about ourselves. Surely, though, you will be more confident in your reasons for why your friend likes the beach than for why a stranger likes the beach.

Although this seems obvious, keep in mind that there is no guarantee that your reasons for your friend's feelings will be any more accurate than your reasons for a stranger's feelings, because extra information does not always give people an accuracy advantage. Recall the propensity with which P. S.'s left hemisphere could explain actions by the right hemisphere, by drawing on his knowledge of shovels, chickens, and chicken coops. P. S. had lots of information from which to generate an answer, but none of it was relevant to the real reason he picked a shovel with his right hand.

Another way to reduce the authenticity illusion is to limit the amount of inside information people have about themselves, thereby lowering their confidence in their own reasons. Of course, the mind is not like a hard disk that can be reformatted to erase all its current contents. We have private information that is more relevant to some judgments than to others, however. Suppose I asked you, "Why do you feel the way you do about the cover of this book?" and "Why do you think a stranger feels the way that he or she does about the cover of this book?" Compared to information about vacations at the beach, you probably have less personal information relevant to your judgment of something as esoteric as a particular book cover. Consequently, you are more likely to rely on general theories about why people like book covers—the same theories you will use to explain the stranger's reaction ("I don't know, I guess I like it because it's mysterious and eye-catching."). Of course, we can bring to bear personal information about virtually anything; it is possible that the book cover reminds you of your Uncle Henry or a photograph you once saw in an antique shop. Still, people use less personal information to explain some responses than they do to explain others. In these cases their reasons probably seem a little less compelling and more like the reasons they would offer for a stranger's responses.

In short, the authenticity illusion varies with the amount of private information people use when generating reasons. But as we have seen, the accuracy of people's explanations seems not to vary much with the amount of private information they use.

It is not welcome news, I suspect, that strangers may know as much about the true causes of our responses as we do. We turn now to a bastion of self-knowledge that is harder to assail, people's feelings and emotions. Even if we do not know the causes of our feelings, surely we know that we have them. Or do we?

6

Knowing How We Feel

We must never take a person's testimony, however sincere, that he has
felt nothing, as proof positive that no feeling has been there.
—*William James, Principles of Psychology (1890)*

Ben liked to joke that he was his own invention and therefore never
could be certain how he really felt about anything or anybody. I won-
dered whether he did not sometimes try to solve the problem, and put
an end to tormenting doubts, by also inventing various experimental
versions of his feelings.
—*Louis Begley, The Man Who Was Late (1992)*

As the old cliché says, "I may not know why but I know
what I like." Several contemporary theories of emotion
argue that whereas the mental processes that produce emotions may be unconscious, the emotions themselves are
not. Affective reactions such as evaluations, moods, and
emotions may be the specialty of the house of consciousness. As the quotations above indicate, however, the story is
not quite so simple. Feelings are often conscious, but they
can also reside elsewhere in the mental neighborhood.

The Incorrigibility of Feelings

Of all the issues I discuss in this book, the idea of unconscious feelings is perhaps the most controversial. In fact

some philosophers and psychologists reject this idea out of hand, arguing that an "unconscious feeling" is an oxymoron. Suppose I were to tell you honestly that I feel a sharp pain in my left knee right now. Do you believe me? "What a strange question to ask," you might think. "As long as he is not joking or lying, then of course he must be experiencing the pain he describes." If this is what you thought, you are in good company. Quite a few philosophers, including Descartes and Wittgenstein, have argued that reports about sensations and feelings are incorrigible. Simply put, people's beliefs about their feelings cannot be doubted. If I say my knee hurts, then it does and that is all there is to it. I am the final authority on my sensations and feelings, and you have no grounds on which to doubt me.

Or do you? Consider this example, from a short story by Mary Kierstead. Two cousins are reminiscing about their childhood summers on the family farm, when their thoughts turn to Topper, the resident pony:

> "You know, it wasn't until I was about thirty that I realized that I'd always hated that goddamn pony. He had a mean disposition, and he was fat and spoiled. He would roll on me, and then step on my foot before I could get up."
>
> "And he bit you when you tried to give him lumps of sugar," Kate added. It wasn't until Blake said it that Kate realized that she, too, had always hated Topper. For years they had been conned into loving him, because children love their pony, and their dog, and their parents, and picnics, and the ocean, and the lovely chocolate cake.[1]

Suppose we had asked Blake and Kate, when they were twelve, if they loved Topper. "Of course we do," they would have answered honestly. But Blake and Kate are now convinced that they never loved the beast. They *believed* that they did, but in truth they hated him. If so, then Cartesian and Wittgensteinian incorrigibility is false. People can be wrong when they honestly report a feeling ("I love Topper").

A longstanding philosophical debate over the incorrigibility issue often focuses on interesting conundrums. For example, suppose my knee started hurting at 2:00, when I banged it on the corner of my desk.

At 2:05 I get a phone call and during the conversation, I do not notice that my knee hurts. When I hang up the phone at 2:10, my knee hurts again. What happened to the pain during the phone call? Is it possible to be in pain but not to know we are in pain? Or did the pain stop while I was on the phone and restart afterward?[2]

Although I think the incorrigibility argument is wrong, there are two good reasons why it has persisted: the measurement problem and the theory problem. The measurement problem is that even if people can be wrong about their feelings in principle, we have no way of knowing if and when this is the case, because we do not have a pipeline to people's feelings that is independent of their self-reports. The theory problem is the question of how and why the mind would be organized in such a way that people can be wrong about their feelings. Why on earth would humans be built this way? Although both the measurement and theory problem are formidable, I believe they can be overcome.

THE MEASUREMENT PROBLEM

What kind of independent criterion could we call upon to doubt people's statements that they love someone or that their knee hurts? Short of the fanciful Inner Self Detector, there is no perfect, independent measure of such internal states such as how much pain I am feeling in my knee or how much Blake and Kate love Topper. There is no physiological "pain detector," for example, on which a dial points to the precise amount of pain someone feels in his or her knee.

But the fact that it is difficult to prove that a self-reported feeling is inaccurate is no reason to accept the incorrigibility argument. This would be like saying that there are no other planets outside our solar system, because we did not (until recently) have powerful enough telescopes to observe them, or that when I take off my glasses, nothing exists beyond the few feet I can see. We should not let measurement issues drive theoretical ones.

Furthermore, although there are no error-free, independent measures of people's internal states such as the Inner Self Detector, there are grounds on which we might at least be highly suspicious of the accuracy of people's reports about their feelings. It might be clear from a person's behavior, and how that behavior is interpreted by others, that he or she possesses a nonconscious feeling. A number of writers on this topic have used jealousy as an example. Sam observes his wife chatting with an attractive man at a party. The man asks his wife for a dance and she accepts. On the way home, Sam is curt and remote toward his wife. When she asks if anything is wrong, he sincerely replies, "No, I'm just tired." Sam truly believes he is not jealous, even though anyone who observed his behavior would say otherwise. The next day Sam recognizes that he did feel threatened by his wife's attention to the other man.[3]

This example highlights another way in which we might doubt people's reports about their feelings: when people themselves later acknowledge that they were wrong about what they were feeling. The fact that Sam later agrees that he was jealous, and that Blake and Kate acknowledged, years later, that they had always hated Topper, is not definitive proof that they had been wrong about their feelings. After all, their reconstructions of their feelings could be in error. Examples such as these, however, meet what we might call the "strong suspicion" criterion. The fact that observers disagreed with the person about his or her feelings (e.g., all the partygoers but Sam believed that he was jealous), and the fact that Sam later believed he had been jealous are strong grounds on which to doubt the veracity of his original denial of jealousy.

Finally, just as astronomers are developing more powerful tools to peek into the distant universe, so are psychologists developing better instruments to measure people's internal states. True, we do not yet have an Inner Self Detector, but increasingly sophisticated techniques are being developed, such as measures of the neurological correlates of emotion and affect.

THE THEORY PROBLEM

Suppose we were given the job of designing the optimal human being (in our spare time). Should we endow humans with feelings and emotions? If so, should we make these feelings conscious or unconscious? It would seem pretty odd to say, "Okay, human, you can have feelings, but sometimes you are not going to be aware of them." What function could this possibly serve?

Such a functional approach can be dangerous, because it is easy to fall into the trap of assuming that every feature of the human mind serves a useful purpose. Nonetheless, the fact that it is easy to tell a story about why conscious feelings are adaptive, and difficult to tell a story about why unconscious feelings are adaptive, seems to favor the incorrigibility argument.

There are two solutions to the theory problem, one old and one new. The old solution is psychoanalytic theory, which argues that the reason feelings can be unconscious is repression. The newer solution is our friend the adaptive unconscious, which might produce feelings independently of people's conscious constructions of their feelings.

Psychoanalysis and repressed feelings. According to Freud, feelings can be kept out of awareness because they are anxiety-provoking, such as failing to recognize sexual attraction toward one's parents. The most dramatic case of repressed feelings is reaction formation, whereby unconscious desires are disguised as their opposite. Erotic attraction toward a member of the same sex, for example, might be so threatening to people that they unconsciously transform their desire into homophobia.[4]

The psychoanalytic view of repressed feelings has proved difficult to test in a rigorous way. Not only would researchers have to demonstrate that people have a feeling of which they are unaware—which, as we have seen, is no easy matter—they would also have to show that the reason people are unaware of the feeling is that they have repressed it. A number of writers have reviewed the evidence for repression and found it wanting.[5]

One recent study, however, is quite suggestive. This study examined the psychoanalytic idea that people who are extremely homophobic may be repressing homosexual urges; that is, that their dread of homosexuality may be a means of disguising sexual attraction toward members of the same sex. The researchers recruited male college students who had scored low or high on a questionnaire measure of homophobia. They asked the men to watch sexually explicit videos while they were attached to a device that measured how much of an erection they had. Now, you might be wondering how the researchers did this, and how they got men to *agree* to do it. In answer to the first question, they used a device called a plethysmograph, a rubber ring placed around the penis that measures changes in its circumference. The plethysmograph is quite sensitive to changes in penis size and has been used extensively as a measure of male sexual arousal. In answer to the second question, the men watched the videos alone in a room and were allowed to attach the plethysmograph themselves; there was no mad scientist demanding that the men drop their trousers in public.

All the videos the men watched depicted consensual sexual behavior between two adults. One film showed heterosexual sex between a man and a woman, one showed lesbian sex between two women, and one showed homosexual sex between two men. The two groups of men showed similar levels of arousal (as measured by the plethysmograph) to the heterosexual and lesbian videos. Consistent with the psychoanalytic hypothesis of reaction formation, however, the homophobic men showed significantly greater increases in penile erection to the male homosexual film than did nonhomophobic men—even though the homophobic men claimed that they were no more aroused by the homosexual film than nonhomophobic men said they were.

This study does not provide airtight proof that the homophobic men had a feeling (sexual attraction toward other men) of which they were unaware. As the authors of the study note, there is some evidence that anxiety can increase sexual arousal; thus the greater increases in erections may have been the result of anxiety in the homophobic men, not sexual attraction. Though not definitive, the study is at least consistent with the psychoanalytic idea of reaction formation, whereby conscious feelings (homophobia) served the purpose of disguising unconscious ones (homosexual attraction).[6]

Emotions are functional; but do they need to be conscious? Even if we assume that repression is alive and well, the theory problem would not be completely solved. An advocate of incorrigibility might respond, "I am willing to concede that in rare, neurotic cases, people can keep a painful feeling out of consciousness. This is by far the exception, however. In the vast majority of cases, people are fully aware of their feelings, evaluations, and emotions. In fact it is highly functional for people to be aware of their own feelings. Imagine if we had no idea whether we were attracted to or repulsed by a new acquaintance. Not a good way to ensure procreation." This argument suggests that not only is there no compelling theory to explain why people would be unaware of their own feelings (save for unusual cases of repression), but there is a compelling reason why it is to people's advantage to be aware of their own feelings.

The view that emotions serve important functions is an old one with many supporters. Charles Darwin, for example, pointed to the social, communicative functions of emotions. The expression of disgust signals other members of the same species to avoid a certain food; the expression of fear signals our compatriots that danger is near. Emotions may also further the survival of the individuals who have them. An animal that is angry or afraid reacts in ways that make it appear more dangerous to its foes; a cat, for example, displays bared teeth, an arched back, and raised body hair. Fear makes people flee from dangers, and pain teaches them not to touch hot stoves.[7]

A close look at the functional argument, however, raises a question that has seldom been asked: Does an emotion have to be conscious to be functional? Most theorists have said yes, assuming that events occur in this order: People encounter something in their environment that is dangerous, such as a ferocious bear. The perception of the bear triggers an emotion, namely fear. The conscious experience of this emotion causes the person to act in an adaptive way, such as running in the opposite direction.

As reasonable as this sequence may seem, it is not the only possible explanation of emotional reactions. One problem is that emotions are often slow to develop and occur after people have taken steps to deal with dangerous events. Consider something that happened to me several years ago, when I was driving a rental car during a thunderstorm. Unbeknownst to me, the car had severely worn, bald tires. When I went under a highway bridge and drove from the dry pavement back onto the rain-slicked highway, the tires lost their grip, and the rear of the car fishtailed dangerously from left to right. For a few tense seconds, I fought to regain control of the car and avoid slamming into the guardrail. Fortunately I came out of the skid without incident and continued on my way.

The interesting thing is the point at which I experienced a conscious emotion. According to the standard, functional view, the perception that I was in danger triggered fear, which caused me to take action to regain control of the car. In fact, I did not experience any emotion as I felt the car go into a skid and began tapping the brakes furiously. It was only after the car stopped fishtailing and I was no longer in danger that I experienced the "whoosh" of emotion. ("Oh my God, I could have been killed!") How could my fear have been a signal to act in a lifesaving manner, when it did not occur until after the danger had been averted?

Examples like this were familiar to William James, who proposed a different sequence of events from the standard, evolutionary explanation of emotions. James argued that the perception of environmental events triggers bodily responses, which then trigger conscious emotions; "we feel sorry because we cry, angry because we strike, afraid because we tremble." In his famous example, we do not meet a bear and run because we are afraid; we meet a bear, run, and then experience a post-hoc fear that played no causal role in our fleeing—much like the "whoosh" of fear I experienced after regaining control of the rental car.

James's theory triggered a debate on the relationship between bodily responses and emotions that continues to this day. For our purposes, the issue is whether the conscious experience of emotion is necessary for adaptive responses to environmental threats. James's theory suggests that it may not be, and thus turns the entire issue of the function of emotions on its head. Maybe conscious emotions serve no function at all, but are a by-product of nonconscious cognitive processes that size up the environment and trigger adaptive behaviors—like heat that is released as a by-product of a chemical reaction, but does not cause the reaction.[8]

A similar argument could be applied to the social function of emotions. It might well be adaptive for a cat to rear its back and hiss when it encounters Rex, the Doberman next door, but perhaps it can do so without the conscious experience of fear. The cat might perceive danger (Rex slipped off of his chain again) and react appropriately, without any conscious experience at all.

But if it is not a conscious emotion that triggers adaptive behaviors, what does? How does the perception of a bear lead to fleeing, without any intervening emotional response? One reason James's theory of emotion was so controversial is that it did not explain how the perception of an environmental event could lead directly to behavioral responses to that event. One possibility is that emotions and feelings do precede adaptive behaviors, but that people are not always aware of these emotions and feelings.

The Adaptive Unconscious Feels

From the nonconscious mental processes we have considered so far, it is a small leap to argue that the adaptive unconscious can have its own beliefs and feelings—not because these beliefs and feelings are so threatening that the forces of repression keep them hidden, but because the adaptive unconscious operates independently of consciousness.

Almost by definition, emotions are states that inundate consciousness. They are often accompanied by bodily changes that are hard to ignore, such as increased heart rate and shortness of breath. How could such a state exist outside of awareness? How could we have a feeling and not feel it? The answer, I suggest, is that we need to adjust our definition of feelings, to allow for the possibility that people can have them without knowing it.

THE NONCONSCIOUS EARLY WARNING SYSTEM

One example of such nonconscious feelings is a danger-detection system documented by Joseph LeDoux. Evolution has endowed mammals (e.g.,

humans and rats) with two pathways in the brain that process information from the environment differently, dubbed by LeDoux the low road
and the high road of emotion. Both roads start at the same place, namely
at the point at which information from the environment reaches the
sensory receptors and from there travels to the sensory thalamus. The
roads also end up at the same place—the amygdala, an almond-shaped
region of the forebrain (*amygdala* means "almond" in Greek) long
believed to be involved in the control of emotional responses. The amygdala has neural pathways to the areas of the brain that control heart rate,
blood pressure, and other autonomic nervous system responses associated with emotion.

The two roads, however, get to the amygdala via different routes. The
low road consists of neural pathways that go directly from the sensory
thalamus to the amygdala, allowing information to reach it very quickly,
but with only minimal processing of the information. The high road
goes first to the cortex, the area of the brain responsible for information
processing and thinking, and then to the amygdala. The high road is
slower but allows for a more detailed analysis of the information in the
cortex.

Why do mammals have these two emotional pathways? One possibility is that the low road evolved first in organisms that did not have a
sophisticated cortex. Once the cortex expanded, perhaps it took over the
role of emotional processing and superseded the more primitive low
road. In LeDoux's words, the low road may be "the brain's version of an
appendix" that no longer has any function. LeDoux rejects this view,
however, arguing that the low and high roads work in tandem in a quite
adaptive manner. The low road operates as an early warning system that
quickly alerts people to signs of danger, whereas the high road analyzes
information more slowly and thoroughly, allowing people to make more
informed judgments about the environment.

To use one of LeDoux's examples, suppose you are walking in the
woods and suddenly see a long, snakelike object lying in the middle of
the path. You stop instantly and think "Snake!" as your heart begins to

beat rapidly. You then realize that the shape is not a snake after all but a fallen branch from a hickory tree, and you go on your way.

What happened, according to LeDoux, is that the image of the stick was sent directly from the sensory thalamus to the amygdala, with a crude analysis that said, "Snake ahead!" This "low road" processing caused you to stop abruptly. Meanwhile, the image was also sent to the cortex, where it was analyzed in more detail, revealing that the object had bark and knotholes. This "high road" processing overrode the initial, low-road response, recognizing that it was a false alarm. The early warning system (the low road) errs on the side of seeing danger ahead; as LeDoux puts it, "The cost of treating a stick as a snake is less, in the long run, than the cost of treating a snake as a stick." High-road processing serves to put our fears to rest (at least much of the time), saying, "Hey, calm down, snakes don't have knotholes and bark."

The low road of emotional processing operates outside of conscious awareness. We see the stick and freeze, without any conscious feeling or thought. Does this prove, however, that people have nonconscious emotions, or simply mental processes of which they are unaware? This seems to be largely a semantic issue. If what we mean by fear is how we experience it consciously, with its concomitant shortness of breath and the feeling that our hearts are traveling to our throats, then it is very difficult to have these feelings and not be aware of them. But if we mean "Does the person have a nonconscious evaluation that something dangerous lurks ahead?" then the answer seems to be yes: people believe that something is scary and act accordingly. This seems pretty close to saying that people experience an evaluation or emotion of which they are unaware. LeDoux endorses this latter point of view, arguing that "The brain states and bodily responses are the fundamental facts of an emotion, and the conscious feelings are the frills that have added icing to the emotional cake."[9]

LeDoux has amassed an impressive amount of evidence consistent with his low-road/high-road picture of emotional processing. As a theory of nonconscious feelings, however, it is limited in three ways. First, all the research has concerned a single emotion, fear. It makes sense to endow humans with an early warning system that makes them freeze at the slightest sign of danger. But what about other emotions and feelings? Can they exist nonconsciously as well? Second, the dichotomy of rudimentary low-road processing and complex high-road processing may not be the full story. I believe it is useful to distinguish between different kinds of "high road" processing, namely processing by the adaptive unconscious and the conscious system.

Third, the theory does not allow for the simultaneous existence of different feelings, one conscious and one nonconscious. In the Topper example, Blake and Kate believed they loved their pony when at some level they also hated him (or so my argument goes). As compelling as LeDoux's early warning system model is, it cannot account for examples such as these. Once the high road has time to analyze the situation it overrules the low road, saying that "sometimes a stick is just a stick." In contrast, the adaptive unconscious may evaluate the environment in one way, while people believe (consciously) that they feel differently.

LOVING AND HATING TOPPER

Why did Blake and Kate both love and hate Topper when they were children? It is possible that this is an example of psychoanalytic repression. Admitting to themselves that they hated a pet they were supposed to love may have raised anxieties about parental approval, for example, triggering the mechanism of repression. But although such an explanation is possible, there may be a simpler one for this type of unacknowledged feeling.

The adaptive unconscious is an active evaluator of its environment, and when a pony bites us and steps on our feet, it infers that the pony is mean and evaluates it negatively. However, people also have an active, conscious self that simultaneously forms inferences and evaluations. Often the conscious system gets it right. We notice that we have been avoiding Topper and that we are apprehensive in his presence, and infer correctly that we can't stand him.

Sometimes, though, the conscious system gets it wrong. One way this can happen is that people fail to notice that a feeling has changed until their attention is drawn to it. Over a century ago, William Carpenter argued for the existence of such "unnoticed" feelings, such as "the growing up of a powerful attachment between individuals of opposite sexes, without either being aware of the fact." Carpenter noted that "The existence of a mutual attachment, indeed, is often recognised by a bystander . . . before either of the parties has made the discovery . . . the Cerebral state manifests itself in action, although no distinct consciousness of that state has been attained, chiefly because, the whole attention being attracted by the present enjoyment, there is little disposition to introspection."[10]

This example meets our "strong suspicion" criterion of a nonconscious feeling, in that people act as if they have a feeling of which they are unaware, observers believe they have the unacknowledged feeling, and the people themselves later acknowledge that they had the feeling (assuming that Carpenter's lovers come to recognize their mutual attraction). Surely, though, the lack of awareness of such strong feelings is temporary. Once people take the time to introspect, they recognize their attraction for another person. In Carpenter's words, the feeling "suddenly bursts forth, like a smouldering fire, into full flame."[11]

There may be other times when it is more difficult to recognize the feelings generated by the adaptive unconscious, even when people introspect about their feelings. The conscious system is quite sensitive to personal and cultural prescriptions about how one is supposed to feel, such as "children love their pony, and their dog, and their parents, and picnics, and the ocean, and the lovely chocolate cake." People might assume that their feelings conform to these prescriptions and fail to notice instances in which they do not. These "feeling rules" can make it difficult to perceive how one's adaptive unconscious feels about the matter. Because everyone knows that "children love their pony," it is difficult for them to notice that Topper is a nasty brute—not because it would be especially anxiety-provoking to do so, but because it is difficult to see through the smokescreen of cultural and personal feeling rules.[12]

Remember my friend Susan from Chapter 1? She was convinced that she was in love with Stephen, because he fitted her definition of the kind of man she ought to love. He shared many of her interests, he was kind, and he clearly loved her. And yet it was obvious to those of us who knew Susan that she did not love him. Why was she the last one to figure this out? Her conscious "feeling rules" seemed to get in the way. The fact that he conformed to her image of the kind of man she *ought* to love made it difficult for her to realize that she did not.

BEYOND ANECDOTES

As compelling as these examples are, they are just anecdotes. Is there empirical evidence for the idea that people can possess one feeling while believing they have another? As it happens, there is a fair amount of support for this idea in the social psychological literature. One source of evidence comes from the literature on self-perception and attribution theories, in which people have been found to infer the existence of new attitudes and emotions by observing their behavior and the situation in which it occurs.

According to these theories, when people are uncertain about how they feel, they use their behavior and bodily reactions as a guide. Many studies have found, for example, that people infer their emotions from the level of arousal they are experiencing and the nature of the social situation. We saw an example of this in Chapter 5 in the "love on the bridge" study. Men interpreted their arousal as a sign of attraction to the woman who approached them. They overestimated their attraction to the woman, failing to note that they were aroused, at least in part, because of the scary bridge.

In another experiment, Stanley Schachter and Ladd Wheeler asked participants to take part in a study of the effects of a vitamin compound on vision. Participants received an injection and then watched a fifteen-minute comedy film. Unbeknownst to the participants, the "vitamin" was actually epinephrine in one condition, a placebo in another, and chlorpromazine in a third. Epinephrine produces physiological arousal in the sympathetic nervous system, such as increased heart rate and slight tremors in the arms and legs. Chlorpromazine is a tranquilizer that acts as a depressant of the sympathetic nervous system. The researchers reasoned that because the participants did not know that they had received a drug, they would infer that the film was causing their bodily reactions. Consistent with this hypothesis, people injected with the epinephrine seemed to find the film the funniest; they laughed and smiled the most while watching it. People injected with the chlorpromazine seemed to find the film the least funny; they laughed and smiled little while watching it.[13]

Richard Nisbett and I reviewed the dozens of studies like this and found that although there is ample evidence from people's behavior that they have changed their attitudes or emotions (e.g., the laughing during the film), people seldom report that they have these new attitudes or emotions. For example, Schachter and Wheeler asked participants to rate how funny the film was and how much they enjoyed it, and found no difference between the conditions. On average, people in the epinephrine condition (who had smiled and laughed a lot) did not rate the film as any funnier than people in the chlorpromazine condition did (who had smiled and laughed very little). This pattern of results—whereby people act as if they have a certain emotion or evaluation, but do not report the existence of this emotion or evaluation—is quite common in studies like Schachter and Wheeler's.[14]

These results raise some intriguing questions: When people infer their feelings from their behavior, who is doing the inferring, and what happens to the feelings that are inferred? We saw the answer to the first question in Chapter 5: the attribution process, whereby people observe their behavior and make inferences about its causes, typically occurs in the adaptive unconscious. This process *can* occur consciously; the conscious self is an active analyzer and planner, and sometimes people mull over why they did what they did (e.g., "Why on earth didn't I begin the project sooner so that I didn't miss the deadline?"). The kinds of self-attributions studied by Schachter and Wheeler, however, are typically made quickly and nonconsciously. The participants in the epinephrine condition did not sit there scratching their heads thinking, "How funny is this film? Well, my heart is beating fast and my hands are shaking a little, so I guess it's hilarious." Instead, they made quick, nonconscious inferences that the film was funny, which caused them to laugh a lot. Similarly, the men in the "love on the bridge" study did not say to themselves, "Hm, I wonder why my heart is pounding? Let's see, I'd say I'm feeling 37 percent fear and 63 percent love—no, wait a minute, it's 34 percent fear and 66 percent love." Rather, they made a quick, nonconscious inference that their arousal was due, at least in part, to attraction to the woman.

But what happens to the feelings that result from these nonconscious inferences? Why didn't Schachter and Wheeler's epinephrine participants rate the film as funnier than the other participants did? After all, these participants laughed and smiled the most during the film, as if they had inferred it was hilarious. Schachter and Wheeler suggested an answer: when rating the film, people based their responses more on their long-term preferences for the type of film they had watched (a slapstick film with the actor Jack Carson). As one of their participants put it, "I just couldn't understand why I was laughing during the movie. Usually, I hate Jack Carson and this kind of nonsense and that's the way I checked the scales [in the questionnaire]."[15]

In short, people's adaptive unconscious inferred that the film was funny, which caused them to laugh a lot. When asked how funny the film was, people based their response on their personal theories about their liking for this type of film. The adaptive unconscious felt one way, whereas people's conscious selves felt differently—just like Blake and Kate's attitudes toward Topper, and my friend Susan's feelings about Stephen.

I have referred to the phenomenon in which people have two feelings toward the same topic, one more conscious than the other, as "dual attitudes." One of the most interesting cases is people's attitudes toward minority groups, where it is generally assumed that people know whether they are prejudiced. For example, Title VII of the United States

Civil Rights Act, which prohibits discrimination in employment on the basis of race, color, sex, national origin, and religion, assumes that such discrimination is conscious, deliberate, and intentional. The law was written to prevent flagrant, conscious racism, with no acknowledgment that there might be such things as "unconscious prejudice" or "unintentional discrimination."[16]

It is becoming increasingly clear, however, that prejudice can exist at both an explicit level (people's conscious beliefs and feelings about other groups) and an implicit level (people's automatic evaluations of other groups of which they might not be aware). People can sincerely believe that they are not prejudiced and yet possess negative attitudes at an implicit level. To demonstrate this, social psychologists have developed some quite clever methods of measuring implicit prejudice, which I discuss in Chapter 9.[17]

An unresolved issue is whether these quick, implicit, negative reactions are unconscious. I believe that people often are not aware of these feelings, but can become so under the right circumstances. John, a white liberal, may sincerely believe that he is completely nonprejudiced, and that he treats blacks the same way as he treats whites, unaware that he harbors negative feelings. There is evidence that such well-intentioned people can possess negative feelings and act more negatively toward blacks in ways that blacks notice but they do not.[18] But even though people are often unaware of these negative feelings, they might recognize them if they looked carefully. If John were to take an honest look at his feelings and carefully monitor how he responded to blacks, he might come to recognize his negative implicit attitude.

This example raises an important question about nonconscious feelings and attitudes. In previous chapters, we have portrayed the adaptive unconscious as a system of mental processes that are inaccessible, no matter how much people try to observe them. Whereas feelings and attitudes can reside out of sight, they appear to have a greater potential to reach awareness—if people can succeed in finding them through the smoke screen of their conscious theories about how they feel. This is often a matter of being a good observer of how one acts (e.g., how one responds in the presence of African Americans), rather than a matter of looking inward and introspecting about one's feelings.

TOWARD A THEORY OF NONCONSCIOUS FEELINGS AND ATTITUDES

At the beginning of the chapter I mentioned a standard view of the adaptive unconscious: it consists of a vast array of mental processes that can result in feelings, which emerge into consciousness. Imagine a compact disc player that can be programmed to search for and play various kinds of musical selections. The hardware and software that find and play the music operate out of view; but the end product—the sweet melody of an early Beatles song, say—is what we hear (what reaches awareness). Similarly, mental selection and interpretation can be nonconscious, but the feelings they produce are conscious.

In contrast, I have argued that even the products of the adaptive unconscious—the melody itself—can fail to reach consciousness. Nonetheless, I think that feelings differ from the rest of the adaptive unconscious in their potential to reach awareness. The mental processes that produce them, such as the kinds of features of the adaptive unconscious detailed in Chapters 3, 4, and 5, are inaccessible, like the hardware and software in the compact disc player. Under some circumstances, however, people are aware of the feelings they produce.

It might even be the case that the default is for feelings to emerge into awareness, and that it takes special circumstances to prevent them from doing so. We have seen three such circumstances. The first is repression, whereby forces are brought into play to hide a threatening feeling (as in the case of homophobia). The second is inattention, or the failure to notice that a feeling has changed (as in Carpenter's example of falling in love). The third is the obscuring of feelings by the smoke screen of people's conscious theories and confabulations. People fail to recognize a feeling or evaluation if it conflicts with a cultural feeling rule ("people love their ponies," "my wedding day will be the happiest time of my life"), a personal standard ("I am not prejudiced at all toward African Americans"), or conscious theories and inferences about how one feels ("I must love him because he conforms to my idea of Mr. Right").

Cases such as these, in which people fail to recognize a feeling produced by the adaptive unconscious, may not be very common. People typically recognize that they feel lust toward the person who sits in the third row of their American literature class, sad when their cat dies, and nauseous after riding the Big Thunder roller coaster for the third time. Nonetheless, the conditions under which people fail to recognize a feeling are probably not all that rare.

Further, people differ in the frequency with which they recognize their own feelings; indeed, one definition of emotional intelligence is the ability to recognize our wants, needs, joys, and sorrows. Some people are good at seeing through the smoke screen of their personal and cultural theories, recognizing when their feelings are at odds with these theories and standards. Other people are less skilled at this kind of self-awareness.[19]

In extreme cases people are unable to recognize even their most basic and extreme emotions, a psychiatric condition called alexithymia (from the Greek words for "lacking words for emotions"). Although alexithymics do have emotions, they find it difficult to describe what these emotions are or where they came from. One woman reported that she often cried but did not know why; "It just makes my body feel better." Once, she said, she cried herself to sleep after watching a movie in which a mother of eight died of cancer. When her therapist pointed out that she might have been feeling sadness and grief about the fact that her own mother was dying of cancer, the woman looked bewildered and said she did not see the connection.[20]

Clearly, alexithymia is the most extreme case of unawareness. Few of us are that confused when trying to understand our own feelings. But all of us are alexithymic to a degree; there are times when our adaptive unconscious possesses feelings that we do not recognize. What about our knowledge of how we will feel in the future, and how long we will feel that way? It is often as important to know how we will feel about future events (e.g., "How happy will I be if Steve asks me to marry him?") as to know how we feel in the present. If people sometimes have difficulty knowing how they feel right now, however, they might also have difficulty predicting their feelings.

7

Knowing How We Will Feel

How often is it the case, that, when impossibilities have come to pass, and dreams have condensed their misty substance into tangible realities, we find ourselves calm . . . amid circumstances which it would have been a delirium of joy to anticipate!

—*Nathaniel Hawthorne, "Rappaccini's Daughter" (1846)*

The only thing standing in the way of lasting happiness, most of us think, is the inability to get what we want. People often say, "If only I had _____ , I would be much happier." For one person it is "true love," for another "a million dollars," for a third "an appearance in Las Vegas as an Elvis impersonator." Whatever our dreams, we all tend to think that we would be significantly happier if they were to come true.

To achieve lasting happiness, however, it is not enough for our wishes to come true. We also have to know what to wish for. Will an appearance as an Elvis impersonator or a trip to Disney World make us happier? Obviously, we have to know the answer to this question in order to know what to work toward. We have to make correct *affective forecasts*, predictions about our emotional reactions to future events.

Affective forecasts are a crucial form of self-knowledge. Decisions big and small—whom to marry, what job to accept, whether to have children, whether to invest in the Elvis outfit—are based on predictions about how gratifying and pleasurable these events would be. Just as our emotional reactions to current events have a special status and often reach consciousness, so may emotional reactions to future events be an important form of self-knowledge that people achieve much of the time. Most of us know that good health, a million dollars, and a happy marriage would make us happier than chronic pain, poverty, and a messy divorce. It would be difficult to survive in a world in which people had no clue as to what would make them feel good versus bad. Even rats can make accurate affective forecasts, learning to avoid pressing a bar that will have unpleasant results (electric shock) and learning to press the bar that will have pleasant results (yummy rat treats).

Often, however, it is not enough to know what our initial reaction to an event will be. We also need to know how long that reaction will last. Life-altering decisions such as whom to marry and whether to have children are based on the assumption that they will cause enduring happiness and not just a moment's pleasure. But people's affective forecasts often involve a *durability bias,* a tendency to overestimate the duration of reactions to future emotional events. Research on this bias raises questions about the nature of happiness and why external events do not seem to influence it for as long as we think. It does not uncover the secret of how to attain everlasting happiness, but it does suggest a few hints.[1]

The Fleetingness of Emotional Reactions

Suppose that I asked you to imagine the best and worst things that could happen to you in the next week. Common answers to this question are "winning the lottery jackpot" and "the death of a loved one." How long would your emotional reactions to these extreme events last? Most of us would respond by saying, "I would be thrilled for months or even years if I won the lottery" and "I would be devastated forever by the death of a loved one." For many of us, these affective forecasts would be wrong.

MONEY CAN'T BUY ME LOVE—OR HAPPINESS

Imagine that you are one of ten finalists in your state lottery. You and the other finalists are onstage waiting for the name of the winner to be drawn on live television. Beads of sweat form on your brow as the lottery official picks an envelope from a bin. He seems to take forever to open the envelope and unfold the piece of paper. But then he pauses, looks directly at you, and calls out your name. Yes, it has really happened: you have beaten the odds and are a million dollars richer.

How happy do you think you would be at that moment? How happy would you be over the next few months? the next few years? Most of us would guess correctly that it would be thrilling to find out that we were the winner. When Paul McNabb's name was picked as the first million-dollar winner in the Maryland State Lottery, in July 1973, he fell to the floor and mumbled, "Oh my God," over and over. Governor Marvin Mandel had to bend over to hand McNabb the check for his first installment of $50,000. McNabb probably thought he was on easy street and that all his problems were over.

Fast forward to 1993, after McNabb had received the last of his annual $50,000 lottery checks. When interviewed by a reporter from the *Washington Post*, he was smoking generic-brand cigarettes and nursing a free soda at a bar in Las Vegas. He lived in a two-bedroom apartment and did not own a car. When the reporter asked him how he felt about winning the lottery, he laughed and said, "Would I do it all again? Hell, no."

Soon after he appeared on television in 1973, McNabb was besieged by people demanding a share of the winnings. One person threatened his daughters; another broke into his house. "If you had gone through what I went through that first year, you wouldn't have trusted your own mother," he told the reporter. McNabb eventually moved to Nevada to escape the attention, but he did not find lasting happiness there either. "Do you realize I've lost 20 years of social life, of being human? I never got over the point that I always had to be on my guard."[2]

Well, you might think, not everyone knows how to handle money, and there are bound to be people for whom it causes more problems than it solves. If you are like me, you think that you would deal with it just fine, thank you very much. Surely, for us, the opportunities the money opened would far outweigh the hassles. More than likely, we would both be wrong. McNabb's experiences may seem extreme, but they are not at all uncommon. One study found that virtually all the million-dollar winners in New Jersey experienced harassment and threats and that many lived in fear. Most ended up moving to avoid the unending phone calls and unexpected visitors, often to strange neighborhoods where they felt isolated from their friends and family. Salvatore Lenochi, for example, was bombarded with annoying phone calls from strangers, including one from a man who phoned every day demanding money for his invalid wife and himself. Someone threatened Lenochi's children with a knife. Family members became resentful of his good fortune. "Now I have the money and I'm not sure if I wasn't better off before," Lenochi said. A sociologist who interviewed lottery winners summarized it this way: "They have won the battle against poverty and deprivation, but are losing the war; they are financial successes but social and psychological causalities."[3]

If people knew that winning the lottery would not make them any happier, and might even cause substantial misery, they might think twice before plunking down their hard-earned dollars for lottery tickets. And yet state lotteries continue to earn billions of dollars, which is testimony to the conviction so many people have money can, indeed, buy them love (and happiness).

"I'LL NEVER GET OVER IT"

A few years ago, my friend Carolyn's mother died suddenly of a heart attack at the age of fifty-nine. Carolyn was devastated and she said she was sure that she would never get over her grief. And in some ways she was right. Five years later, Carolyn still misses her mother and often feels sad when she thinks about her. But the stomach-gnawing anguish she experienced in the days after her mother's death subsided little by little, more quickly than she expected. Before long, Carolyn was the funny, energetic, outgoing person she always was, who loves to solve difficult problems at work, spend time with her children, and play tennis.

If Carolyn could wave a magic wand and bring her mother back to life, she surely would. Nonetheless, she would be the first to admit that she recovered from her mother's death more quickly than she anticipated. She would also agree that, as tragic as her mother's early death was, good things came out of it, such as becoming closer to her father. After her mother's funeral she taught her father how to use e-mail and now keeps in much closer touch with him, exchanging e-mail several times a week.

Carolyn's experiences are consistent with research that finds that the bereavement process often unfolds in ways people do not anticipate. Many people either are not affected at all by the loss of a loved one or recover surprisingly quickly from intense grief. One study found that 30 percent of parents who lost babies as a result of sudden infant death syndrome never experienced significant depression. Another found that 82 percent of bereaved spouses were doing well two years after the death.[4]

To be sure, many people are devastated by the death of loved ones, especially if the death occurs unexpectedly. One study found that in the week after a spouse dies, the suicide rate increases by 70 times for men and 10 times for women. Another found that four to seven years after losing a spouse or child in a motor vehicle crash, a significant proportion of people were depressed. Thirty-two percent said that they could not "shake off the blues" on at least three to four days in the past week, compared with 11 percent of people who had not lost a spouse or child.[5]

Why do some people recover quickly whereas others do not? One important factor is the extent to which people are able to find some meaning in the loss. People who find meaning, such as believing that the death was God's will, that their loved one had accepted dying, or that death is a natural part of the life cycle, recover more quickly than people who are unable to find any meaning in the loss. Another important factor is the extent to which people find something positive in the experience, such as the belief that they have grown as a person, gained perspective, or, like Carolyn, that the death has brought other family members closer together.

The death of a loved one, for example, can create new opportunities for people to help others. When Candy Lightner's thirteen-year-old daughter was killed by a drunk driver in 1980, she channeled her rage and grief into a national movement to remove drunk drivers from the road, founding Mothers Against Drunk Driving (MADD). In July 1981, six-year-old Adam Walsh was abducted from a shopping mall and brutally murdered. His parents, John and Reve Walsh, became national advocates for missing children and were the driving force behind acts of Congress that established a center for missing children with a computerized database. John Walsh helped establish the television program *America's Most Wanted*, of which he is host. The people who recover the quickest from traumas are those who feel that it led to some good things, such as their ability to help others.[6]

This last finding is particularly interesting from the perspective of people's beliefs about grief before they lose a loved one. Most people imagine that it is a uniformly negative, devastating experience. They might be surprised to learn that most people experience frequent positive emotions after a loss, even if they also feel substantial grief. They might be even more surprised to learn that a loss or trauma might well change them in beneficial ways. I doubt that many of us have ever thought, "It would be terrible if he or she died, but at least I'll become a better person as a result." And yet many of us would. Ronnie Janoff-Bulman has studied victims of several different kinds of trauma, including the death of loved ones, rape, and debilitating injuries. As she puts it, "The victimization certainly would not have been chosen, but it is ultimately seen by many as a powerful, even to some extent worthwhile, teacher of life's most important lessons."[7]

People are surprisingly resilient not only in response to major life events like winning the lottery or losing a loved one, but also to everyday emotional events. One study assessed college students' happiness over a two-year period. Many good and bad things happened to the participants during this time. About a third lost a close family member, more than half broke up with a romantic partner, and more than half gained at least ten pounds. Over 80 percent were involved in a romantic relationship for at least two months, almost everyone made a new close friend, and over a quarter were admitted to graduate school. As important as these events were, they had only temporary effects on people's happiness. As the authors put it, "only recent events matter." This is even more true of adolescents than of adults. One study found that when adolescents were in extremely good or bad moods, it took them only forty-five minutes, on average, to return to their baseline level of happiness. (This finding will come to no surprise to anyone living with a teenager.)[8]

The literatures on lottery winners, bereavement, and reactions to everyday life events all converge to show that people are more resilient than they know. As Adam Smith observed, "The mind of every man, in a longer or shorter time, returns to its natural and usual state of tranquillity. In prosperity, after a certain time, it falls back to that state; in adversity, after a certain time, it rises up to it."[9]

Why Are People So Resilient?

One possible reason for people's resilience is that, as noted by La Rochefoucauld four centuries ago, "Happiness and misery depend as much on temperament as on fortune." There are happy people who see a silver lining in every cloud, and disgruntled people who always see a rain cloud on the horizon. There is indeed evidence that happiness is a personality trait, and a heritable one at that. Monozygotic twins, for example, have fairly similar levels of happiness, even when they have been reared in separate families.[10]

Clearly, though, happy people are sometimes sad, and chronically grumpy people sometimes manage a smile. The fact that happiness is partly heritable does not mean that people are stuck at one level of happiness that never varies. The trick is to explain why people return to their normal level of happiness relatively quickly after they experience events that make them happy or sad. Paul McNabb was ecstatic when he learned he had won a million dollars, but the thrill did not last very long. Why not?

IT'S THE CHASE THAT MATTERS

One possibility is that the pursuit of a goal is as enjoyable as achieving it—if not more so. I often spend months or years collecting data on a research project, analyzing the data, writing an article reporting the results, and sending the article to a psychology journal. It might seem that the crowning moment would be when I get the letter in the mail saying that the article has been accepted for publication. After all, that is the culmination of a great deal of work and is what I've been working toward for all those months. And indeed, I am quite happy to receive such a letter—more so, certainly, than one saying that my article was rejected. But the pleasure does not last very long. I am happiest, I think, when I am making progress toward the goal—when one of my graduate students tells me that our most recent data look great or when I have had a good day of writing. Once the project is completed and the article accepted, my attention turns to the next project.

It is very important in life to have something to work toward, and once we achieve one goal, we shift our sights and work toward a new one. In fact when things are going really well, we achieve a state of "flow" in which we lose our sense of self and time. One composer described the experience of writing music like this: "You are in an ecstatic state to such a point that you feel as though you almost don't exist . . . My hand seems devoid of itself, and I have nothing to do with what is happening. I just sit there watching in a state of awe and wonderment. And the music just flows out by itself." It is not just artists who have these experiences; people can experience flow doing almost anything.[11]

Imagine that you are part of a grand experiment in which you are provided with everything you need. At regular intervals you are given gifts of money, food, love, sex, fame—whatever you want. The only catch is that you can do nothing that increases or decreases the likelihood of obtaining these rewards. In fact, in order to receive the rewards, you have to spend eight hours a day in a room doing nothing—no career to occupy your time, no one to talk to, no books to read, no paintings to paint, no music to compose—in short, nothing to engage you. Even though you can get any reward you want, this would be a hellish life. Compare it to a quite different existence, in which the tangible rewards are modest. You make only enough money to meet your basic needs and have few luxuries. But you get to spend every day absorbed in activities you love.

In such extreme cases few of us would choose the first life over the second. In everyday life, however, I think people sometimes opt for lives more like the first one. I see undergraduates striving for careers that will pay them lots of money but doom them to mind-numbing daily routines (tax law comes to mind, but that might just be me). The second kind of life is that of a struggling artist, a social worker who loves to make a difference in people's lives, or, I suppose, tax attorneys who are really turned on by the latest changes in Roth IRAs. Daily absorption is more important than the paycheck at the end of the month, as long as that paycheck covers our basic needs.

The importance of flow and absorption helps explain why a positive event that people have worked toward—such as the publication of one of my articles—does not cause lasting pleasure: the goal is met, and my thoughts turn to a new problem. The absorption view should predict, however, that the failure to achieve a goal that people have worked toward should cause prolonged sadness, especially if this failure prevents people from becoming absorbed in everyday, pleasurable activities. Although such failures are painful, the distress does not last as long as people think it will. Daniel Gilbert and I, for example, found that assistant professors overestimated the duration of their unhappiness if they failed to achieve tenure at their university, which was a major life goal for many of them.[12]

Further, some important life events would seem to facilitate goal-directed behavior and yet still do not cause lasting happiness. Winning a million dollars allows people to work toward many goals they could not previously pursue, such as traveling, going to law school and studying tax law, or sitting at home and learning to crochet. So why doesn't it make people happier?

SUFFERING BY COMPARISON

A quite different explanation of emotional evanescence is that people's reactions to an event depend on how that event compares with their prior experiences to similar events. According to this view, we constantly compare our experiences with others like it and ask ourselves, "How does it compare?" The first meal we eat at a fancy three-star restaurant is wonderful. But after eating at a lot of fancy restaurants, we change our standard of comparison. A meal at a mere two-star restaurant now doesn't seem that special, because it wasn't as good as the *cassoulet de mer* at Chez Michel. The sad fact is that there may be a cost to extremely pleasurable experiences. They are wonderful when they occur, but they give us a new reference point against which all future experiences are compared, and many of them will suffer by comparison.

One study, for example, compared people who had won from $50,000 to $1 million in the Illinois State Lottery with a control group of non-winners. The winners were no happier than the nonwinners; nor did they say they would be happier in two years. Even worse, the winners reported that they found several everyday activities, such as talking with a friend, watching television, and hearing a funny joke, less pleasurable than nonwinners did. Apparently, life's everyday pleasures paled in comparison with the extreme high of winning a large sum of money.[13]

Surely there is some truth to this notion. My wife and I share a beer at dinner most nights, and I think our standards have risen over the years. One inexpensive brand used to be as good as another; a Blatz or a Falstaff was as good as a Stroh's. Then we spent a sabbatical in Seattle, which is microbrewery heaven. We had a great time sampling all the different brands, and would often choose restaurants on the basis of which beers they served rather than the kind of food they happened to have. Our standard of comparison increased considerably, such that we can no longer enjoy an inexpensive beer with dinner. But, if truth be told, we probably do not enjoy our daily microbrew any more than we used to enjoy a Stroh's, before our standards were raised. What used to be special is now the norm.[14]

A problem with the change-in-standards view, however, is understanding what people use as their comparison point at any given point in time. Sometimes we use our most extreme prior experience as the comparison point. After eating at Chez Michel's, meals at Nick's Diner might never be the same. But sometimes we compartmentalize our experiences and do not compare them with the extremes. A gourmet might have a quite enjoyable meal at Nick's, because he is comparing it with the meal he had yesterday at McDonald's, and not with his meal at Chez Michel in Paris last month.

The choice of a comparison point, and the way in which it influences emotional experiences, is a complex process that is probably determined by such things as how people define a category (e.g., "all meals" versus "meals in Greek diners"), how recent people's experience is in a particular domain (how long ago they ate at Chez Michel), and the amount of experience they have in a particular domain (e.g., one meal or a hundred meals at Chez Michel). For our purposes, the point is that a change in the standard of comparison helps explain why people adapt to life events; the bar is raised, and what was pleasurable (or painful) before seems ordinary now. But it is not the full story.[15]

HAPPINESS IS LIKE BLOOD PRESSURE

Another way to look at emotional evanescence is to compare happiness to physiological systems such as blood pressure. *Allostasis* refers to the process whereby bodily systems react to changes in the environment (as opposed to homeostasis, in which there is a single set point that a system tries to maintain). Blood pressure, for example, has to rise when we get out of bed in the morning, so that there is enough blood flow to the brain to keep us from fainting. When we sit down to read the morning newspaper, it goes down again. There is not a single, ideal level of blood pressure that our body tries to maintain. At the same time, it is obviously not to our benefit for blood pressure to get too low or too high, and there are mechanisms in place to keep it within a limited range.

I believe that an analogous process occurs with human emotions. It is to people's advantage to react emotionally to their environments, such that emotions vary from moment to moment. It is also to people's advantage to have mechanisms in place to keep them away from the emotional extremes.

Think, for example, about the last time you experienced a state of euphoria. Maybe it was the day you were married, the day a child of yours was born, or the day you attained some other life goal, such as being admitted to the college of your choice. You probably felt on top of the world and experienced a wave of pleasure rushing through your body. Your heart was beating rapidly, your blood pressure went up, and you were short of breath.

Now imagine what it would be like to feel this way for an hour, a day, or a week. Sounds exhausting, doesn't it? No one has the stamina to maintain such an extreme emotional state. If our blood pressure and heart rate were elevated for several days, we might well keel over from a heart attack. Surely, there have to be mechanisms in place that prevent our bodies from being that revved up for too long.

Prolonged positive (or negative) emotions might also have psychological costs, making it difficult to concentrate and to notice new emotional information. One function of emotions is to signal people quickly which things in their environments are dangerous and should be avoided and which are positive and should be approached. People have very fast emotional reactions to events that serve as signals, informing them what to do. A problem with prolonged emotional reactions to past events is that it might be more difficult for these signals to get through. If people are still in a state of bliss over yesterday's success, today's dangers and hazards might be more difficult to recognize.

In short, it is not good for us to be depressed or euphoric for long. This state of affairs might seem dismaying, because it implies that there are limits to the happiness any event can bring us. Actually, there is both good news and bad news. The good news is that if humans are programmed to avoid prolonged emotional swings to the positive or negative ends, then there are protective mechanisms that keep us from experiencing prolonged negative states. Sometimes these mechanisms go awry, of course, as evidenced by the incidence of chronic depression. Most people, however, have built-in mechanisms that help them cope with negative life events. The bad news is that these mechanisms might also make it difficult to prolong our pleasurable reactions to positive events. People possess physiological and psychological mechanisms that, basically, rain on their parades.[16]

One such mechanism occurs at the physiological, neurochemical level, in response to internal changes that cause affective responses. According to opponent process theory, physical events that cause extreme affective responses are disruptive, and the body must have some means of restoring equilibrium. It does so by initiating an "opponent process," which produces the opposite affective response. The ingestion of cocaine, for example, triggers negative, opponent processes to neutralize the positive feelings caused by the drug. Touching a hot stove triggers positive, opponent processes to neutralize the resulting pain.

Opponent process theory has become a popular way of accounting for responses to physical stimuli such as drugs. One interesting feature of the theory is the idea that over time, with repeated exposure to a stimulus, the opponent process becomes stronger and longer in duration. A stimulus that initially causes a great deal of pleasure, such as cocaine, causes less and less pleasure over time, because the opponent process it triggers grows in strength.

Opponent process theory helps explain what happens at a physiological level when bodily systems are disrupted, such as neurochemical responses to drug ingestion. It does not deal as well with psychological responses to complex emotional events such as winning a lottery, falling in love, or losing a loved one. In order to explain why the emotions such complex events trigger are often short-lived, we need to examine the kinds of psychological and behavioral responses people have to them.[17]

One type of response is a quite conscious, deliberative one, whereby people take steps to keep their emotions in check. This is obvious when it comes to negative emotions; we don't like to feel bad and often try to improve our moods, such as renting a funny movie. It is less obvious with positive emotions—why would we deliberately spoil a good feeling? Although such cases may be rare, they do exist. Laughing uproariously at a funeral is unlikely to engender goodwill, and people might take steps to lower their mood before entering the funeral parlor (e.g., by thinking sad thoughts). Similarly, if people know they have to concentrate on something, such as working with another person on a task, they purposefully avoid putting themselves in too good a mood.[18]

Thus, there are both physiological processes (the opponent process) and deliberative behavioral strategies that serve to moderate positive and negative emotions. Neither of these processes, however, can account fully for people's amazing resilience to positive and negative life events. I believe an important set of psychological processes has been overlooked, processes that I call making sense through psychological "ordinization."

MAKING SENSE

Imagine that a high school student named Sarah finds out that she has been accepted by the University of Virginia, her first choice of college. When she opens the acceptance letter and reads the words "We are happy to inform you . . . ," she feels a rush of extreme pleasure and excitement, much like Paul McNabb when his name was announced as the million-dollar winner. Soon, however, she finds herself thinking about her acceptance less and less. When it does come to mind, she does not experience the same "ping" of pleasure; indeed, "I will be a UVa student" becomes part of the background of her identity—something that is normal and ordinary, not novel and exciting.

The same kind of psychological ordinization occurs after negative events. When a life-changing negative event occurs, such as the death of a loved one, we can hardly think of anything else. The person dominates our thoughts, and, like my friend Carolyn, we feel like we will never get over the loss. It seems impossible that the person is gone. Consider a character named Francie in a short story by D. Eisenberg, who has just learned that her mother has died: "If you were to break, for example, your hip, there would be the pain, the proof, telling you all the time it was true: *that's then and this is now.* But this thing—each second it had to be true all over again; she was getting hurled against each second. *Now. And now again—twack!* Maybe one of these seconds she'd smash right through and find herself in the clear place where her mother was alive, scowling, criticizing."[19]

We have all had this "twack" experience after major positive and negative life events. We can hardly think about anything else, and when we do, the event suddenly slams back into our consciousness. "No, it can't be! But wait, it is!" (Sudden rush of positive or negative feelings). Little by little, however, the "twacks" diminish, and the event no longer has so much emotional power. How does this happen?

Psychological processes are triggered, I suggest, that transform the events from the extraordinary to the ordinary, in a way that robs them of their emotional power. We weave events into our knowledge of ourselves and the world, in a way that makes the event seem normal, ordinary, even expected. When something happens that is novel or inconsistent with people's expectations about the world, they engage in mental work to come to terms with and explain the new event. If possible, people assimilate it into their current theories and expectations. Doing this often involves a reconstrual of the event to make it seem more understandable and predictable.

Sometimes events are so unexpected and so discrepant from our worldviews that they are very difficult to assimilate. Our loved ones die suddenly, or we discover, after thinking we are terminally ill, that the diagnosis was wrong and we are in good health. When an event is not easily explained by what we know, we alter what we know to accommodate the new event. We change our worldview in ways that make the event seem relatively normal and predictable. To be sure, this can take awhile. When major, life-changing events occur, we experience repeated "twacks," when the event dominates our thoughts. Gradually, however, the twack attacks diminish in frequency and power. Our worldview has changed to accommodate the event, and we do not think about it very often.

There is nothing particularly novel about my description of the processes of assimilation and accommodation. The developmental psychologist Jean Piaget described this process over fifty years ago, to explain how children come to understand their physical and social environments. Many other psychologists have discussed how prone people are to reduce uncertainty, find meaning, and explain novel events—in short, to make sense of their worlds. The emotional consequences of making sense, however, have seldom been discussed. I suggest that once emotional events have been explained, tied into a neat little package, and stored away in our minds, we think about them less, and they lose much of their emotional power. Hence, a fundamental paradox: people try to make sense of novel events so that they can repeat the good ones and avoid the bad ones, but in the process the experiences lose their future hedonic power.

"I KNEW IT ALL ALONG . . ."

One way the human sense maker works is by coming to view an event as more predictable and inevitable after it occurs. Think back, for example, to the impeachment of President Clinton in late 1998 and early 1999. As the events unfolded, whereby the House of Representatives voted to impeach the president and the Senate held a trial to see if he should be removed from office, it was not at all clear what the outcome would be. Some felt that the Senate would vote to convict the president because enough Democrats were so outraged by his behavior that they would cross party lines and vote against him. Others felt that Clinton, like President Nixon before him, would resign before undergoing a humiliating trial in the Senate, or that a trial would be averted by a plea bargain, whereby the Senate would vote to censure the president for his conduct in return for avoiding a trial. Most people believed that even if a trial were held and Clinton was acquitted, his presidency would be crippled and he would find it extremely difficult to govern.

The president was acquitted, and, strangely, the government went on pretty much as it did before—an outcome that few predicted. In retrospect, however, this outcome seems like something we should have expected. Surely few Democrats would vote to convict a president in their own party, especially in the highly partisan atmosphere of the impeachment proceedings. And who could be surprised that such a resilient politician as Bill Clinton would survive the whole process relatively untarnished? Once people know what the outcome of an event is, they construct explanations that make it seem inevitable, much more so than before it occurred, when many other outcomes seemed just as likely. This hindsight bias is not a conscious process. If we knew that we were exaggerating the predictability of an event, it seems unlikely that we would do so. It is not as if people say, "I've explained why Clinton survived the impeachment process relatively unscathed, so now I'll change my view of how predictable I thought this was before the trial." Rather, this change of perspective happens quickly and nonconsciously. And because the event now seems predictable—ho hum, anyone could have seen it coming—it does not seem as novel and exciting, and its emotional power is reduced.

If people's proclivity to make sense of the world spoils the pleasure they experience from novel events, then it follows that those who have difficulty making sense should obtain more long-lasting pleasure. This seems to be a small benefit of the tragedy of Alzheimer's disease. People who suffer from Alzheimer's lose the ability to form new memories and thus cannot explain novel events in any lasting way. Because everything is experienced for the first time, novel pleasures do not fade as quickly as they do for the rest of us.

Alzheimer's keeps things new. After onset, the unfamiliar can never become familiar. The Alzheimer's mind is constantly flooded with new stimuli; everything is always in the moment, a rich, resonant, overwhelming feeling. "I've noticed that I have a large amount of appreciation for whatever I'm focused on," commented [one Alzheimer's sufferer]. "It is very clear and real. Look away and it is gone. Look back and it is fresh and new . . ." Ever-freshness, then, may be considered an Alzheimer's consolation prize.[20]

THE PSYCHOLOGICAL IMMUNE SYSTEM

Although the ordinization process operates on both positive and negative events, serving to keep our emotions within a useful, adaptive range, it works harder to minimize the impact of negative occurrences. We want to get over our setbacks, failures, and disappointments as quickly as possible, and to wallow in our achievements and successes. The paradox is that as much as we want to maintain our reactions to positive events, there are nonconscious processes in place that make us "recover" from them quickly. In contrast, people want to recover from negative events, and there are extra defenses people have to accomplish this.

Some of these defenses are quite conscious and deliberate. All of us have strategies we use to cheer ourselves up when we are feeling blue, such as commiserating with a friend, going to the movies, playing basketball, or seeking solace in a box of chocolates. These strategies often have only short-term effects, however. When we get back from playing basketball or wipe the final smear of chocolate off of our lips, our failures are still staring us in the face.

Fortunately, people also are equipped with powerful psychological defenses that operate offstage, rationalizing, reinterpreting, and distorting negative information in ways that ameliorate its impact. When someone tells us that our hair looks like a poorly trimmed hedge, we assume they are joking and can't be serious. When someone turns us down for a date, we convince ourselves that he or she was not right for us after all. When a journal editor rejects one of our articles for publication, we decide that the editor must have extremely poor judgment. These events hurt when they first occur, but very quickly we find ways of warding off the pain by reinterpreting or rationalizing them. Just as we have a physiological immune system that identifies dangerous foreign bodies and minimizes their impact, so do we have a psychological immune system that identifies threats to our self-esteem and finds ways of neutralizing these threats.

In short, the ordinization process operates on both positive and negative emotions, but the psychological immune system is an extra weapon people use to fight negative emotions. The psychological immune system uses the "feel good" criterion discussed in Chapter 2, namely selecting, interpreting, and evaluating incoming information in ways that maintain our self-esteem. One of the most important lessons from social psychology is that people are masterful spin doctors, rationalizers, and justifiers of threatening information and go to great lengths to maintain a sense of well-being. And the psychological immune system operates largely outside of awareness.[21]

Why Don't People Realize That They Are So Resilient?

Given all the evidence for how resilient people are, it is striking that people don't realize this when predicting their emotional reactions to future events. Daniel Gilbert and I have found evidence for this lack of appreciation of resilience—the durability bias—in numerous studies. In one, college football fans predicted how happy they would be in the days following a victory or loss by their favorite team. They anticipated that the outcome of the game would influence their overall happiness for two to three days, but it did not. By the following day, people were back to their normal level of happiness. In another, assistant professors predicted that the outcome of their tenure decision would have a large impact on their overall happiness for five years after the decision. In fact, professors who had received tenure in the previous five years were not significantly happier than professors who had been denied tenure.[22]

INCORRECT PREDICTIONS ABOUT HOW OUR
INTERNAL WORLDS WILL CHANGE

Why don't people realize how resilient they are? The short answer is that the ordinization process operates out of view, and thus people overlook it when predicting their emotional reactions. People do not take into account how much their internal worlds will change in ways that will make the event seem normal, expected, or even mundane.

In the case of predicting negative events, Daniel Gilbert and I have referred to this lack of knowledge as "immune neglect," because people fail to appreciate how much their psychological immune system will kick into action and rationalize the event. We demonstrated this in a study in which people interviewed for a desirable job and predicted how unhappy they would be if they were turned down. In one condition, they were interviewed by a single, capricious interviewer who asked irrelevant questions, whereas in another they were interviewed by a team of experts who asked quite relevant questions. People predicted they would be equally unhappy in these two conditions if they did not get the job. When told they had not got the job, however, people in the capricious interview condition recovered more quickly. It was easy for them to rationalize their failure by blaming the interviewer and not themselves, but difficult for the others to blame the expert interviewers. The interesting finding from our perspective is that people did not take into account how easy it would be to rationalize when making their predictions; they thought that not getting the job would hurt just as long in both conditions.

INCORRECT PREDICTIONS ABOUT HOW OUR EXTERNAL
WORLDS WILL CHANGE

Another cause of the durability bias is that people fail to take into account the ways in which their external worlds will change after an emotional event. One version of this error is misunderstanding the nature of the event itself. When people imagine what it would be like to win a million dollars, they think about vacations to exotic places and new cars. If they understood that winning the lottery would also entail family feuds, lost friendships, and harassing phone calls in the middle of the night, they would make more accurate predictions about how they would feel. Psychologists refer to this as the misconstrual problem: people make inaccurate predictions about their reactions to emotional events because they are thinking about the event in the wrong way.[23]

But there are times when people know exactly what an event will entail and still commit the durability bias, such as in the failure-to-get-the-job and football studies mentioned earlier. The misconstrual problem cannot explain these examples, because there were no unexpected consequences of the events that people failed to anticipate. College football fans have lived through many games and can probably anticipate pretty well what will happen when their team wins or loses another one. They still overestimate the duration of their emotional reactions, however, because they forget to take into account the fact that as time goes by, many other events will influence their thoughts and feelings. People tend to think about a future event as occurring in a vacuum, without reminding themselves that their life will be full of other activities that will compete for their attention and influence their happiness—a tendency that we have called *focalism*.[24]

People are not clairvoyant, of course, and cannot know with certainty what the future will bring. The point is that whatever happens after the event will compete for people's attention, regardless of whether these events are unpredictable (our long-lost cousin shows up on the doorstep and asks to stay with us for a month) or predictable (we go to work, attend meetings, come home, play with our kids). By forgetting this fact, and viewing the future in a vacuum, people overestimate how long the event will influence their happiness. The philosopher Wladyslaw Tatarkiewicz put it like this: "The pleasures and pains, joys and sufferings, which people actually experience, often fall short of what they had anticipated . . . In anticipating a coming event we have it alone in mind, and make no provision for other occurrences."[25]

If so, then it should be possible to reduce the durability bias by asking people to think about the many other events that will occur in the future. This is what we found in the study of college football fans. As mentioned earlier, we found the standard durability bias, whereby people predicted that the outcome of the game would influence their overall happiness for longer than it actually did. Another group first took part in what they thought was an unrelated study, in which they were asked to describe in detail what they would be doing on a randomly chosen day in the future, such as how much time they would spend going to class, socializing with friends, studying, and so on. Then these students took part in the study in which they predicted how happy they would be after a future football victory or loss.

Reminding people that the football game would not occur in a vacuum, and that the subsequent days would be filled with many events that would compete for their attention, succeeded in reducing the durability bias. The people who first completed the prospective "diary" predicted that they would think less about the football game than did the other participants, and that the outcome of the game would have less of an impact on their overall happiness.

Why people overestimate the duration of their emotional reactions to future events is now clear. First, they fail to take into account the extent to which external events will influence their thoughts and feelings (the focalism bias). Perhaps more importantly, they also fail to anticipate how quickly novel events will come to seem mundane through the psychological process of ordinization. This is especially difficult to do because at the time people make their predictions, the event *is* novel and powerful. When people imagine winning the lottery, a death in the family, or even the purchase of a new car or television, they are thinking about out-of-the-ordinary, emotion-producing events. Even if they know in the abstract that they will "normalize" these events over time, it is difficult to ignore how novel and attention-grabbing they seem now.

The portrait I have drawn of self-knowledge has not been very encouraging. People have limited access to their own personalities, the reasons for their responses, their own feelings, and how they will feel in the future. Is there hope for improvement? What strategies work the best? Is it always wise to improve self-insight, or is a little self-delusion a good thing?

8

Introspection and Self-Narratives

> Of all studies, the one he would rather have avoided was that of his own mind. He knew no tragedy so heartrending as introspection.
>
> —*Henry Adams, The Education of Henry Adams (1918)*

There is a lot about ourselves that is difficult to know, such as our nonconscious preferences, personality traits, goals, and feelings. How might people gain insight into the hidden corners of their minds? What better place to start than with introspection, which many of us assume opens an inner path that, if followed carefully, leads to important self-insights. Introspection can be quite useful, but not always in the way that most people think.

"Introspection" is a very broad term, covering many different ways of examining the contents of one's own mind. It can involve brief, off-the-cuff attempts to figure out how we feel about something ("Do I really want the trout amandine or would I rather have a hamburger?") and decades-long self-analyses recorded in lengthy journals. The object of the search varies widely; people can try to decipher their feelings, motives, traits, or values, not to mention what they want for dinner. Usually it is a solitary exercise, but it can be done with a guide such as a psychotherapist.

It might seem pointless to lump together such radically

different kinds of introspection. What do insight therapies have in common with idle thoughts about menu preferences? Actually, I believe that different forms of introspection have a lot in common, even when viewed through the lenses of such diverse approaches as psychoanalysis, postmodern conceptions of the self, and social psychological research on self-contemplation.

Flashlights, Archaeological Digs, and Self-Narratives

Introspection is often thought of as a flashlight that illuminates thoughts and feelings that were not previously the object of a person's conscious attention. The mind can be thought of as a cave, with consciousness constituting those objects that are currently in the beam of the flashlight. Anything in the cave can become conscious simply by pointing the light in the right direction. According to this view, there are no thoughts or feelings that are buried so deeply that they cannot be illuminated.

This approach is similar to part of Freud's topographical model of the mind, namely the preconscious and conscious chambers. People have many ideas and feelings that are not repressed, but do not happen to be the current focus of attention. These are the contents of the preconscious, which according to Freud can "succeed in attracting the eye of consciousness." The conscious self need only point the flashlight in the right direction to bring a particular thought or feeling into consciousness, such as "the name of my hometown is _____" or "Oglethorp is a curious name."[1]

The flashlight metaphor also captures the case of unnoticed feelings. Sometimes people's feelings change before they are consciously aware that they have, such as William Carpenter's example of "the growing up of a powerful attachment between individuals of opposite sexes, without either being aware of the fact." Feelings may have popped up in the darkness like mushrooms. With a little introspection, however, the flashlight can find them.

But the flashlight metaphor goes only so far, because not everything in the cave can be so easily illuminated. The case of unnoticed feelings, for example, may be the exception rather than the rule. Although feelings are the one output of the adaptive unconscious that is likely to reach consciousness, sometimes even feelings are unconscious. And other contents of the adaptive unconscious, such as personality traits and goals, are likely to remain beneath the surface, unavailable to conscious scrutiny (the beam of the flashlight).

Freud, of course, recognized this limitation, which is why the unconscious was the biggest chamber in the topographical model. As a collector of antiquities, Freud was fond of the metaphor of psychoanalysis as an archaeological dig, whereby clues to the past are buried under many mental strata. With great difficulty the clues can be excavated one by one, and put together to reveal the nature of the person's unconscious drives and feelings.

An important part of the archaeology metaphor is the idea that what is unconscious can be made conscious. It is much more difficult than simply pointing the beam of a flashlight, for two reasons. Unconscious thoughts and feelings are often quite old, dating back to early childhood, and thus considerable excavation is necessary. Second, there are active forces attempting to prevent the dig from taking place (i.e., repression and resistance), which is why it is very difficult to perform a self-analysis, unaided by a trained therapist. The chief differences between the archaeology and flashlight metaphors are thus the location of hidden thoughts (in the unconscious or preconscious) and the difficulty of uncovering them. These metaphors share, however, the idea that there are truths that can be uncovered through introspection. As the psychoanalyst Donald Spence put it,

Freud had a fondness for thinking of himself as a kind of archeologist, believing that in the process of psychoanalysis he was always uncovering pieces of the past. If the patient is assumed, by virtue of his free-associating stance, to have privileged access to the past, and if the story we hear is assumed to be the same as the story he is telling, then it is tempting to conclude that we are hearing a piece of history, an account of "the way things were."[2]

What if introspection is an altogether different kind of activity from pointing a flashlight or going on an archaeological dig? The adaptive unconscious is a pervasive yet hidden engine humming beneath the surface of the mind, and there is no engine hatch that we can open to take a direct look at its operation. Just as we cannot observe the workings of our perceptual system—how binocular vision works, say—we cannot observe directly our nonconscious traits and motives. Although it may feel as though we are discovering important truths about ourselves when we introspect, we are not gaining direct access to the adaptive unconscious. Introspection is more like literary criticism in which we are the text to be understood. Just as there is no single truth that lies within a literary text, but many truths, so are there many truths about a person that can be constructed.[3]

The analogy I favor is introspection as a personal narrative, whereby people construct stories about their lives, much as a biographer would. We weave what we can observe (our conscious thoughts, feelings, and memories, our own behavior, the reactions of other people to us) into a story that, with luck, captures at least a part what we cannot observe (our nonconscious personality traits, goals, and feelings).[4]

One version of the narrative viewpoint is perfectly compatible with the archaeology metaphor: people can excavate many things about themselves through introspection, which they then weave into a story. Any archaeological dig is incomplete; one can never uncover all there is to know about the past. There has to be some means of filling in the blanks and figuring out what all the artifacts mean, and that is where the narrative comes in. According to this view, introspection is a pipeline to people's true feelings and motives, but the "raw data" still must be combined into a coherent self-story, of which there might be several versions. This view is not incompatible with Freud's approach to psychotherapy, particularly as expressed in his later writings. The process of free association and interpretation is not just an uncovering of the client's true past, but a construction of a narrative that provides a healthy, coherent explanation of the client's life.[5]

But we need to be more radical. Introspection itself involves the construction of a story; many of the facts for the biography must be inferred, rather than directly observed. Construction occurs at all levels, from off-the-cuff introspections about one's motives to long-term psychotherapy. Introspection is best thought of not as illumination or archaeology but as writing a self-biography, with limited source information.

The flashlight metaphor works well when it comes to illuminating the contents of consciousness; I may not be thinking of my dentist's name right now or how I feel about root canals, but with a little introspection I can bring these thoughts and feelings to mind. No amount of introspection, however, can illuminate the contents of the adaptive unconscious, no matter how hard I try. Trying to access unconscious goals and motives results not in a direct pipeline to these states, but in a constructive process whereby the conscious self infers the nature of these states.[6]

In a short story by Julian Barnes, for example, Anders Bodén travels by steamboat every two weeks to inspect the seasoning sheds of his sawmill. By chance, the wife of the town pharmacist, Barbro, makes the same biweekly trip to visit her sister, and the two discover that they enjoy each other's company as they stand at the rail of the ship watching the forest go by.

One might think that Anders would know exactly how he feels about Barbro through simple introspection whereby he attends closely to his feelings. The yearnings of the adaptive unconscious are not always so easy to discern, however, and Anders has to construct how he feels. Prior to their meetings he has never taken much note of Barbro, and at first he finds her a pleasant traveling companion who is attentive to his stories about the history of the sites they pass, but nothing more. It is only when Anders' wife accuses him of having an affair with Barbro (town gossip has reached her about the meetings on the steamboat) that Anders wonders if he feels something more deeply:

> Anders Bodén lined up the insults he had received from his wife and stacked them as neatly as any woodpile. If this is what she is capable of believing, he thought, then this is what is capable of happening . . . Of

course, now I see: the fact is I have been in love with her since we first met on the steamboat. I would not have come to it so soon if Gertrud had not helped me there.[7]

Anders' self-narrative takes a crucial turn because of his wife's suspicions, not because he succeeded, through introspection, in discerning a previously unnoticed set of feelings. He *infers* that he loves Barbro, and this inference becomes a central part of his narrative. Barbro, too, decides that she loves Anders, but their meetings end when Barbro's sister moves away and she no longer has a reason to take the steamboat trip. Their lives go on, and the two rarely see each other. The tragedy of the story is that as the years pass, the would-be lovers embellish and cherish their private narratives about their love for the other, only to see these narratives collapse when they finally try to act on them in a fateful meeting. It turns out that Anders and Barbro really did not know each other very well and that, like an anaerobic organism that has adapted to a lack of oxygen, their private narratives about their love for each other cannot withstand the fresh air of an actual meeting.

Like Anders and Barbro, is it possible that people can introspect too much, to the point at which they construct a false picture of their feelings? Do some kinds of introspection result in better stories than others?

Everyday Introspection

A few years ago some friends of mine, both research psychologists, moved to a new city and began looking for a house. They took a rather unusual approach to their house hunt. First, they made a list of all the attributes of a house they cared about, such as the neighborhood, school district, number of rooms, layout of the kitchen, and so on. The list was quite exhaustive, taking up several pages. Then, when they visited houses with their real estate agent, they took out a copy of the list and rated each house on every attribute. They used the familiar tool of the social psychologist, the 7-point scale. Is the kitchen in this house a 5 or a 6 on the scale? What about the broom closet? After seeing several houses, my friends figured, they would have a good way of quantifying and remembering how they had felt about each one. They could simply compute the average rating of each house and know which one to buy.

Contrast this to the way my real estate agent determines the kind of house her clients want. When she meets with her clients for the first time, she listens patiently as they describe their preferences, nodding her head sympathetically. Many people, like my psychologist friends, go into exhaustive detail. Then, my agent ignores everything the clients just said. She takes them to a wide variety of houses—some modern, some old; some with large yards, some with small; some in town, some in the country—even if the clients have just told her that they would never consider houses in some of these categories.

On the initial visits, the agent pays close attention to her clients' emotional reactions as they walk through the houses, trying to *deduce* what they are really looking for. Often, she says, she determines that people like something quite different from what they have described. One couple said they had to have an older house with charm and would not even consider a newer house. My agent noticed, however, that the couple perked up and seemed happiest when she took them to modern houses. The couple eventually bought a house in a new development outside of town, rather than the older house in the city they said they had always wanted. My agent's wisdom is shared by other real estate professionals, so much so that there is a common saying in the business: "Buyers Lie."

Buyers, of course, do not deliberately misrepresent what they want. Rather, they may not be fully aware of their preferences or have difficulty articulating them. One reason my real estate agent is so successful is that she is quite skilled at inferring what her clients want and often knows their preferences better than the clients themselves do.

Is there a way that people can introspect more carefully about these nonconscious states in order to figure them out? A lot of time would be saved if people could articulate their preferences exactly. Real estate agents would not have to drive clients around to different kinds of houses and figure out what they really wanted.

Perhaps my psychologist friends are onto something. If people approached their preferences more carefully and analytically, using 7-point scales to rate every attribute of a new house or car or potential mate, maybe they could determine better what they really liked. This strategy has been recommended by many very smart people, such as Benjamin Franklin, in a letter to the scientist Joseph Priestley:

> My way is to divide half a sheet of paper by a line into two columns, writing over the one Pro, and over the other Con. Then, during three or four days of consideration, I put down under the different heads short hints of the different motives, that at different times occur to me, for or against each measure . . . When each [reason] is thus considered, separately and comparatively, and the whole lies before me, I think I can judge better, and am less likely to make a rash step.[8]

Other people have suggested that the analytic "pluses and minuses" approach is not very useful. Even worse, as the writer Mario Vargas Llosa discovered when he was a judge at the Berlin film festival, it might actually obscure how one really feels:

> I went to every screening with a fresh pack of notecards that I would dutifully cover with my impressions of each and every film. The result, of course, was that the movies ceased to be fun and turned into problems, a struggle against time, darkness and my own esthetic emotions, which these autopsies confused. I was so worried about evaluating every aspect of every film that my entire system of values went into shock, and I quickly realized that I could no longer easily tell what I liked or didn't or why.[9]

A well-known social psychologist had a similar experience when trying to decide whether to accept a job offer from another university. It was a difficult decision, because there were many attractive features of both her current position and the new one—as well as some minuses. One of her colleagues, Irving Janis, had written a book advising people to complete detailed "balance sheets," listing the pros and cons of each alternative (much as Benjamin Franklin recommended), so she decided to give it a try. Here is her report of what happened: "I get half way through my Irv Janis balance sheet and say, 'Oh hell, it's not coming out right! Have to find a way to get some pluses over on the other side.'"[10]

And finally, I should report on what happened to my psychologist friends who carried their exhaustive list of 7-point scales to every house they visited. After dutifully filling out the scales for a few houses, they found that they were even more confused than before about which houses they liked and why. "We finally threw away the list," they said, "and went with our gut feelings about which house we liked the best." They bought a lovely house in which they have been living happily for the past fifteen years. Perhaps introspection is not always fruitful, and may even mislead people about how they feel. As the poet Theodore Roethke put it, "Self-contemplation is a curse / That makes an old confusion worse."[11]

Does this mean that introspection is a useless exercise that is best avoided? that we should advise against all navel-gazing, tell insight therapists to take down their shingles, and recommend that people focus on anything but themselves? It would be odd for a psychologist to tell people never to think about themselves, and this is not my message. The key is to understand that introspection does not open magic doors to the unconscious, but is a process of construction and inference. Once this is understood, the question becomes when this process of construction is likely to be helpful and when it is not.

OURS IS NOT TO REASON WHY

Consider what happens when people engage in the Franklinesque type of introspection, whereby they analyze the reasons for their preferences. Sometimes people do this formally, as Franklin suggested, by making lists of the pluses and minuses of the alternatives. At other times they do it less formally, such as when they think, "Why do I feel the way I do about this person I'm dating, anyway?" My colleagues and I have investigated what happens when people introspect in this manner. We typically ask people to spend about ten minutes writing down their reasons for a particular feeling. We tell them that the purpose of this exercise is to organize their thoughts and that no one will read what they write, and then see what effect this introspection has on their subsequent attitudes.

We have asked people to analyze a wide range of attitudes, including their feelings toward someone they have just met, romantic partners, political candidates, social issues, consumer products, works of art, and college courses. We have been struck by the fact that people have no difficulty in coming up with a list of reasons for their feelings. Almost never has anyone said, "Sorry, I just don't know why I feel the way I do." Instead, people freely and readily write quite detailed reasons for their feelings.

The accuracy of people's reasons, however, is suspect. People are not always wrong—if they say they love their romantic partner because he is extremely kind, or because he has a great sense of humor, they might be right. People do not have access to all the determinants of their feelings, however, and their reasons are often a function of cultural or personal theories that can be wrong or, at best, incomplete. In the panty-hose study discussed in Chapter 5, for example, people did not recognize that the order in which they examined four pairs of panty hose helped determine which one they liked the best. Instead, people constructed stories to explain their feelings, and these stories were often incorrect. As Immanuel Kant put it, "We can never, even by the strictest examination, get completely behind the secret springs of action."[12]

If people recognized that their explanations were sometimes inaccurate, there would be no danger in making a list of the reasons why they felt the way they did. "I'll do the best I can," they might say, "but keep in mind that my list is undoubtedly incomplete and that some of the things I put down are probably wrong. Hey, I took psychology in college, Doc." As seen in Chapter 5, however, there is an illusion of authenticity such that the reasons people give feel more accurate than they are.

Because people have too much faith in their explanations, they come to believe that their feelings match the reasons they list. If they generate several reasons why their dating partner is pretty unexciting ("He has really nice taste in upholstery"), they infer that they are not all that in love—even if they were in love before. In other words, they construct a story about how they feel that is based on reasons that are not entirely trustworthy. The story has the ring of truth to people, but because they have used faulty information (reasons that happened to be on their minds), it often misrepresents how they really feel.

We have found evidence of just this sequence of events. For example, Dolores Kraft and I asked college students involved in dating relationships to write down, privately and anonymously, why their relationship was going the way it was, and then to rate how happy they were with their relationship. Compared to people in a control condition who did not analyze reasons, these students tended to change their attitudes toward their relationship. Some became happier with it, some less happy.

Why? First, we assumed that people did not know exactly why they felt the way they did. It is not as if people can say with any accuracy, "Okay, here are my reasons: her basic integrity and kindness account for 43 percent of my love, her sense of humor 16 percent, her political views 12 percent, that endearing way she brushes the hair out of her eyes 2 percent, and the rest is pheromones." Instead, people brought to mind reasons that conformed to their cultural and personal theories about why people love others and that happened to be on their minds ("I was just looking at the paisley pattern on his couch and thinking about what a great decorator he is"). Because there is a certain arbitrariness to these reasons, they often do not match people's prior feelings perfectly. In fact the reasons people gave bore almost no relationship to how happy they said they were with their relationship a few weeks earlier. But because people do not recognize this fact, they assume that their reasons are an accurate reflection of their feelings, leading to attitude change. In short, people construct a new story about their feelings based on the reasons that happen to come to mind.[13]

This is what seems to have happened to Proust's Marcel in *Remembrance of Things Past*. As seen in Chapter 1, Marcel becomes convinced that he no longer loves Albertine, after analyzing and introspecting about his feelings: "As I compared the mediocrity of the pleasures that

Albertine afforded me with the richness of the desires which she prevented me from realizing . . . [I] concluded that I did not wish to see her again, that I no longer loved her."

I should point out that analyzing reasons does not always lead to attitude change in a negative direction. In our study of dating couples, not all people who listed reasons became more negative toward their relationship. Rather, the direction of the attitude change depended on the nature of the reasons that happened to come to each person's mind. People who found it easiest to think of positive reasons ("He's a great friend and easy to talk to") changed their attitude in a positive direction, whereas those who thought of lukewarm or negative reasons ("He has a fine fashion sense, though it would be nice if he didn't wear that pink shirt quite so often") changed in a negative direction. Marcel found it easiest to think of negative aspects of his relationship with Albertine, and thus concluded that he no longer loved her.

If Benjamin Franklin picked up a psychology journal and read about these findings, he might respond, "Just as I thought—when people step back and think about the pros and cons, they come up with a better-informed, more reasoned point of view. After people analyze reasons, their attitude is superior to the quick, possibly rash judgments they would have otherwise made."

The story people construct on the basis of their reasons analysis, however, can misrepresent how they really feel. Such was the case with Marcel, who discovers, only after learning that Albertine has left him, how wrong he was about his overanalyzed feelings. We have found that the feelings people report after analyzing reasons are often incorrect, in the sense that they lead to decisions that people later regret, do not predict their later behavior very well, and correspond poorly with the opinion of experts.

For example, in another study we compared people who were asked to list reasons about why their relationship was going the way it was with people who did not list reasons. Whose feelings did the best job of predicting the longevity of the relationship? It was the latter group, who did not analyze reasons. This is consistent with the notion that when people analyzed reasons, they constructed stories based on faulty data, such as which aspects of the relationship were easiest to put into words, were on their minds, or were consistent with their theories about how they should feel, leading to attitudes that were less well informed than those of people in the control group, who just gave their unanalyzed, gut feelings. As Goethe put it, "He who deliberates lengthily will not always choose the best."

A study of people's attitudes toward works of art tested Goethe's hunch. Some people analyzed exactly why they liked or disliked five art posters and some did not. Then, all participants chose one of the posters to take home. Two weeks later, we called people up and asked them how happy they were with the poster they had chosen. Benjamin Franklin might predict that the people who analyzed their reasons would make the best choices, by carefully laying out the pros and cons of each option. We found the opposite: the people who did not list reasons, and presumably based their choices on their unanalyzed gut feelings, were happier with their posters than were the people who had listed reasons. Like Mario Vargas Llosa, who found it difficult to tell how he felt about the films when he analyzed each one, the students in the reasons analysis group seemed to lose sight of which poster they really liked the best.[14]

A few years ago I was interviewed by a reporter about this line of research. After we chatted for a while the reporter said she had one final question: "So, Dr. Wilson, I gather you are saying that people should never think about why they feel the way they do and should simply act on their first impulses?" I was horrified and had images of people following the reporter's conclusions about my research, leading to increases in teen pregnancy, drug relapses, and fistfights.

It is important to distinguish between informed and uninformed gut feelings. We should gather as much information as possible, to allow our adaptive unconscious to make a stable, informed evaluation rather than an ill-informed one. Most of us would agree that it would not be wise to marry the first person we are attracted to. If we spend a lot of time with someone and get to know him or her very well, and still have a very positive gut feeling, that is a good sign.

The trick is to gather enough information to develop an informed gut feeling and then not analyze that feeling too much. There is a great deal of information we need in order to know whether someone would make a good partner, much of it processed by our adaptive unconscious. The point is that we should not analyze the information in an overly deliberate, conscious manner, constantly making explicit lists of pluses and minuses. We should let our adaptive unconscious do the job of forming reliable feelings and then trust those feelings, even if we cannot explain them entirely.

IS IT ALWAYS SO BAD TO THINK ABOUT REASONS?

Another thing I told the reporter is that there are some exceptions to the danger of analyzing reasons, which follow from our explanation of why it can be harmful. As we have seen, people often change their minds about how they feel because the reasons they think of do not match their prior feelings very well. There is a group of people for whom this is not true, namely people who are quite knowledgeable about the topic they are analyzing. In the study with the art posters, for example, people who knew a lot about art—those who had taken high school and college art courses—tended to list reasons that matched their prior feelings well. Consequently, the act of listing reasons did not lead to any attitude change in this group. It was the unknowledgeable people who were most likely to bring to mind reasons that conflicted with their initial feelings, causing them to revise their stories about how they felt. Contrary to Benjamin Franklin's advice, the knowledgeable people in our studies do not seem to gain anything by analyzing reasons. The art experts did not like the posters they chose more than unknowledgeable people, but neither did they like them more.

But surely, you might argue, we have not done a fair test of the kind of introspection Franklin recommended. He suggested that people write down pros and cons "during three or four days consideration," whereas in our studies people typically write about reasons only once for ten minutes or so. Might people better decipher their feelings with a longer self-analysis? To find out, Dolores Kraft and I asked the people in our dating couples study to come back to our lab and analyze reasons again, once a week for four weeks. We found that a fair amount of attitude change occurred the first time people analyzed reasons (as discussed earlier), and then people tended to stick to this new attitude when they came back and analyzed reasons again. There did not seem to be any advantage to analyzing reasons more than once; rather, people brought to mind reasons that conflicted with their initial attitude, changed their attitudes to match those reasons, and then stuck to that new attitude.

It is possible, of course, that people would have benefited from an even longer reasons analysis or from one that was not spread out over so much time. My hunch, though, is that if people are not very knowledgeable about the topic they are analyzing, it is an exercise best avoided—at least in the way we have studied it, whereby people sit down by themselves and think about why they feel the way they do.

RECOGNIZING GUT FEELINGS

Suppose you take my advice and let your adaptive unconscious develop feelings about somebody or something, and avoid the kind of introspection in which you try to put into words exactly why you feel the way they do. What if you are still not certain how you feel? Sometimes people have mistaken beliefs about the nature of their feelings, particularly when their feelings conflict with cultural feeling rules ("people love their ponies," "my wedding day will be the happiest time of my life"), personal standards ("I am not prejudiced at all toward African Americans"), or conscious theories ("I must love him because he conforms to my idea of Mr. Right"). Is there a kind of introspection by which you can gain access to feelings that are hidden in this manner?

Introspection should not be viewed as a process whereby people open the door to a hidden room, giving them direct access to something they could not see before. The trick is to allow the feelings to surface and to see them through the haze of one's theories and expectations.

A recent study by Oliver Schultheiss and Joachim Brunstein suggests one way people might accomplish this. They measured people's implicit motives, using the Thematic Apperception Test technique described in

Chapter 4, whereby people make up stories about a set of standard pictures and these stories are coded for how people express motives such as the need for affiliation or power. They then told participants that they would play the role of a therapist who would use directive techniques to counsel a client. Because people were instructed to be directive and keep control of the situation, and to focus on ways of helping the client, those who were high in both the need for power and the need for affiliation were expected to react especially positively.

The question is, did people know that this was a situation that was well suited or not well suited to their implicit motives? The answer was no when the researchers simply described the counseling situation to participants, and then asked them how they would feel. Consistent with many studies that find that people are not very aware of their implicit motives, people who were high in the need for affiliation and power did not anticipate that the counseling session would make them any happier or feel more engaged than other participants.

In another condition, however, people first underwent a goal imagery procedure whereby they listened to a detailed, tape recorded description of the counseling session and imagined how they would be likely to feel in that situation. Under these circumstances people high in the need for affiliation and power were more likely to recognize that the situation would be one that they would enjoy, and they reported that they would be much happier and more engaged in that situation than other participants did.[15]

Thus, hearing a detailed, image-laden description of the situation was sufficient to trigger feelings generated by people's implicit motives, and people were able to pay attention to these feelings and use them to predict how they would feel in the real situation. I would not call this "introspection" as normally defined, because people were not opening doors to hidden rooms in order to see feelings of which they were unaware. Instead, they were able to imagine a future situation well enough that the feelings it would invoke were actually experienced, and were able to avoid the kinds of introspection we have studied (analyzing reasons) that might obscure how they would really feel.

It remains to be seen how well people can use this technique in everyday life. The suggestion, at least, is that if people took the time to imagine future situations in great detail (e.g., "How would I feel if my housekeeper rushed in with the news that Albertine has left me?"), they might be better able to recognize the feelings generated by their adaptive unconscious, and to see through the smoke screen created by analyzing reasons or by the adoption of cultural feeling rules and conscious theories. They would have better data on which to base their narrative about their feelings and reactions.

Introspecting about Personal Problems

Although some of the studies on introspection considered so far dealt with topics that were very important to people, such as why a romantic relationship is going the way it is, they are generally not topics that are causing people distress (most of the participants in our studies were reasonably happy with their relationships). Perhaps people are more adept at introspecting about things that have gone wrong in their lives. There are many ways to introspect about one's source of distress, however, some of which are more helpful than others.

RUMINATING WHEN DISTRESSED

One way is to ruminate about a problem, which Susan Nolen-Hoeksema defines as thinking about one's feelings and their causes repetitively without taking action to improve one's situation. In numerous studies, she has found that rumination leads to a negative, self-defeating pattern of thought that makes matters worse, especially when people are depressed or in bad moods to start with. Ruminators are worse at solving problems related to their distress, focus more on negative aspects of their past, explain their behavior in more self-defeating ways, and predict a more negative future for themselves.

In one study, for example, the participants were college students who were either moderately depressed or nondepressed. In the rumination condition, the students were asked to spend eight minutes thinking about their emotions and traits—that is, to try to understand their feelings, why they felt that way, their character, why they turned out the way they did, and who they strived to be. In a distraction condition, the students spent eight minutes thinking about mundane topics unrelated to themselves, such as "clouds forming in the sky" and "the shiny surface of a trumpet." People's moods were measured before and after they completed the rumination or distraction task. Rumination caused depressed participants to become even more depressed, whereas the distraction task made them less depressed. Rumination had little effect on people who were not depressed.

When the depressed students ruminated they focused on the negative side of things, as if their dysphoria was a filter that kept out any positive thoughts. Compared with the other groups—such as the nondepressed students who ruminated and the depressed students who did not ruminate—they brought to mind more negative memories from their pasts (e.g., "Everyone passed the test except me") and felt that negative events in their current lives, such as getting into arguments with their friends, were more common. In another study, people who reported that they often ruminated when they felt depressed were more likely to be depressed a year later, even after their initial levels of depression were controlled for. In short, unhappiness and ruminating about your unhappiness is a bad combination that leads to more depression.[16]

FINDING MEANING THROUGH INTROSPECTION

Imagine that you received these instructions:

> For the next three days, I would like for you to write about your very deepest thoughts and feelings about an extremely important emotional issue that has affected you and your life. In your writing, I'd like you to really let go and explore your very deepest emotions and thoughts. You might tie your topic to your relationships with others, including parents, lovers, friends, or relatives; to your past, your present, or your future; or to who you have been, who you would like to be, or who you are now.[17]

Jamie Pennebaker and his colleagues have given these instructions to hundreds of people, including college students, community members, maximum-security prisoners, people laid off from their jobs, and new mothers. Most people take it quite seriously and write about personal, often deeply troubling incidents, such as the death of a loved one, the end of a relationship, or sexual and physical abuse. Not surprisingly, people find it upsetting to write about such events and, right after doing so, report more distress than do control participants who write about superficial topics (such as their plans for their day).

As time goes by, however, people show remarkable benefits from the writing exercise. Compared with people in the control condition, those who write about emotional experiences report better moods, get better grades in college, miss fewer days of work, show improved immune system functioning, and are less likely to visit physicians. Writing about emotional experiences is distressing in the short run but has quite positive long-term effects.[18]

Why does writing about emotional experiences—often very painful ones—have more beneficial effects than the other kinds of introspection we have discussed? One possibility is that people tend to hide or suppress their negative emotional experiences, and that the stress caused by constant inhibition takes its toll on their mental and physical health. Having the opportunity to express traumatic events might have a cathartic effect, improving people's well-being by removing the stress caused by inhibition. Although inhibition may well cause stress and contribute to health problems, there is no evidence that Pennebaker's writing exercise works by lowering inhibition. For example, people who write about events that they have already discussed with others do as well as people who write about events they have kept secret.

Rather, writing seems to work by helping people make sense of a negative event by constructing a meaningful narrative that explains it. Pennebaker has analyzed the hundreds of pages of writing his participants provided, and found that the people who improved the most were those who began with rather incoherent, disorganized descriptions of their problem and ended with coherent, organized stories that explained the event and gave it meaning.

Why is rumination harmful whereas Pennebaker's writing exercise is beneficial? One key is that people often ruminate when they are depressed, and the depression focuses their attention on negative thoughts and memories, making it difficult to construct a meaningful, adaptive narrative about the problems. Rumination is a repetitive, spiraling kind of thought whereby people can't stop thinking about things in a negative light, like Mr. Dimmesdale in *The Scarlet Letter:* "He kept vigils, likewise, night after night, sometimes in utter darkness; sometimes with a glimmering lamp; and sometimes, viewing his own face in a looking-glass, by the most powerful light which he could throw upon it. He thus typified the constant introspection wherewith he tortured, but could not purify, himself."[19] In contrast, Pennebaker's participants, who are typically not depressed, are able to take a more objective look at their problems and to construct a narrative that helps explain it in a more adaptive manner. In fact, Pennebaker's technique does not work as well right after a severe trauma, when people are too upset to examine their situation objectively.[20]

Constructing a meaningful narrative can also keep people from trying to suppress their thoughts about a distressing topic. If an event has no coherent explanation it is likely to keep coming to mind, leading to further rumination, or possibly to an attempt to push the thoughts away. Deliberate attempts at thought suppression is a losing exercise, as Daniel Wegner and his colleagues found. People may be able to succeed in not thinking about something for a short time, but often thoughts about the unwanted topic come flooding back. Under some circumstances, such as when people are tired or preoccupied, thought suppression backfires, leading to even more thought about the unwanted topic. An event that has been explained and assimilated into one's life story is less likely to keep coming to mind, triggering attempts to suppress it.[21]

The narrative metaphor helps explain all the examples of everyday introspection we have considered. Analyzing reasons focuses people on bad "data," information that is easy to verbalize but may have little to do with true feelings. Consequently, people construct stories about their feelings from faulty information. Rumination and thought suppression can be harmful in at least two ways: they can make it difficult to engage in the construction of a new narrative, because people are preoccupied with uncontrollable, unwanted thoughts; and, to the extent that people do construct new narratives, they can focus people's attention on negative, pejorative thoughts. Pennebaker's writing exercise is the only kind of introspection we have seen so far in which people are able to construct meaningful stories that have beneficial effects.

PSYCHOTHERAPY: THE CONSTRUCTION OF BETTER NARRATIVES

The psychiatrist Anna Fels relates the story of an elderly patient who came to see her, not with the common complaint of being depressed or anxious, but of having difficulty coping with his impending death. He was suffering from terminal cancer and claimed that it was not thoughts of dying that bothered him, but the process of dying itself. The narrative that he had used to explain his normal life no longer applied, and he was struggling with the construction of a new story to explain his final days. "I'm becoming someone else," he said. "But I don't want to endlessly talk about it, particularly with my wife. She's got enough to deal with."

Dr. Fels asked him to tell the story of his illness, beginning with his diagnoses and leading up to the present time. Gradually the man found meaning and coherence in his final challenge: "Over several sessions his story continued, and I think both the patient and I were surprised at how much better he began to feel . . . What were we doing? Surely it was not classic, psychodynamic psychotherapy aimed at insight into unconscious motives and wishes. Nor was I doing the psychological equivalent of hand-holding. Something else was going on."[22]

Part of what was happening, Fels relates, is that the man had become extremely isolated, with no one to speak openly with about his disease. The bond he was able to form with Fels, as he spoke openly of his new life, was extremely comforting. In her words, their sessions "brought him back into the shared social world."

I suspect that there was more to it than forming new social ties, as important as this surely was. By talking freely about his struggles with his disease, the man was able to construct a coherent narrative that made better sense of his new life, much like the people in Pennebaker's studies who benefited from writing about traumatic events. I do not mean to imply that psychotherapy and the Pennebaker writing exercise are interchangeable. It would be absurd to suggest that writing about a trauma by oneself, fifteen minutes at a time for three days, is a substitute for intensive psychotherapy, in which people spend months or years exploring their problems with the help of a trained therapist. For one thing, psychotherapy is an intensely social experience, allowing for the kinds of social bonding that Fels discusses. Nonetheless, psychotherapy and the writing process have an important commonality. In both cases, people succeed in developing new narratives about themselves that are more beneficial than the narratives they held before.

The evidence that psychotherapy works by changing people's narratives can be summarized quite succinctly. First, psychotherapy has been proved to be beneficial in well-controlled studies, but the exact form of psychotherapy does not matter much. This is true even for therapies that, on the face of it, hold fundamentally conflicting views about how to treat psychological problems, such as psychodynamic therapy (with its emphasis on childhood memories, unconscious thoughts and feelings, and insight) and behavior therapy (with its emphasis on current behavior and what maintains it). In a classic study of the treatment of depression, for example, Bruce Sloane and colleagues found that psychodynamic and behavior therapies were equally effective (both were superior to a no-treatment control group).

Second, therapists of all persuasions provide their clients with a new narrative to explain their problems. A key finding in Sloane's study was that the psychodynamic and behavior therapists offered their clients the same number of interpretations about the causes of the clients' problems (albeit quite different interpretations). Finally, clients who adopt the views and interpretations offered by their therapist improve the most in therapy.[23]

In short, psychotherapy seems to be a beneficial process whereby clients adopt a new narrative about their problem that is more helpful than the story they told before, like Fels's patient who was able to find meaning in his struggles with cancer. To be sure, a major revision of one's life narrative can be a difficult journey that requires the guidance of a skilled therapist. There may not be one "true" story that people must adopt to get better, however; there may be a range of healthy narratives.

On what basis can we say that one self-story is healthier than another? Self-stories should be accurate, I believe, in a simple sense: they should capture the nature of the person's nonconscious goals, feelings, and temperaments. But how can people go about constructing stories that correspond to their adaptive unconscious? What kinds of information should they use?

9

Looking Outward to Know Ourselves

O wad some Power the giftie gie us
To see oursels as ithers see us!
It wad frae monie a blunder free us
An foolish notion
    —*Robert Burns, "To a Louse" (1786)*

How *do* people know what story to tell? "Inside information" is not the only source material for self-biographies. There are various kinds of "outside information" that people might use as well—information that, in some cases, might be superior to what people can learn by looking inward.

Knowing Ourselves by Studying Psychological Science

Many people learn about their bodies by reading about medical research, such as studies on the dangers of tobacco, saturated fat, and ultraviolet radiation. Given that we have no direct, privileged access to how our pulmonary or cardiovascular systems work, we are at the mercy of such outside sources of information to inform us about how things like smoking tobacco influence our health. I suggest that the same is true in the psychological realm. People can

183

learn a lot about themselves from reading reports of controlled psychological studies.

It can be quite a leap, of course, to infer something about ourselves from research that reports the mean response of a large group of people, especially if the group is unlike us in important respects. Many of us do not want to think that we are like "the average person." But the same problem exists when we read about medical research. We cannot be certain that we will respond the same way to tobacco or saturated fat as the average person did in a study conducted in Norway, and in fact might prefer to believe that we are not "average" in this respect. In many medical and psychological studies, however, the amount of individual variation is relatively small, such that the findings hold true for most people. In other cases there is a considerable amount of individual variation; for example, some people can smoke cigarettes their entire lives and not get cancer, whereas other smokers get cancer at an early age. But even in these studies, the response of the average person is informative in a probabilistic sense. We cannot be certain that we will get cancer if we smoke, but we know that smoking increases the odds that we will.

By the same token, there is a lot to be learned by reading about psychological research, even if it reports the responses of the average person. I offer two different examples: the extent to which people are influenced by advertising and whether people are prejudiced toward members of minority groups.

ARE YOU INFLUENCED BY ADVERTISING?

Suppose a new kind of television broadcasting is introduced from which all advertising as we know it has been eliminated. Yes, it's really true; you can watch your favorite television programs with absolutely no interruptions. Sounds great, doesn't it? The catch is that advertisements are still present in the form of subliminal messages. Pictures and slogans, such as images of political candidates and the message "Vote for Binkley" are flashed so quickly that you do not consciously see them.

Recognizing that such a drastic change in advertising will be controversial, the networks give you a choice. By pushing a button on your remote control, you can watch programs the old-fashioned way, in which regular, everyday advertisements interrupt the program every fifteen minutes or so, or the new, futuristic way, in which all the ads are broadcast subliminally. Which kind of advertisements would you choose to watch?

When I posed this question to a sample of college students, 74 percent said they would prefer the old-fashioned advertisements. A typical response was "I want to be aware of the choices I make instead of letting other people make the choices for me." Makes sense, doesn't it? Why would we want to let messages enter our minds that could influence us in ways we can't control, without even knowing that we are being influenced? Sounds like an Orwellian nightmare come true.

The only problem is that if people want to avoid being controlled by advertising, then they are making precisely the wrong choice. Subliminal messages have little or no effect on consumer behavior or attitudes when used in ad campaigns, whereas there is considerable evidence that everyday, run-of-the-mill advertising does.

But how could individual consumers possibly know this? By definition they could not know whether they were influenced by subliminal ads, because they would not even know when they had "seen" one. However, it is also difficult to know how much we are influenced by everyday ads we see on television and in the print media, for all the reasons I have discussed. People cannot discover through simple introspection the extent to which seeing an ad for Tylenol influences their purchases the next time they go to the grocery store, just as they cannot easily judge, through introspection, whether smoking cigarettes will give them cancer. It is quite possible that they are being influenced more than they think.

What can we learn from psychological research? Words hidden in movies do not cause people to line up at the concession stand, and subliminal messages in self-help tapes do not (unfortunately!) help us to quit smoking or lose weight. Nor is there any evidence that implanting sexual images in cake icing increases sales, despite popular claims to the contrary.[1]

This is not to say that subliminal messages never have an effect—just that they have not been shown to do so in everyday advertising. Under very carefully controlled laboratory conditions, subliminally presented information can have subtle effects on people's emotions and judgments. We encountered such a case in Chapter 2, in a study by John Bargh and Paula Pietromonaco. The researchers flashed words having to do with certain personality traits on a computer screen at subliminal levels, and found that people used these traits when subsequently interpreting another person's behavior. When the words "hostile," "insult," and "unkind" were flashed, for example, people were more likely to interpret another person's behavior in a negative light than when these words were not flashed—even though people had no awareness of having seen the words. Indeed, studies such as this demonstrate the ability of the adaptive unconscious to guide people's interpretations of the world behind the mental scenes.

Replicating such effects in everyday life, however, in ways that would influence people's consumer behavior has proved very difficult, because the conditions necessary to get subliminal effects in the laboratory are very hard to duplicate in advertisements. The illumination of the room has to be exactly right, people have to be seated just the right distance from the screen, and there can be nothing else competing for their attention. I am unaware of any well-controlled study that succeeded in influencing people's behavior by placing subliminal messages in everyday advertising or audiotapes, despite many efforts to do so.

Maybe clever advertisers will figure out a way of getting subliminal ads to work. Even if they do, however, the effects of their ads are unlikely to be as powerful as everyday ads presented at conscious levels. Despite people's blasé attitude toward ads that they see on television, hear on the radio, and see in the print media, these ads can shape their behavior in powerful ways. Perhaps the best evidence for this comes from studies that use split cable market tests. Advertisers, working in conjunction with cable television companies and grocery stores, show different versions of commercials to randomly selected groups of cable subscribers. The subscribers agree to use a special identification card when they shop, allowing the grocery stores to keep track of exactly what they buy. The advertisers can thus tell whether people who see a particular commercial are in fact more likely to buy the advertised product. The answer is that they often are.[2]

People fear subliminal advertisements (which have no effect) more than everyday advertising (which often has powerful effects) because they worry that they will be influenced without knowing it. But ironically, everyday advertisements are more likely to influence us without our fully recognizing that we are being influenced. It is not as if we go to the drugstore and think, "Should I buy the house brand or Advil? Well, if Advil is good enough for Nolan Ryan, it's good enough for me . . ." Instead, we might find a name brand more comforting or familiar and not realize why we feel that way. So we shell out the extra cash for something that is no different from the house brand. Nor does a teenager say, "I think I'll start smoking because I want to be like the Marlboro man I saw on a billboard." Instead, adolescents learn to associate smoking with independence and rebellion, with little recognition that it was advertising that helped create this association. Even when we consciously see and hear something such as an advertisement, we can be unaware of the way in which it influences us.

I do not mean to portray people as automatons, marching mindlessly to the commands of Madison Avenue. The failure to recognize the power of advertising makes us more susceptible to it, though, because we are likely to lower our guard while watching commercials or fail to avoid them altogether. Consequently, we can be influenced in unwanted ways without being aware that we are being influenced. Nancy Brekke and I termed this "mental contamination," because our minds can unknowingly become "polluted" with information we would rather not have influence us.[3]

Given that many studies find that advertising often influences people in unwanted ways, we might entertain the hypothesis that it has the same effect on us. There is lots of good psychological science out there, and by considering it carefully we might gain insight into our own minds. We can then make more informed decisions, such as whether we should worry more about the word "SEX" in ice cubes or everyday TV ads for painkillers. We would also know which button to push on the remote control, if we ever are given the choice between watching subliminal ads versus regular ads.

By some measures, racial prejudice has decreased dramatically over the past few decades in the United States. As recently as 1945, many states and localities had laws that denied African Americans basic freedoms such as whom they could marry, where they could live, and where they could send their children to school. These laws began to change, notably with the 1954 Supreme Court decision to ban segregation in schools and with the 1964 federal Civil Rights Act. Opinions voiced by Americans in polls have improved over the same period. In 1942 only 2 percent of southerners and 40 percent of northerners believed that blacks and whites should attend the same schools, whereas by 1970 these percentages had increased to 40 percent and 83 percent, respectively. In a 1997 Gallup poll, 93 percent of whites said they would vote for a qualified black candidate for president, compared with 35 percent in 1958. Sixty-one percent said they approved of interracial marriage, compared with 4 percent in 1958.

Though encouraging, these figures belie the fact that racial prejudice persists in the United States and elsewhere throughout the world. In 1989 researchers conducted a sobering study to see if there was still racial discrimination in housing in the United States. In twenty locations throughout the country, accomplices of the researchers met with real estate agents to inquire about buying or renting homes and apartments. The accomplices presented themselves as similarly as possible except for their race; some were white, some were black, and some were Hispanic. In a discouragingly large number of cases, the real estate agents discriminated against their minority clients. They presented them with fewer options than their white clients and were less likely to follow up the meeting with phone calls. The amount of discrimination the minorities encountered was about the same as found in a similar study conducted twelve years earlier, suggesting that there has been little or no reduction in housing discrimination over that period.[4]

It is not hard to find other signs of continuing prejudice. Hate crimes are all too common, such as the brutal 1998 murder of James Byrd Jr. in Jasper, Texas, who was chained to a pickup truck and dragged, simply because he was black. In 1999 four white police officers shot Amadou Diallo forty-one times when he reached for his wallet, mistaking him for a suspect in a rape case. Many believe that the fact that Diallo was black played a role in the officers' readiness to pull the trigger. Although such tragic cases may be rare, blacks continue to experience many forms of discrimination. Approximately half of the African Americans sampled in a 1997 Gallup poll reported that they had experienced discrimination on the basis of their race in the past thirty days, such as while shopping, eating out, or at work.

How can we reconcile the advances that have been made with such stark evidence for lingering bias? To what extent are Americans still prejudiced, and what form does this prejudice take? One possibility is that people are as prejudiced as they ever were, but have learned to hide it better because it has become less culturally acceptable to be openly racist. Although there might be some truth to this, the very fact that cultural norms have changed is a sign of progress. Further, it is not just what people say that has changed. The percentage of people who chose to marry someone of a different race was more than six times higher in 1992 than in 1960. Another possibility is that prejudice has decreased in segments of the American population but persists in a sizable number of people, accounting for the fact that there are still hate crimes, housing discrimination, and bias in the workplace.

A great deal of research in social psychology, however, suggests another possibility: the same person can be both prejudiced and non-prejudiced. A number of researchers have argued that many people abhor prejudice and discrimination and try their best, at a conscious level, to adopt egalitarian attitudes—more so, perhaps, than at any other point in American history. At a more nonconscious, automatic level, however, many of these same people have unknowingly adopted the racist viewpoint that still pervades American culture.

The adaptive unconscious might have learned to respond in prejudiced ways, on the basis of thousands of exposures to racist views in the media or exposure to role models such as one's parents. Some people learn to reject such attitudes at a conscious level, and egalitarian views become a central part of their self-stories. They will act on their conscious, nonprejudiced views when they are monitoring and controlling their behavior, but will act on the more racist disposition of their adaptive unconscious when they are not monitoring or cannot control their actions.

In one study, for example, white college students reported their opinions of an African-American and a white interviewer. The researchers also measured any nonverbal signs of discomfort during the interviews (e.g., the amount of eye contact the students had with each interviewer). The students' opinions were predicted by their conscious beliefs about how prejudiced they were. The less prejudiced people believed themselves to be, the less likely they were to favor the white interviewer over the black interviewer. Their nonverbal reactions, however, told a different story. People's discomfort during the interviews (e.g., the amount of eye contact, how often they blinked) was not related to their conscious beliefs, but was predicted by a measure of their implicit, automatic prejudice (more on how this was measured in a moment). People who were prejudiced at the automatic level exhibited more negative nonverbal behavior toward the black interviewer, even if they were not at all prejudiced at the conscious level.[5]

This research might tell us something about ourselves. How can we know if we are prejudiced toward members of various groups, be they African Americans, Hispanics, Asians, whites, women, men, lesbians, gays, or Rotary Club members? Consciously, we might not be prejudiced at all toward these groups, and if it were not for social psychological research on the topic, that would be all there is to it. But on the basis of the research, we might at least entertain the possibility that we have automatic, habitual prejudiced responses toward members of some of these groups of which we are not fully aware.

How can we measure people's level of implicit prejudice, bypassing their conscious beliefs and desires? Most of the techniques rely on computer presentations that time how long it takes people to respond to words and pictures. In one version, people think they are taking part in a study of how well they can do two things at the same time, namely memorizing faces and responding to the meaning of words. A photograph of a face is flashed on a computer screen for about a third of a second, which is quite fast but long enough for people to see consciously. The face is followed almost immediately by an adjective. People are asked to memorize the face and then press one button if the adjective has a positive meaning (e.g., "likable," "wonderful") and another if it has a negative meaning (e.g., "annoying," "disgusting"). The computer times how long it takes them to respond. *SMILING?* *WHAT KIND OF FACE?*

It just so happens that some of the pictures that are flashed before the words are of white people and some are of black people. The assumption is that if people are prejudiced at an automatic level, then the race of the face will trigger affective reactions that influence the speed with which they can respond to the words. If people have a negative reaction to a black face, for example, it should be easier to press the "bad" key when a negative word appears, because the negative feelings that are already there will facilitate this response. By the same reasoning, the negative feelings should make people take longer to press the "good" key when a positive word appears, given that the bad feelings are inconsistent with the meaning of the words. The opposite pattern of results should occur when a white face is flashed: because the face triggers positive feelings, *NEUTRAL* people should respond relatively quickly to the good words and slowly to the bad words. On the other hand, if people are not prejudiced, then the race of the face should not influence the speed with which they respond to the words.

The pace of this task is very fast, and people cannot control their responses consciously. There is not enough time for people to say, "Oh, that's a black face; even though I feel a little negatively toward it, I should respond quickly to the positive word that just appeared." Moreover, people do not know that this task has anything to do with their attitudes or stereotypes; they think it is a test of how well they can do two things at once. By observing the speed with which people respond to the words, depending on the race of the face that preceded them, researchers can assess the existence of a pattern of automatic, habitual prejudice.

But can such an artificial task conducted in a psychology laboratory really tap deep-seated feelings toward members of other groups? Well, the proof is in the pudding, namely whether responses on this task predict anything of interest. And indeed they do. The study assessing non-verbal discomfort toward an interviewer used a measure of automatic prejudice much like this one, and other studies have similarly found that responses on the computer task predict how people act toward people of different races. In one study, participants who responded in a prejudiced manner on the computer task were more likely to avoid physical contact with a black student, by placing a pen on the table when it was his turn to use it instead of handing it to him.

Do the measures of automatic prejudice predict more important behaviors than eye blinks and pen passing? An intriguing study by Keith Payne suggests that they might. Participants saw a picture of a white or black face on a computer screen, flashed for a fifth of a second. Then a picture of either a hand tool (such as a pair of pliers) or a handgun appeared, and people had half a second to indicate which type of object it was by pressing a button labeled "tool" or "gun." Given how little time people had to respond, they often made errors by pressing the wrong key.

The interesting questions are what kind of mistakes people (who were nonblack college students) made and whether these mistakes were influenced by the race of the face that preceded the object. Payne hypothesized that many people have an automatic association between blacks and violence, which might make them more prone to mistake a tool for a weapon when it was preceded by a black face. This is in fact what happened. People were significantly more likely to press the "weapon" button when they saw a tool preceded by a black face than when they saw a tool preceded by a white face. The extent to which people made this error was not predicted by a standard, paper-and-pencil measure of racial prejudice; it was an automatic association of which people were not fully aware.

This was, of course, only a laboratory study in which people were seated in front of a computer, pressing buttons in response to pictures of faces and objects, not in response to real people. The parallels of the findings to the Amadou Diallo shooting, however, are sobering. When the police officers saw Diallo reach into his pocket for his wallet, they had about the same amount of time as participants in Payne's study to make a critical decision: Did he have a gun? Tragically, they decided he did, when in fact he was unarmed. We will never know if, had Diallo been white, they would have made a different decision. The Payne study, however, suggests that such errors are influenced by the race of the victim.[6]

It is important to remember that the police officers had to act extremely quickly. It is not as if they stood around and thought, "Well, let's see, he's black, so he is probably armed." They didn't have time to think at all, at least not consciously. In fact the police officers might well hold completely egalitarian and nonracist beliefs at the conscious level, and would not have been influenced by Diallo's race if they had had time to think. A number of studies have found that there can be a dissociation between people's automatic attitudes rooted in the adaptive unconscious and their conscious beliefs. The person who believes that he or she holds completely egalitarian views might have deeper, automatic reactions toward minorities that are quite negative. Fooling ones self

Research on automatic prejudice is in its infancy, and we need to discover a lot more about how best to measure it and what it predicts. From the point of view of self-knowledge, though, this research might make us question and, perhaps, monitor better our own beliefs and behavior. In fact we might not have to speculate about whether these findings apply to ourselves as tests of automatic prejudice become more widely available. It is possible to take one version of these tests on the Internet and to receive a score that is, purportedly, an index of your automatic prejudice.[7] Clearly, a lot more research is needed to understand fully what these tests are measuring. Nonetheless there is something to the idea that people can be nonprejudiced at a conscious level while their adaptive unconscious feels otherwise, and we should at least question whether this is true of us.

Before individual tests of nonconscious prejudice and other states are perfected and made widely available, the question remains how people can gain greater access to their own idiosyncratic feelings and traits, and not just the general tendencies of participants in research studies. Are there other forms of "self-outsight" that can inform us more directly about our own nonconscious yearnings and motives?

Seeing Ourselves through the Eyes of Others

I have a friend, Mike, who insists that he is shy, to the surprise of everyone who knows him. He appears to meet people easily and has always had plenty of friends. When he travels, he invariably strikes up a conversation with his fellow passengers. He is a great storyteller and enjoys regaling people at parties with tales of his childhood in New Jersey. He is an engaging college teacher and appears quite comfortable lecturing in front of hundreds of students.

How can Mike possibly think he is shy, when he clearly possesses such great people skills? Maybe Mike experiences anxiety when he is around other people, despite looking so comfortable and relaxed in social settings. Mike's friends can't get inside his skin to see whether he feels nervous and sweaty before each lecture, or whether he has to force himself to be outgoing and gregarious at parties, when he would really rather be home reading a book.

People's friends are, in fact, less likely to see them as shy than people are to see themselves as shy, precisely because people are good at masking the social anxiety they often feel. If you ask Mike, however, he reports—quite honestly—that he does not feel particularly anxious when he teaches or when telling stories at parties, and that he genuinely enjoys being around large groups of people. Why, then, does he claim that he is a shy person?

From what Mike has told me, he was an introverted child. While most of his classmates were running around the playground shouting and yelling, he was likely to be off to the side drawing in the dirt with a stick. He did not have many friends, though he always had one best buddy. He gravitated toward solitary activities such as writing and computer games, avoiding more social ones such as team sports.

Mike outgrew his introversion by the time he was in college. Beginning in high school he had a wide circle of friends and began taking drama classes. It is not uncommon for children to become less introverted as they age; for example, 50 to 60 percent of college students who say they were shy at ages eight to fourteen report that they are no longer shy. This is what seems to have happened to Mike, except for one thing: he never changed his self-theory that he was shy. We have a case of someone who has a self-theory about his personality ("I am shy and introverted") that is at odds with his adaptive unconscious, which has become more extraverted.[8]

We can all probably think of similar cases in which we disagreed with a friend about his or her feelings, motives, or personality traits, and honestly felt that we were right. Parents might feel that their daughter is giving up on herself too easily, and is much more talented at math than she thinks she is. Many of us felt that our friend Susan was not in love with her partner Stephen, even though she sincerely believed she was. In each of these examples, people believe that they feel one way or have a certain disposition (e.g., "I'm shy," "I love Stephen"), but people who know them well disagree. In at least some of these cases, people might be wise to abandon their self-theory and adopt the view that other people have of them, like a Dennis the Menace cartoon in which Dennis asks his mother, "Mom, what do I feel like doing?"

George Cooley labeled this form of self-knowledge the "looking glass self": we see our reflection in other people's eyes, namely how they view our personalities, preferences, and behaviors, and often adopt that reflection—called the *reflected appraisal*—as part of our self-concept. The beauty of this approach is that it avoids many of the pitfalls we have seen with looking inward. We don't have to have any special access to our own feelings or traits; it is self-knowledge by consensus, whereby we adopt the majority opinion of what we are like.[9]

There are many obstacles, however, to recognizing that people see us differently than we see ourselves, and to admitting that they are right and we are wrong. Further, it is not clear that we always *should* base our self-views on what others think, especially if those others do not share our high opinion of ourselves.

HOW WELL DO WE SEE WHAT OTHER PEOPLE THINK ABOUT US?

People have a fairly accurate picture of how others view their personalities (e.g., how sociable, intelligent, and competent they are) and how much other people like them. But this accuracy mostly reflects the fact that we project our self-theories onto other people, and not because we are good at reading what other people really think about us. Suppose that Sarah believes that she is highly intelligent and assumes that other people think so too. She is correct because she is, in fact, intelligent, and this is apparent to other people. Sarah does not have to see her reflection in other people's eyes at all; she is accurate about her reflected appraisals simply because other people agree with her self-theory.

But what happens when people's self-theories and reflected appraisals disagree, as in Mike's case? In order to learn from others, we would first have to recognize that there is a discrepancy, by watching and listening to other people to determine what they really think of us. Lots of studies have shown that this is quite difficult. For one thing, other people often hide their impressions from us, particularly if these impressions are negative. What is there to gain from telling a valued coworker that she has hideous taste in clothes, or that her new haircut makes her look ten years older? If people always said exactly what they think about their friends, they would have fewer friends.

Even when people are giving us signals about what they really think, we often have a hard time seeing them. If Bob believes that he is a great storyteller, he is likely to overlook or misinterpret signs that other people do not agree, such as the fact that Sue keeps looking at her watch during his yarn about his vegetable garden. This is especially true when reading other people correctly would threaten a positive self-theory. Rather than interpreting Sue's behavior as a sign that he is not the raconteur that he thinks he is, Bob is likely to put a positive spin on it ("Sue can't tear herself away from my great story even though she is late for an appointment").

I don't mean to imply that we are completely clueless or delusional about how others view us. Sometimes we are forced to confront other people's views directly, such as when students receive grades from their teachers or employees receive performance evaluations from their bosses. In everyday life it is more difficult to determine what other people think of us, but people sometimes manage to get at least a glimmer. In one study, for example, air force recruits who had gone through six weeks of basic training were asked to rate their own personalities, one another's personalities, and how they thought the other recruits viewed their personalities.

The researchers were particularly interested in how accurate people were in guessing the extent to which their fellow recruits believed they had personality disorders such as narcissism, obsessive-compulsiveness, and dependency. For our purposes, the key question is the extent to which people's reflected appraisals were accurate, after controlling for their self-views. For example, if people thought that most of their peers viewed them as dependent, were they in fact viewed this way by their peers? Importantly, the researchers statistically eliminated people's self-views from this correlation, to eliminate the possibility that people were simply basing their reflected appraisal on their self-views. As noted earlier, people often think, "Well, I think I'm dependent, so others probably do too." By controlling for people's self-views, the researchers examined the accuracy of people's appraisals independently of these self-views.

It turned out that people did recognize, at least to some extent, how they were viewed by others, even if they did not view themselves in this manner. However, the extent of this accuracy was not very impressive; the average correlation between people's guesses about how others felt about them and how they really felt about them was about .20 (where a correlation of 0 would indicate no accuracy, and a correlation of 1 perfect accuracy).[10]

How can we improve our accuracy? Here's an idea: when we send out our holiday cards next December, perhaps we should include a questionnaire that asks our friends to provide a detailed description of what they really think of us, such as how much they like us and how intelligent, kind, honest, sensitive, and athletic they think we are. To ensure honesty, we should provide stamped, self-addressed envelopes in which our friends can return the questionnaire anonymously. But would we really be better off by tabulating the results and revising our self-views accordingly?

SHOULD WE USE OTHERS TO REVISE OUR SELF-THEORIES?

It is not always in our best interests to use others to revise our self-theories, because discovering our friends' true opinions about us might puncture some adaptive illusions. What's the harm in believing that people like us a little more than they actually do? Revising our self-theories in a downward direction ("Okay, so I'm not the most popular person at the dance") might not be particularly useful in leading to self-improvement or changes in behavior that make us happier. In fact people are often better off having an inflated view of how others feel about them. Most people, for example, think that they are more popular, talented, attractive, and intelligent than the average person, which of course can't be true of everyone (except in Garrison Keillor's mythical Lake Wobegon, in which all the children are above average). People who have positive illusions are less likely to be depressed than those who do not, are likely to persist longer at difficult tasks, and are more likely to succeed on difficult tasks.[11]

There are risks, however, in maintaining illusions that are too out of whack. There is a name (and restraining order) for people who refuse to believe that a loved one does not love them in return, and follow that person around relentlessly. People who refuse to believe that they are not suited for a career in medicine are likely to experience a lot of anguish if they continue to do poorly in their premed courses. There are times when it is to our benefit to pay close attention to what others think of us and to consider revising our self-views accordingly, even if this means adopting a more negative view of ourselves.

One such time is when an important life decision is at stake, such as whether to pursue a career in medicine (despite repeatedly failing chemistry). Surely people should not always heed other people's opinions about their career options. There are well-known instances in which people succeeded in spite of the general opinion of others that they never would. Albert Einstein, for example, had an inauspicious beginning to his academic career: at age sixteen he failed an entrance examination to an engineering school. Instead of giving up, he continued his schooling, applied again, and was finally admitted. No one was particularly impressed by his accomplishments at the engineering school; when he graduated in 1900 he failed to receive any job offers. He finally accepted a temporary position as director of the patent office in Bern, Switzerland, where he stayed for seven years. It was there that he wrote his first articles on relativity theory, in his spare time, eventually earning a doctorate from the University of Zurich in 1905.

For every Einstein, however, there are many people who wasted years pursuing careers for which they were ill suited, despite the advice of experts in their area. Unless we are so passionate about a career that we are willing to tolerate failure and frustration, it is often wise to heed the view that experts have of our abilities.

This is especially true if other people have a very discrepant view from our own, which brings us to another case in which we should at least consider adopting other people's viewpoint. Though there is little harm in having a slightly more positive view of our own abilities than other people do, problems can arise when the gap gets large.

Consider an example in which people regularly receive clear feedback about what others think of their abilities, namely college professors who receive end-of-the-semester course evaluations. In my department, as in most, students are asked to rate professors on a number of dimensions (e.g., their overall teaching effectiveness) and to provide detailed comments about what they thought of the course. Most professors have strong beliefs about their strengths and weaknesses in the classroom, and course evaluations are a unique opportunity to see how much other people (their students) agree with these beliefs. Clearly, the feedback would be useful if a professor's beliefs were seriously out of whack. If Professor Jones thinks he is a scintillating lecturer who keeps his students on the edge of their seats for the entire semester, and the students report that going to his class was preferable only to having a root canal, then clearly Jones needs to change both his self-theory and his teaching methods. Such discrepancies are especially likely to occur with new professors who have not received much feedback about their abilities.

After teaching many courses, though, most professors develop a pretty good idea of their teaching strengths and weaknesses. Consistent with the literature on positive illusions, these ideas are probably reasonably accurate, though skewed in an overly positive direction. How useful is it for these professors to examine their evaluations at the end of every semester, realizing that they are not quite as good a teacher as they thought they were? It would be extremely useful if they are teaching a new course or trying a new approach. It might not be all that useful if they have a pretty good idea of their strengths and weaknesses and continue to try to improve. In fact, if professors go into class believing that they are about to wow everyone in the room, their lectures are probably better than if they go in with head down, thinking, "Some of the students would rather be at the dentist."

Or, consider this example. In my forties I began to play in a men's senior baseball league, which is limited to people thirty or older. There are some quite talented players in the league, including some who played professionally or in college. Alas, few of these stars are on my team, which has a disproportionate number of over-the-hill players with dysfunctional joints and muscles.

Despite our lack of success in the win column, it is clear that most of my teammates have a somewhat inflated view of their own abilities. If we did something like the holiday card experiment on my team, I have little doubt that most people would be surprised to find that their teammates do not think they are as good a player as they believe they are. (I am sure that I am no exception.)

Would it be useful for my teammates and me to do periodic reality checks, polling one another about what we think of each other's abilities? It would if our self-theories were so delusional that we were constantly at odds with the coach, wondering why we were not the starting pitcher and clean-up hitter every game. Most of us, however, are not that blind to our talents (or lack thereof), while maintaining our illusions that we are better than we really are. Indeed, if all of us realized our true level of skill, we would probably pack up the bats and go home. It is life's positive illusions that make us show up for the next game.

Sometimes, though, important life decisions are at stake, and in these cases illusions are not so harmless. If one of my teammates were convinced that he still had a shot to play professionally and was about to quit his day job and head for a major league tryout camp, it would behoove him to poll the rest of us in the dugout to see if this was a good career move.

All these examples are ones in which people have a more positive view of themselves than other people do. Although people usually have somewhat inflated views of themselves, sometimes their views are too negative, and this is another case in which we should seriously consider adopting other people's views of us.

Consider Katherine Dirks, a University of Virginia undergraduate who won a prestigious Marshall Scholarship in 2001, allowing her to study at Oxford University for two years. Dirks had an outstanding record of achievement. She was both a Jefferson and Echols Scholar at Virginia, the two most prestigious undergraduate scholarships; she maintained a grade-point average of 3.9; and she was president of the Raven Society, the oldest Virginia honorary organization. And yet she was quoted in the newspaper as saying that she did not think she had much of a chance to win a Marshall Scholarship and had decided not to apply, until two of her professors talked her into it. It is a good thing that she heeded her professors' advice instead of acting on her self-theory.

At times, then, we should be more attuned to other people's views of us, as well as being good consumers of psychological research. Surely, however, these are not the only means of discovering the nature of our adaptive unconscious.

10

Observing and Changing Our Behavior

It seems to me, that if you tried hard, you would in time find it possible to become what you yourself would approve; and that if from this day you began with resolution to correct your thoughts and actions, you would in a few years have laid up a new and stainless store of recollections, to which you might revert with pleasure.
—*Charlotte Brontë, Jane Eyre (1847)*

We are what we pretend to be, so we must be careful about what we pretend to be.
—*Kurt Vonnegut, Mother Night (1966)*

Observing other people's reactions to us and reading the relevant psychological literature are not the only means of discovering the nature of our adaptive unconscious. Our own behavior is another source of information that can be quite telling. By being careful observers of our own actions, we can learn a lot about ourselves. In addition, if we want to change some aspect of our adaptive unconscious, a good place to start is deliberately to begin acting like the person we want to be.

The author Marcia Muller, for example, created a fictional heroine, Sharon McCone, who bore little resemblance to herself:

She was taller, thinner and braver than I. She had a job, while I had no prospects of one. She commanded an amazing variety of skills—marksmanship, judo, bread making, automotive repair—while I could barely type. She would go anywhere, safe or dangerous, and ask anyone questions, while I had been known to become nervous when dialing the phone for the correct time.

Muller wanted to become more like her heroine, and eventually did so by deliberately acting more like her.

> I didn't grow taller, but I did lose weight and become braver. Not to the point of facing down criminals with a .38 or subduing them with judo, but I was definitely more confident. In the course of my research for subsequent novels, I would learn to walk into places safe and dangerous and ask anyone questions. Finally I'd declared my own independence.[1]

Sue Grafton, another well-known author of detective novels, also created a fictional alter ego who she came to emulate, at least in some ways. Before Grafton wrote her novels she was a dissatisfied admissions clerk at a hospital who was fed up with the plainness and predictability of her life. "I needed out," she says. "This was not enough to contain me. I needed freedom. Air." She succeeded in becoming a new person in part by creating her fictional heroine Kinsey Milhone, a brassy, independent, profane, fast-food-eating, jeans-wearing private investigator. By imagining Kinsey on paper, Sue Grafton found it easier to act like her and, eventually, to acquire some of her traits.[2]

But how do people recognize in the first place that there are parts of their adaptive unconscious that they want to change? And, short of writing detective novels with a tailor-made hero, how do we change who we are?

Knowing Ourselves by Observing Our Own Behavior

To learn about the true nature of our personalities or how we really feel, sometimes it is useful to observe what we do. In the words of E. M. Forster, "How can I tell what I think 'till I see what I say?"[3]

According to the psychologist Daryl Bem, observations of our own behavior are a major source of self-knowledge. The central proposition of his self-perception theory is that people infer their internal states just as an outside observer would, by seeing how they behave and guessing what feelings or traits must underlie that behavior. In so doing, people make note of the conditions under which the behavior occurs, such as the extent to which it was influenced by the surrounding circumstances. A professional musician at a wedding is likely to infer that she is performing because it is a paying job, not because she has particularly fond feelings for the bride and groom or enjoys religious services. The key, said Bem, is to analyze our behavior in the same way an outside observer would: we look at our behavior and make an educated guess about why we did it.

This is a truly radical proposition. Can it really be the case that when trying to decide what is in our hearts and minds, we are in no better position than a stranger who observes us from the outside? Bem's theory is a hybrid of radical behaviorism that treats the mind as a black box unworthy of scientific study. Not only is the mind a black box for scientists, Bem argued; it is often a black box to the person who owns that mind. The only way to determine the contents of the box is to make an educated guess, based on what people do—and that goes for scientists, people observing each other, and for people observing themselves.

Bem's theory caused quite a furor, partly because it seems, on the basis of simple introspection, so absurd. When I stub my toe I know right away that I feel pain; I do not have to observe myself hopping around the room howling to figure it out. When I haven't eaten in a while, I do not have to watch myself go to the refrigerator and make a sandwich to realize that I am hungry. It's like the old joke about two behaviorists who have just made love. One says to the other, "I know it was good for you, but was it good for me?" This is funny precisely because it is so silly to assume that people do not directly experience feelings such as their own sexual pleasure.

Bem acknowledged, however, that there are times when we know directly that we feel pain or love or sexual pleasure and do not need to observe our behavior to figure this out. The point is that there are many other times when it is not so clear how we feel, and it is then that we are forced to be outside observers of our behavior, so that we can decipher our feelings, attitudes, and traits.[4]

Despite years of research on self-perception theory, there is an enduring question: Is the self-perception process one of self-revelation, whereby people come to know better their true feelings by observing their behavior, or one of self-fabrication, whereby people infer internal states that did not exist before?

When Sarah met Peter at a party, for example, she did not think she liked him very much; in many ways he was not her type. She found herself thinking about him a lot, however, and when Peter telephoned and asked her out on a date, she said yes. Now that she has agreed to the date, she discovers that she likes him more than she knew. This is an example of self-perception as self-revelation, because Sarah uses her behavior to bring to light a prior feeling of which she was unaware, until she agreed to go out with Peter.

Another possibility is that Sarah really did not like Peter all that much when she first met him. She felt obligated to go out with him because he is the son of her mother's best friend, and her mother thought they would be a good match. Sarah does not fully realize that this is the reason she said yes, however, and mistakenly thinks, "Hm, I guess I like Peter more than I thought I did if I agreed to go out with him." This would be an example of self-fabrication: Sarah misses the real reason for her behavior (the desire to please her mother), and infers that she feels more positively toward Peter than she did before.

The difference between self-revelation and self-fabrication is crucial from the point of view of gaining self-knowledge. Inferring our internal states from our behavior is a good strategy if it reveals feelings of which we were previously unaware. It is not such a good strategy if it results in the fabrication of new feelings.

Self-fabrication would not be an issue if people were adept at knowing exactly why they behaved the way they did. If Sarah recognized that the reason she agreed to go out with Peter was a sense of family obligation, she would not make the mistake of thinking she liked Peter more than she did. As we have seen, however, people are not always skilled at knowing exactly why they respond the way they do and often make precisely this kind of mistake.

In fact almost all the experiments on self-perception theory are examples of self-fabrication, whereby people misunderstand the real reason for their behavior and make mistaken inferences about their internal states. Many of these studies are ones in which people, like Sarah, underestimate the power of the situation over their behavior and mistakenly infer that they did what they did because of their inner feelings or attitudes. In a study conducted at Yale University, for example, students agreed to go to a street corner and gather signatures on a petition to reduce air pollution in New Haven. In one condition participants heard an experimental accomplice also agree to the request, and remark that he did so because he "wouldn't mind convincing people about something I really believe in." What, if anything, should the students learn about themselves from the fact that they, too, agreed to collect the signatures?

The real reason most people agreed was that the experimenter was quite persuasive and made it hard to say no, as evidenced by the fact that all students did agree to the onerous request. Instead of saying, "I did it because the guy twisted my arm," though, people mistakenly inferred that their behavior was a reflection of a strong attitude—stronger than they had actually felt before. In other words, they engaged in self-fabrication. It is quite common for people to overlook situational influences on their actions and infer that they acted on the basis of their internal states—so common that this phenomenon is called the *fundamental attribution error.*[5]

In most studies of the fundamental attribution error, the situational influences are rather subtle (such as an experimenter applying pressure to convince us to get signatures for a good cause) and easy to miss. What if the situational constraints or incentives are obvious? In these cases people correctly recognize that their behavior was caused by situational demands and thereby stop themselves from fabricating internal states. If our supervisor asks us to buy Girl Scout Cookies from his daughter's troop, and not-so-subtly implies that our next raise is contingent on saying yes, we will probably attribute our purchase of ten boxes of Thin Mints to his arm-twisting, rather than to the idea that the Girl Scouts are now our favorite charity and Thin Mints our favorite snack.

But if situational influences are too strong, people make a different kind of self-fabrication error: they overattribute their actions to the situation, and underestimate how much they wanted to perform the behavior. Suppose that Bill has always loved to play the guitar and spends hours practicing. What happens when he also has a strong situational reason for the same activity, such as playing at a wedding for an enormous fee? It might seem as if Bill would enjoy the performance all the more, because he now has two reasons for doing it: the money he is earning and his love of guitar playing.

Many studies show that in situations like this, people in fact overattribute their behavior to the situation and underestimate their intrinsic interest in the activity. The more Bill plays professionally, the less he is likely to enjoy playing the guitar, because he infers that he is "doing it for the money," not because he loves it. This is another form of self-fabrication: because of a strong situational incentive or demand, people underestimate the magnitude of their internal interest in the activity.[6]

A final example of self-fabrication is the case in which people's behavior might plausibly result from more than one internal state. Consider the case in which people find that their bodies are revved up; their heart is beating rapidly and they are short of breath. The way in which they interpret this arousal will determine the emotion they experience. If someone has just pointed a gun at them and said, "Give me your wallet," they will correctly interpret their arousal as a sign of fear. Often, however, there is more than one explanation for our arousal. Perhaps we are on a first date with a very attractive man or woman, and just narrowly avoided an automobile accident. How much of our arousal is due to fear over almost losing our lives versus attraction to our date?

Again, if people were perfect at knowing the causes of their responses (in this case their arousal), there wouldn't be any problem. They could say, "Well, 61 percent of my arousal came from the nearly hitting that truck, and 39 percent is due to attraction to my date," and go on their way. Instead, people often make mistakes about the source of their arousal and end up with a self-fabricated feeling. People might underestimate how much their arousal resulted from the close call with the truck, for example, and assume that they are even more attracted to their date than they thought they were.

To the extent that such self-fabrication is common, the self-perception process, whereby people observe their behavior to infer their feelings, is not such a good path to self-knowledge. People misunderstand why they are responding the way they are and wrongly infer that they don't like playing the guitar as much as they believed they did or that they are more in love than they thought.

Sometimes, however, we have feelings of which we are not fully aware, and the self-perception process has the potential to reveal these feelings. Consider the example from the previous chapter, in which people have prejudiced feelings toward members of a minority group, but convince themselves that they actually are not prejudiced at all. Or consider Henry Higgins, who couldn't see through his elaborate smoke screen of himself as a cultured, fair-minded English gentleman that he was in fact a coarse, misogynous brute. In cases such as these, people might be wise to become better observers of their own behavior. If an employer notices that he keeps passing over qualified African Americans, finding excuses to hire less qualified whites, he should begin to question his own level of prejudice. Henry Higgins would have been well advised to pay more attention to how he treated Eliza and Mrs. Pearce. Perhaps my friend Susan would have realized sooner than she did that she did not love Stephen, if she had paid more attention to the fact that she often found excuses not to see him on weekends.

WHO DOES THE INFERRING?

But there is a complication, namely the question of which part of the mind engages in the self-perception process, inferring how we feel from what we do. In the examples above, I assumed that people consciously make the effort to observe their behavior to figure out how they really feel. Although we can surely do this, the fact is that our adaptive unconscious might also be drawing inferences from our behavior, without our knowing it. In fact one of the major roles of the adaptive unconscious is to draw inferences about the nature of ourselves and the social world.

We encountered an example of such nonconscious inference in a study by Stanley Schachter and Ladd Wheeler, in which people watched a comedy film after receiving an injection (see Chapter 6). Those who unknowingly received epinephrine (adrenalin) became physiologically aroused, and thus found themselves with an elevated heart rate and sweaty palms while watching the film. They attributed their arousal at least in part to the assumption that the film was very funny, as shown by the fact that they smiled and laughed a lot more during the film than people who had not received epinephrine. These inferences seem to have been made nonconsciously, however, because when asked how funny the film was, people in the epinephrine condition did not report that it was any funnier than other participants did. Instead, they relied on their conscious theories about how much they liked the kind of comedy they saw, such as the person who said, "I just couldn't understand why I was laughing during the movie. Usually, I hate Jack Carson and this kind of nonsense and that's the way I checked the scales." In other words, the adaptive unconscious inferred from people's level of arousal that the film was funny, causing people to laugh and smile more, whereas people's conscious selves drew different conclusions.

There is not much we can do to control the nonconscious inferences we draw about ourselves. The best approach is to try to perform the self-perception process consciously as well. In this way, people's conscious self-narratives are likely to match better the changes that are occurring nonconsciously, such as what films they find funny, whom they like, and in what situations they are most comfortable. I don't mean to suggest that people should become so self-vigilant that they constantly question the accuracy of their self stories. When faced with an important decision, however—such as whether to marry or have children—people might be wise to be good observers of themselves, and engage less in the kind of fruitless introspection discussed in Chapter 8.

Remember Mike from the previous chapter, who believes he is shy but seems anything but? It would seem to be to his advantage to pay more attention to his own behavior, to see that he often acts in a quite extraverted manner. By so doing he might realize that his theory about his shyness is out of date, and revise it to fit his adaptive unconscious. People's conscious stories about themselves are often too negative or limiting, and it is to their benefit to revise these stories to better match their nonconscious traits, abilities, and feelings. More often, perhaps, people's conscious theories are too positive. Whereas it can be useful for us to maintain positive illusions about ourselves, if we are to grow and change for the better, we need to recognize that we may be more prejudiced than we thought or, like Henry Higgins, less kind.

Do Good, Be Good

If people do have an overly positive view of themselves, they may not want to revise their conscious stories downward to match their more negative unconscious states. Rather, people would be better off changing their nonconscious states to match their more positive self-stories. People who hold nonprejudiced, egalitarian attitudes toward other social groups at a conscious level, but possess more prejudiced attitudes at an automatic, nonconscious level, do not want to revise their conscious narratives to match their nonconscious states. They prefer to do the reverse, changing their nonconscious, prejudiced attitudes to match their conscious, egalitarian ones. Similarly, if Henry Higgins were to recognize that he had an inflated view of himself, he would presumably want to change for the better.

But how? It is not easy to know what our nonconscious states are, much less to change them. Aristotle suggested that "We acquire [virtues] by first having put them into action ... we become just by the practice of just actions, self-controlled by exercising self-control, and courageous by performing acts of courage." William James offered similar advice: "Seize the very first possible opportunity to act on every resolution you make, and on every emotional prompting you may experience in the direction of habits you aspire to gain."[7] In other words, the first step to changing our nonconscious inclinations is to change our behavior. People who are concerned that they might be prejudiced at a nonconscious level could try their best to act in nonprejudiced ways as often as possible. Doing so can lead to change at the automatic level in two ways. First, it provides the opportunity for people to infer from their behavior, nonconsciously, that they are nonprejudiced people, according to the self-perception process discussed earlier. That is, it provides the adaptive unconscious with new "data" from which to infer attitudes and feelings.

Second, as suggested by William James, the more frequently people perform a behavior, the more habitual and automatic it becomes, requiring little effort or conscious attention. One of the most enduring lessons of social psychology is that behavior change often precedes changes in attitudes and feelings. Changing our behavior to match our conscious conceptions of ourselves is thus a good way to bring about changes in the adaptive unconscious.

But why stop with trying to mold the adaptive unconscious to our conscious conceptions of ourselves? Sometimes people are dissatisfied with both their conscious and nonconscious feelings or traits in a particular area. Their goal is not one of self-knowledge, whereby they bring their conscious narratives more into line with their nonconscious states, but self-improvement, whereby they change both. Perhaps the "alter your behavior first" strategy can work here as well, bringing about desired changes in people's conscious narratives and their adaptive unconscious. In short, if we want to become a better person, we should follow a "do good, be good" strategy. By acting in ways that are helpful and caring toward others, we will come to view ourselves as more helpful and caring people.

Now, I know that this sounds simplistic. People do not transform themselves into saints by doing one kind act. People who no longer love their partners cannot make themselves fall in love again simply by acting as if it were so. An extremely shy person cannot suddenly become the life of the party by deciding to chat with a few strangers. I think we underestimate, however, how much we *can* change feelings and traits by changing our behavior.

I have always considered myself to be a bit introverted, for example, and I think this conscious conception is true, in the sense that my nonconscious dispositions and inclinations are on the shy side. I have often wished I were more comfortable in large groups, and a few years ago I decided that the answer was simply to act in a more extraverted way whenever possible. I made more of an effort to chat with people, such as someone at a party whom I had never met, rather than talking only with my friends or sticking close to the buffet table. The more I did so, the more comfortable I became in such situations. I will never be like my wife, who can chat with anyone, anytime, with great ease and charm. But I think I have become more extraverted as a result of my little experiment.

Some of this change is simply due to practice, of course. The more I have made the effort to chat with people, the better I have become at small talk. This practice effect has also been true with my teaching; when I first taught large lecture courses to hundreds of people I was a basket case, but little by little I learned how to do it without my teeth chattering. After years of teaching, large lecture courses are now my favorites. My stand-up skills will never earn me a spot as the guest host of *The Tonight Show,* but they're better than they used to be.

Deliberately changing our behavior is beneficial beyond the practice it gives in a new way of acting. It also promotes a new self-definition. The more I find myself chatting comfortably with a new acquaintance at a party, or gathering steam in a lecture to a large class, the more my view of myself changes. This can happen at both a nonconscious and a conscious level. My adaptive unconscious is more likely to draw the inference that I am an outgoing person, and this inference has become a part of my conscious self-narrative as well. The more my self-definition changes, the easier it becomes to act in yet more extraverted ways automatically, rather than having to force myself to make the effort. Automatic selves produce automatic actions. The new "extraverted" Tim takes the controls and steers me in directions I never would have gone before, like chatting amiably with the person sitting next to me on a plane, rather than keeping my nose in a book.

The idea that deliberately changing our behavior can change our self-conceptions has been used to help people experiencing significant problems. Part of the credo of Alcoholics Anonymous, for example, is "Fake it until you make it." Because an addiction to alcohol can seem so overwhelming and hard to overcome that people do not know where to begin, it is often useful to start small by acting as if one had the problem under control. Obviously, avoiding a drink on one occasion is not a cure for alcoholism. Small changes in behavior can lead to small changes in one's self-concept, however, and small changes in one's self-concept can make the next behavior change easier.

The same strategy has been used to treat people who are chronically depressed. A number of effective therapies are available for depression, including antidepressant drugs and several kinds of psychotherapy. The psychotherapist Terrence Real notes that an important part of the therapeutic process is to "do the behavior first and let the feelings follow." This is especially true of men, he suggests, in whom depression often takes the form of social isolation and a lack of intimacy. It can be quite helpful for depressed men to make the effort to act more sociably instead of isolating themselves. As Real advises, "Do the dishes, help the kids with their homework," because repeated efforts in this direction can help people form social ties and change their self-definitions.[8]

As another example, think for a moment how you might design an intervention to lower the high pregnancy rate in adolescents in the United States. If you are like many researchers in this area, your approach would be to tackle the problem head-on, such as by educating adolescent boys and girls about abstinence and birth control, and perhaps by making contraceptives more easily available. Such programs have been tried and have resulted in somewhat lower pregnancy rates.

Rather than trying to change adolescents' sexual behavior directly, though, maybe we should try to change their self-conceptions. If we could find a way to make them feel more connected to their communities, more competent, and more adultlike, perhaps they would be more likely to avoid risky sexual behavior. An appeal of such a broad approach is that it might help adolescents avoid other self-defeating behaviors besides early pregnancy, such as dropping out of school.

This all sounds well and good, but how can we get adolescents to change their view of themselves? It seems like an insurmountable task to try to change people's personalities and self-views with a large-scale intervention. The answer might actually be rather straightforward: first change the adolescents' behavior, getting them to *act* in competent, adultlike ways, with the assumption that their self-views will fall in line with their behavior.

This is the approach taken by a national program called Teen Outreach. Although it is multifaceted, including classroom discussions and guest speakers, the central component of the program is to involve adolescents in volunteer work of their choice. There is no direct attempt to educate people about teen pregnancy or contraception; instead, students in grades nine through twelve engage in supervised volunteer work, such as working as aides in hospitals and nursing homes or as peer tutors. The results have been remarkable. In one large-scale study in which teens were randomly assigned to the Teen Outreach program or a control group, those who participated in the program were less likely to fail a course, less likely to be suspended from school, and, if female, less likely to become pregnant.[9]

The success of interventions such as these is undoubtedly due to multiple causes, such as gaining social skills through practice, obtaining positive feedback from others, and connecting to a social network of supportive adults who act as role models. I suspect that another critical component, however, is the change in self-image that the volunteer work promotes. Teens who used to view themselves as alienated and ineffective come to see themselves as caring, helpful, competent people with a stake in their community, a self-view that is much less compatible with becoming pregnant or dropping out of school.

The "do good, be good" principle is one of the most important lessons psychology has to offer. If you do not like something about yourself or are feeling down, it can be helpful to alter your behavior in a more positive way. Behavior change is often quite difficult, especially when it involves overcoming an addiction (e.g., quitting smoking) or changing a behavior that is rewarding in other ways (e.g., eating). It is often possible, however, to act in more outgoing ways when we are shy, happy ways when we are sad, or kind ways when we feel unkind. This simple lesson was known to Emily Post, who gave the following advice in her 1922 etiquette manual: "There is one thing every girl who would really be popular should learn, in fact, she must learn—self-unconsciousness! The best advice might be to follow somewhat the precepts of mental science and make herself believe that a good time exists in her own mind. If she can become possessed with the idea that she is having a good time and look as though she were, the psychological effect is astonishing."[10]

It may seem odd to end a book on self-knowledge with the advice that people should think less about themselves and try to change their behavior instead. To fashion a satisfying, functional, self-narrative, however, and to establish a desirable pattern of habitual, nonconscious responses, the best advice is to practice, practice, practice.

Judging the "Goodness" of a Self-Story

But what is it that makes a self-narrative satisfying, functional, and adaptive? Accuracy is the most obvious criterion; it is not to people's advantage to believe that they are the reincarnation of Attila the Hun or that they can fly after jumping off tall buildings. Nonetheless, the modernist assumption that there is one, true account of a person's life and problems is rejected by most narrative theorists. Indeed, the use of the term "narrative" is meant to convey that there are many ways of telling a person's story, and not just one historical truth that must be discovered before positive self-change can be achieved.[11]

But although many narrative theorists *say* that the truth of the story does not matter, I don't think they really mean it. Imagine, for example, that we brought together a psychoanalyst, cognitive therapist, and behavior therapist who all agreed with the basic narrative metaphor and viewed their practice as a matter of helping their clients to adopt more adaptive self-stories. "So you would agree," we might ask, "that the truth of the narrative is less important than that people find a useful and adaptive story that relieves their suffering?" True to the narrative tradition, each therapist nods enthusiastically. "So what you are saying," we continue, "is that the stories that your colleagues' clients adopt are as good as the stories your clients adopt?" Our three therapists begin to shift uncomfortably in their seats. "In other words, the psychoanalytic story is as good as the behaviorist or cognitive one, and each of you could use the other disciplines' stories to good effect?" "Now wait just a minute," our therapists respond, "when we said that one narrative is as good as another, we weren't going *that* far."

There are, of course, eclectic therapists who would agree that different approaches can be effective. Many psychotherapists, however—even those who favor the narrative metaphor—believe that some narratives are truer than others, and that it is to their clients' benefit to adopt the valid ones (e.g., Freudian, Kleinian, Rogerian, Skinnerian). But, as we saw from our earlier discussion of psychotherapy outcome research, this assumption is questionable. Psychotherapy clients benefit by adopting their therapists' stories, but the content of these stories can differ radically.

Perhaps the answer is to adopt the postmodernist perspective that it is pointless to judge self-narratives by their accuracy or historical truth. According to this view, there is no "true self"; rather, in modern life people live in multiple crosscurrents of conflicting social forces, and they construct many narratives specific to particular relationships and cultural circumstances. It makes no sense to judge one of these narratives as "truer" than another.

The postmodernist perspective has been useful in highlighting the influence of culture and society on self-constructions and the extent to which people can adopt different personas in different circumstances. But if truth is not the proper criterion by which to judge a narrative, what is? Even within a given social and cultural context, some narratives are more adaptive than others; most postmodernists would agree that the self-view of a depressed, suicidal person, or of an alienated, socio-pathic high school student on his way to school with an automatic weapon, is not adaptive.

It is difficult, however, to define "adaptive" with no reference to accuracy, and many postmodern accounts of psychotherapy fall into this trap. Kenneth Gergen and John Kaye, for example, note that many postmodernist accounts attempt to avoid an accuracy criterion by arguing that the goal of psychotherapy is to "re-orient the individual, to open new courses of action that are more fulfilling and more adequately suited to the individual's experiences, capacities, and proclivities."[12] But by saying that a narrative should be "suited" to a person's "capacities and proclivities" is to use an accuracy criterion. What is a "proclivity" or "capacity" but an enduring aspect of personality that is best captured in a narrative?

Gergen and Kaye attempt to avoid this trap by arguing for a different definition of narrative utility, namely the idea that narratives exist within specific "games of language, one or more cultural dances," and can be judged only "within the confines of a particular game or dance." "Utility," they argue, "is to be derived from their success as moves within these arenas—in terms of their adequacy as reactions to previous moves or as instigators to what follows."[13]

But surely postmodernists go too far in their disavowal of a truth criterion. As long as we are clear about what it is a narrative should represent, it makes perfect sense to say that the narrative should be accurate. The confusion over this issue has stemmed from a lack of understanding of what that criterion should be.

Self-stories should be accurate in a simple sense: they should capture the nature of the person's nonconscious goals, feelings, and temperaments. In short, there must be some correspondence between the story and the person's adaptive unconscious. As we have seen, people whose conscious conceptions of themselves are "in synch"—that represent their nonconscious motives well—are better off emotionally. Joachim Brunstein, Oliver Schultheiss, and Ruth Grässmann measured people's explicit goals—those contained in their conscious self-narratives—and the implicit goals that were part of the adaptive unconscious. People whose conscious goals matched their nonconscious goals were happier than people who showed a mismatch between their conscious and nonconscious goals.[14]

As with any biography, there are multiple ways of telling the story. A good biography, though, has to account for the facts of the person's life and capture his or her inner goals and traits. The better a story does at accounting for the "data" of the person's adaptive unconscious, the better off the person is. By recognizing their nonconscious goals, people are in a better position to act in ways to fulfill them, or to try to change them.

It may seem that we have come full circle back to Freud, by arguing that people's conscious beliefs about themselves should match their unconscious goals and drives. Isn't this the same thing as saying that the goal of therapy is to "make the unconscious conscious?" In a sense it is. But as should now be clear, the nature of the unconscious that should be captured in a narrative differs radically from the Freudian one. And there are clear differences between the viewpoints in how to make the unconscious conscious. There is no direct pipeline to the adaptive unconscious; it must be inferred by being a good self-biographer (perhaps with the aid of a skilled therapist), not by removing repression and taking a peek at the bubbling cauldron below.

Further, accurate stories can differ radically, much as different paradigms in science can explain the same facts in very different ways. This is why different forms of psychotherapy can be effective: both the psychoanalytic and cognitive therapy "stories" can provide coherent explanations of why a person has interpersonal difficulties or is emotionally distressed. Both can describe the person's adaptive unconscious, albeit in quite different languages.

Another definition of a good narrative is that it meet a peace-of-mind criterion, or the extent to which people have a story that allows them to stop thinking about themselves so much. The lack of a coherent narrative can be an unsettling experience indeed, as Joan Didion lamented in *The White Album:*

I was supposed to have a script, and had mislaid it. I was supposed to hear cues, and no longer did. I was meant to know the plot, but all I knew was what I saw: flash pictures in variable sequence, images with no "meaning" beyond their temporary arrangement, not a movie but a cutting-room experience . . . Certain of these images did not fit into any narrative I knew.[15]

Once an experience is explained coherently, and assimilated into a life story, people no longer think about it very much. This is not necessarily a good thing when the event is positive, because the event loses its ability to cause pleasure more quickly than we might like. It is a good thing for events that cause pain, because rumination and thought suppression are replaced by a coherent story that requires no further elaboration. This seems to be why Pennebaker's writing exercise, discussed in Chapter 8, works so well. People revise their stories to explain negative events that have not been fully assimilated, allowing them to ruminate less about the events and move on. And people who find meaning in the loss of a loved one, such as believing that the death was God's will or that death is a natural part of the life cycle, recover more quickly than people who are unable to find any meaning in the loss.

Consistent with this view, some psychotherapists argue that the best sign of when therapy should be terminated is when the client stops thinking so much about himself or herself. The biography is completed, and no further revisions are needed, with all the angst and rumination that such revisions can entail.

Finally, there is a believability criterion to which people should aspire. In order to achieve peace of mind, the self-biographer must believe the story that he or she is telling. If people view their life stories as arbitrary constructions, each one as good as the next, they are less likely to satisfy the peace-of-mind criterion. People who constantly question and revise their narratives, particularly about negative life experiences, are likely to dwell on these experiences. They may also be less likely to commit to and pursue life goals, if they view these goals as end points of an arbitrary narrative that could easily be revised.

Even Freud, late in his career, came to adopt this view, arguing that "an assured conviction of the truth of the construction . . . achieves the same therapeutic result as a recaptured memory."[16] What matters is that people commit themselves to a coherent self-narrative that corresponds reasonably well to their adaptive unconscious.

In this changing, postmodern world, such a narrative might well include some compartmentalization of selves, or a recognition that there are vast differences between ourselves as "daughter," "weekend athlete," and "Elvis impersonator." People should not get too stuck in one self and should appreciate the cultural and societal arbitrariness of many of their beliefs. At the same time, they should maintain a sense of self-continuity. There is a lot to be said for a commitment to a coherent self-narrative.

It is possible, of course, for self-narratives to be too rigid and resistant to change. The biography can be completed too soon, with a poor representation of the person's adaptive unconscious. Even good biographies need to be revised as people grow and change. Nonetheless, a self-narrative that meets the accuracy, peace-of-mind, and believability criteria is likely to be a quite useful one, precisely by avoiding too much introspection. Consider Robert Zajonc, an eminent social psychologist who has never quite understood all the fuss about self-psychology. "I don't think of my self, as such," he once said. "I may think of my schedule, my obligations, my meetings, but I don't really spend too much time asking, 'Who am I?' "[17] He may be on to something. A good self-narrative need not be constantly retold.

If we are unhappy with our self-views, there are things we can do to change both our story and our adaptive unconscious. It is not easy, and not many of us have the talent and fortitude of novelists such as Marcia Muller and Sue Grafton, who forged themselves into the image of heroines they created in novels. Little steps can lead to big changes, however, and all of us have the ability to act more like the person we want to be.

Notes

1. Freud's Genius, Freud's Myopia

1. Proust (1934), pp. 675–676.
2. Austen (1813/1996), p. 216.
3. Examples such as these can be found in Nisbett and Wilson (1977).
4. Bargh (1997), for example, notes that automatic processes have one or more of these features: they are nonconscious, unintentional, uncontrollable, and effortless.
5. On the minimal role of consciousness, see Velmanns (1991); Bargh and Chartrand (1999); Wegner (in press).
6. On the varied nature of nonconscious systems: Roediger and McDermott (1993); Schacter (1996); Westen (1998); Willingham and Preuss (1995).
7. Freud (1900/1972), p. 592.
8. Quoted in Miller (1942), p. 157.
9. Damasio (1994), p. 249.
10. Whyte (1978), p. 26; Koestler (1978), p. iii.
11. Hamilton (1865); Carpenter (1874); Laycock (1860).
12. Hamilton (1865), p. 250.
13. Carpenter (1874), p. 539.
14. Carpenter (1874), p. 543.
15. Carpenter (1874), p. 539.
16. See especially Hamilton's (1865) lectures 18 and 19.
17. See Grünbaum (1984) for a discussion of the limits of Freudian methodology.

18. See Erdelyi (1985); Westen (1998).
19. A. Freud (1966), p. 28.

2. The Adaptive Unconscious

Epigraphs: Hamilton (1865), p. 241; Dallas (1866), p. 194.

1. See Cole (1995) for a fascinating discussion of Ian Waterman's case.
2. Proffitt et al. (1995); Rock (1997).
3. See, for example, Simon (1997).
4. Freud (1924/1968), p. 306.
5. James Miller (1942) offered sixteen distinct definitions of the unconscious. This number is rivaled only by the number of definitions many authors have offered for consciousness (see, e.g., Ryle 1949).
6. Others have used the term the "cognitive unconscious" or the "emotional unconscious" to describe processes I ascribe to the adaptive unconscious (e.g., Kihlstrom 1987, 1999). I believe it makes more sense to consider nonconscious processing as a whole, rather than drawing lines between what is cognitive and what is emotional.
7. See Nørretranders (1998) for a detailed discussion of how scientists have measured the capacity of consciousness versus the capacity of our sensory systems.
8. Claparède's (1911/1951) patient may not have been completely amnesiac and thus may have retained some limited abilities to learn things consciously. More typically, amnesiacs are able to learn motor skills, such as tracking a moving target with a stylus, with no conscious memory of ever having performed the task from one day to the next (see Schacter 1996).
9. For a review see Kihlstrom and Schacter (1990).
10. See, e.g., Reber (1993, 1997) and Dulany (1997).
11. Lewicki, Hill, and Bizot (1988), quotation p. 33.
12. Although there is some disagreement on the exact location of the filter in the attentional system (e.g., Deutsch and Deutsch 1963; Treisman 1964; Norman 1968; Marcel 1983), there is agreement that the filter operates largely outside of conscious awareness.
13. Conscious control over the settings of the filter is not perfect. As noted by Daniel Wegner (1994), the desire to attend to something sometimes fails, such that our attention is drawn to precisely what we are trying to ignore.
14. The "cocktail party effect," whereby people recognize their name in an unattended auditory channel, was first demonstrated by Moray (1959).

The nonconscious monitor is not perfect; typically, people notice their name in the unattended channel about a third of the time. The fact that they are able to recognize it at all suggests that nonconscious monitoring is occurring. For theories of preattention, see Broadbent (1958) and Treisman (1993).

15. See Bargh and Pietromonaco (1982); Higgins (1996); Mandler (1997).
16. See Damasio (1994); LeDoux (1996); Bargh (1997); Bechara et al. (1997); Clore, Gasper, and Garvin (2001).
17. Bargh et al. (2002); Bargh and Raymond (1995).
18. Brontë (1847/1984), p. 270.
19. Damasio (1994).
20. Brontë (1847/1984), p. 259.
21. Gilbert and Wilson (2000). See also Vaillant (1993).
22. See Heine, Lehman, Markus, and Kitayama (1999). Even within a culture, the ways in which people make themselves feel good vary. Bill Swann (1996) has observed that in Western cultures, people with high and low self-esteem react differently to positive and negative feedback. People high in self-esteem prefer positive feedback and attempt to avoid or discount negative feedback, as any good spin doctor would. People low in self-esteem sometimes do the opposite: they prefer negative feedback and avoid or discount positive feedback. This does not necessarily mean, however, that people with low self-esteem fail to use the "feel-good" criterion. Swann argues that people often desire predictable, coherent feedback and that it is very unsettling to have their views of themselves challenged. This explains why people with negative self-esteem, who have low opinions of themselves, prefer negative feedback about themselves: it helps them maintain a predicable, coherent self-view. In short, it satisfies the "feel-good" criterion, albeit in a rather paradoxical way.
23. See Taylor and Brown (1988). I discuss work on positive illusions in more detail in Chapter 9.

3. Who's in Charge?

Epigraph: James (1890), p. 122.
1. The extent to which such evolutionary adaptations explain current human behavior, such as gender differences in mate selection, is hugely controversial. In my opinion, evolutionary psychologists sometimes go too far in claiming that much of current social behavior can be traced back to human

adaptations that occurred thousands of years ago. Nonetheless it cannot be denied that the brain has evolved according to the principles of natural selection (see, e.g., Kaas and Collins 2001).

2. See Reber (1992) for an insightful elaboration of this argument.

3. Güzeldere (1997).

4. See Flanagan (1992) for an excellent review of these philosophical positions.

5. See Flanagan (1992), p. 7.

6. Wegner and Wheatley (1999).

7. Flanagan (1992), pp. 7–8.

8. Margolis (1987); LeDoux (1996).

9. See Bargh et al. (2002) for a discussion of the role of consciousness in fulfilling nonconscious needs.

10. Whereas it is true that conscious processes are more controlled than most nonconscious processes, not all nonconscious processing meets all the definitions of automaticity. Arthur Reber (1992), for example, notes that learning an artificial grammar occurs nonconsciously but requires cognitive capacity. Further, we are not always in complete control of our conscious thoughts. Automatic, nonconscious processes can lead to intrusions of unwanted thoughts, as documented by Daniel Wegner (1994). In general, however, it is fair to characterize most nonconscious thinking as automatic and most conscious thinking as controlled.

11. See Rosenthal and Jacobson (1968); Sadker and Sadker (1994).

12. For a review of research on implicit and explicit memory, see Schacter (1996).

13. Lepper, Greene, and Nisbett (1973).

14. Wilson, Hull, and Johnson (1981); Wilson (1985). For recent reviews of research on the effects of rewards on intrinsic interest, see Lepper, Henderlong, and Gingras (1999); Deci, Koestner, and Ryan (1999).

15. Clements and Perner (1994).

16. See Hauser (1998); Perner and Clements (2000), Wellman, Cross, and Watson (2001). For evidence that other implicit, nonconscious memory systems develop at the same rate as explicit memory, see Komatsu, Naito, and Fuke (1996) and Rovee-Collier (1997).

17. For evidence on the difficulty of consciously detecting correlations, see Nisbett and Ross (1980); Crocker (1981); and Alloy and Tabachnik (1984).

18. I thank Jonathan Schooler for pointing out this interpretation of the Bechara et al. (1997) experiment.

19. For evidence that negative and positive information is processed in different regions of the brain, see Davidson (1995) and Cacioppo, Gardner, and Berntson (1997).
20. Draine and Greenwald (1999).
21. See Millward and Reber (1972); Greenwald (1992).

4. Knowing Who We Are

Epigraphs: Amiel (1899/1935), quoted by Whyte (1978), p. 157; Didion (1979), p. 11.

1. Shaw (1913/1979), p. 43.
2. Allport (1961), p. 28.
3. See, e.g., Tellegen et al. (1988); McCrae and Costa (1990); Loehlin (1992); Goldberg (1993); Plomin (1994).
4. Sampson (1989); Gergen (1991).
5. See Mischel (1968, 1973). Subsequent research by Triandis (1989) and Markus and Kitayama (1991) shows that overlooking situational influences is especially predominant in individualistic Western cultures. Cultures with a more collectivist orientation, such as many Asian cultures, recognize more that the social situation is a powerful determinant of behavior.
6. See Nisbett (1980); Ross and Nisbett (1991); Funder (1997).
7. Hogan, Johnson, and Briggs (1997). A more recent handbook of personality includes a chapter on the modern approach to the unconscious (Kihlstrom 1999), but the remaining twenty-seven chapters, save one on psychoanalysis, say little about nonconscious processes and personality.
8. Contrary to my argument, Reber (1992) suggests that there are relatively few individual differences in nonconscious processing. However, Reber focuses exclusively on such invariant systems as implicit learning and memory. He may well be correct that these basic functions of the mind vary little across people, just as there is little variation in our ability to acquire language. I take a broader view of the adaptive unconscious, including people's unique environmental adaptations of which they are not fully aware, including their chronic levels of motivation, their chronic construals of the environment, and their chronic representations of other people.
9. Miller (1995), p. 64.
10. For a review, see Mischel and Shoda (1999). The experiment with boys in the residential camp is described in Shoda, Mischel, and Wright (1994).
11. Kelly (1955).

12. See Higgins, King, and Mavin (1982); Bargh et al. (1986). The experiment on the chronic accessibility of honesty is by Bargh and Thein (1985).

13. Malcolm (1981), p. 76.

14. Malcolm (1981), p. 6.

15. Andersen and Glassman (1996), p. 254; Chen and Andersen (1999); Glassman and Andersen (1999); see also Sullivan (1953).

16. Elicker, Englund, and Sroufe (1992). For a review of evidence that responses in the Strange Situation predict later peer relationships, see Schneider, Atkinson, and Tardif (2001).

17. Hazan and Shaver (1987), p. 515.

18. For research on adult romantic attachment and how it is measured, see Hazan and Shaver (1987) and Tidwell, Reis, and Shaver (1996). For research on the Adult Attachment Interview, see Main, Kaplan, and Cassidy (1985); Cassidy and Shaver (1999). For research on the correlation between the two measures, see Bartholomew and Shaver (1998).

19. For research on implicit motives see Murray (1938); Atkinson (1964); McClelland (1985); Winter et al. (1998). For evidence on the separation of implicit and explicit motives, see McClelland, Koestner, and Weinberger (1992) and Schultheiss (in press). For a review of research on dependency, see Bornstein (1995).

20. Russo (1997), pp. 373–374.

21. The research findings on self-reports versus peer reports are reviewed by Kenny (1994). For more recent research on the relative validity of self- versus peer reports, see Kolar, Funder, and Colvin (1996) and Spain, Eaton, and Funder (2000).

22. The studies on predicting one's own versus other people's behavior were by Epley and Dunning (2000).

23. For research on the self see Epstein (1973); McGuire and Padawer-Singer (1976); Markus (1977); Markus and Nurius (1986); Higgins (1987, 1996); Triandis (1989); Markus and Kitayama (1991); Baumeister (1998).

24. Some researchers have distinguished implicit and explicit personality processes. Wegner and Vallacher (1981), for example, discussed "implicit psychology," or the nonconscious patterns of interpretation and construal that are responsible for people's subjective impressions of the world. These are the distinctive patterns of interpretation and evaluation that are located in the adaptive unconscious and that, as we have seen, are important determinants of behavior. Wegner and Vallacher also discussed explicit commonsense psychology, or people's conscious beliefs about themselves. We

have already encountered examples of such conscious theories, such as people's explicit beliefs about their attachment relationships and their explicit beliefs about their motives, both of which have been found to correlate poorly with nonconscious measures of the same constructs, but to predict interesting behaviors in their own right.

25. See McAdams (1994, 1996, 1999).
26. McCrae (1996), p. 355.
27. For social psychological work on alternative selves, see Markus and Nurius (1986); Higgins (1987); Ruvolo and Markus (1992).
28. McClelland and Pilon (1983); these data are discussed more fully by McClelland, Koestner, and Weinberger (1992).
29. Shaw (1913/1979), p. 42.
30. Brunstein, Schultheiss, and Grässmann (1998); Schultheiss and Brunstein (1999); Schultheiss (in press).

5. Knowing Why

Epigraph: Barnes (1986), pp. 183–184.
1. Sacks (1987), p. 109.
2. Estabrooks (1943), pp. 77–78.
3. Gazzaniga and LeDoux (1978), p. 149.
4. Given the research on split-brain patients and people suffering from brain damage, it is tempting to speculate about the locations in the brain of the adaptive unconscious and the conscious self. Indeed, many neuroscientists are studying the neural correlates of conscious and unconscious processing. The most that can be said about these efforts to date is that complex psychological states such as consciousness are interactions between many areas of the brain and are not located in a single lobe or localized set of neurons.
5. See Milgram (1974). For a general discussion of the power of social influences, and people's failure to recognize these influences, see Aronson, Wilson, and Akert (2002) and Ross and Nisbett (1991).
6. See Schachter and Singer (1962); Dutton and Aron (1974); Zillmann (1978).
7. Nisbett and Wilson (1977), quotation p. 231. Responses include Smith and Miller (1978); Ericsson and Simon (1980); Gavanski and Hoffman (1987).
8. The position I present here is an update of Nisbett and Wilson (1977) by Wilson and Stone (1985).

9. On the difficulty of perceiving covariation, see Nisbett and Ross (1980); Crocker (1981); Alloy and Tabachnik (1984).

10. The mood study, Wilson, Laser, and Stone (1982), was inspired by an unpublished study by Weiss and Brown (1977). Additional evidence for the argument that privileged information both helps and hurts people comes from the fact that in the Wilson, Laser, and Stone study and others like it, there is a positive correlation between participants' reports about the influences on their mood and the actual determinants of their mood, even when the strangers' reports are partialed out (statistically controlled). This result suggests that people achieve some accuracy by relying on privileged information, after shared theories (as measured by the strangers' reports) are subtracted out. However, there is also a positive correlation between the strangers' reports and the actual determinants of the participants' mood, even when the participants' reports were partialed out. This suggests that people lose some accuracy by relying on privileged information and not on shared theories. This and other evidence about the accuracy of people's and strangers' causal reports is reviewed by Wilson and Stone (1985).

6. Knowing How We Feel

Epigraphs: James (1890), p. 211; Begley (1992), p. 35.

1. Kierstead (1981), p. 48.
2. See, e.g., Armstrong (1968); Sheridan (1969); Palmer (1975).
3. For examples of unrecognized jealousy see Hebb (1946); Russell and Barrett (1999).
4. See Freud (1911/1958).
5. See, e.g., Erdelyi (1985) and Holmes (1990); for recent evidence that memories can be deliberately repressed, see Anderson and Green (2001).
6. The study of homosexual attraction in homophobics is by Adams, Wright, and Lohr (1996). The authors are not arguing that the homophobics were latent homosexuals who had no heterosexual feelings. In fact the homophobic men showed a larger increase in erection size in response to the heterosexual video than in response to the homosexual video. Nonetheless they did experience some increase in erection size in response to the male homosexual film, whereas the nonhomophobic men did not.
7. For evolutionary theories of emotion, see Darwin (1872); Tooby and Cosmides (1990); Lazarus (1991); Ekman (1992). For a discussion of the specific functions of emotions, see Frijda (1994); Keltner and Gross (1999).

8. A Danish physiologist named Carl Lange independently came up with a theory quite similar to James's; thus this approach became known as the James-Lange theory of emotion. See James (1894). For recent discussions of the James-Lange theory, see Ellsworth (1994) and Lang (1994).

9. LeDoux (1996), pp. 163, 165, and 302.

10. Carpenter (1874), pp. 539–540.

11. Ibid., p. 540.

12. See Hochschild (1979).

13. Schachter and Wheeler (1962); see also Schachter and Singer (1962).

14. Nisbett and Wilson (1977). For an updated review of this literature, see Wilson (1985).

15. Schachter and Wheeler (1962), p. 126.

16. For a theory of dual attitudes, see Wilson, Lindsey, and Schooler (2000). For an analysis of legal prohibitions against discrimination, see Krieger (1995).

17. Devine (1989); Higgins and King (1991); Fazio et al. (1995); Dovidio et al. (1997).

18. Dovidio (1995); Dovidio et al. (1997).

19. For a discussion of emotional intelligence, see Salovey and Mayer (1990); Goleman (1995).

20. Warnes (1986), p. 99. On emotional intelligence: Salovey, Hsee, and Mayer (1993); Goleman (1995). On alexithymia: Linden, Wen, and Paulhus (1995) Lane et al. (2000).

7. Knowing How We Will Feel

Epigraph: Hawthorne (1846/1937), p. 1055.

1. A lot has been written about how to define and measure happiness. Most of the studies I discuss allow people to define happiness for themselves, asking them straightforward questions such as "How happy would you say you are these days?" People's answers to questions like this have been found to be quite valid; for example, they are correlated with family members' and friends' reports of how happy they are and with the likelihood that they will commit suicide in the next five years. See Diener (2000) for a detailed discussion of measurement issues.

2. Richburg (1993), p. A28.

3. Kaplan (1978), p. 67. See also Brickman, Coates, and Janoff-Bulman (1978); Abrahamson (1980).

4. See Wortman, Silver, and Kessler (1993); Lund, Caserta, and Dimond (1989).

5. Kaprio, Koskenvuo, and Rita (1987); Lehman, Wortman, and Williams (1987).

6. Janoff-Bulman (1992); Davis, Nolen-Hoeksema, and Larson (1998).

7. Janoff-Bulman (1992), p. 133.

8. See Larson, Csikszentmihalhi, and Graef (1980); Suh, Diener, and Fujita (1996), p. 1091.

9. Smith (1759/1853), p. 149.

10. Lykken and Tellegen (1996).

11. Quoted in Csikszentmihalyi (1999), p. 825. Csikszentmihalyi has written extensively about the concept of flow, how to achieve it, and its relationship to happiness. For other work on the pursuit of goals and happiness see Emmons (1986); Ryan et al. (1996); Diener (2000).

12. Gilbert et al. (1998).

13. Brickman, Coates, and Janoff-Bulman (1978).

14. There is a lesson here, which I have applied to wine. I purposefully keep myself from drinking expensive wines too often, so that I do not ruin my enjoyment of cheap ones. I enjoy an occasional fancy wine, but I know that if I get too used to $25 bottles of Cabernet, I'll no longer enjoy the $7.99 specials in the supermarket. Why ruin something that gives me pleasure?

15. For writings on comparison levels, see Helson (1964); Brickman and Campbell (1971); and Parducci (1995).

16. It may be that the optimal state is not a balance of zero, but a moderately positive balance. The body can "handle" mild positive states; and indeed, most people report being above the neutral point of happiness most of the time. Further, mildly positive emotions may well have beneficial effects, such as improving people's ability to think creatively (see Fredrickson 1998). But the body cannot handle prolonged, extreme positive emotions. People rarely experience euphoria for extended periods.

17. On opponent process theory see Solomon (1980). For applications to drug addiction, see Koob et al. (1997). For a demonstration that opponent process theory does not explain well reactions to psychological (as opposed to physical) events, see Sandvik, Diener, and Larson (1985).

18. See Erber (1996).

19. Eisenberg (1994), p. 109.

20. Shenk (2001), pp. 194–195.

21. Gilbert and Wilson (2000). See also Vaillant (1993).

22. See Gilbert et al. (1998); Wilson et al. (2000).

23. See Griffin and Ross (1991); Ross and Nisbett (1991).
24. See Schkade and Kahneman (1998); Wilson et al. (2000).
25. Tatarkiewicz (1976), p. 111.

8. Introspection and Self-Narratives

Epigraph: Adams (1918), p. 432.
1. Freud (1924/1968), p. 306.
2. Spence (1982), p. 27. As we will see later, some modern psychoanalysts have rejected the archaeology metaphor and its implication that what are being unearthed in therapy are ancient truths. For example, object relation theorists downplay the importance of unconscious drives rooted in childhood and focus more on conflicts in current relationships. For some psychoanalysts, the analogy of introspection as espionage works better, whereby a patient and therapist attempt to uncover secrets that are deliberately hidden from view. Unlike the archaeology metaphor, the secrets are not necessarily ancient ones rooted in childhood, but perhaps issues concerning current relationships with others. Like the archaeology metaphor, however, there are truths to be discovered and this discovery can be difficult.
3. For a review of the evidence that introspection does not lead to more accurate reports about the self, see Silvia and Gendolla (2001).
4. The introspection-as-narrative metaphor has become popular in various subdisciplines of psychology and psychiatry, espoused by psychoanalysts such as Roy Schafer (1976) and Donald Spence (1982), postmodernists such as Kenneth Gergen (1991), psychologists such as Jerome Bruner (1990) and Douglas McAdams (1996), and cognitive therapists such as Michael Mahoney (1995). These views have been somewhat parochial, however, with little cross-fertilization or empirical grounding. I believe that a version of the narrative metaphor can be applied to all forms of introspection, including off-the-cuff glances inward, long-term self-examination, and psychotherapy.
5. As Donald Spence put it, "But as he [Freud] became more clinically experienced, he began to back away from this [archaeological] model and adopt a more moderate stand about the historical truth value of his analytic work, and in his final paper on the topic, he seems to have taken the position . . . that 'an assured conviction of the truth of the construction . . . achieves the same therapeutic result as a recaptured memory'"; Spence (1982), p. 289, quoting Freud (1937/1976), p. 266.

6. There is research evidence consistent with this interpretation of the flashlight metaphor. For example, several studies have found that people who introspect about how they feel report feelings that are especially good predictors of their future behavior, suggesting that the introspection focused their attention on feelings that were accessible but not currently the focus of consciousness. For a review of these studies see Wilson and Dunn (1986).

7. Barnes (2000), p. 69.

8. Quoted in Goodman (1945), p. 746.

9. Vargas Llosa (1986), p. 23.

10. Quoted in Zajonc (1980), p. 155.

11. Roethke (1965), p. 249.

12. Kant (1785/1949), Second Section.

13. Wilson and Kraft (1993). In another study we manipulated the kinds of thoughts about a new acquaintance that came to people's mind when people analyzed reasons, by making either positive or negative thoughts about this person easier to remember. As we expected, when positive thoughts were easy to remember people wrote about these thoughts in their reasons and then changed their attitude toward this person in a positive direction. When negative thoughts were easy to remember people wrote about these thoughts in their reasons and then changed their attitudes in a negative direction. A control group of people also found it easier to recall positive or negative information, but didn't analyze why they felt the way they did, and did not change their attitudes toward the person. Rather, it was the act of introspecting about one's reasons that led people to change their minds about how they felt. People assume that there is something particularly diagnostic about the reasons that they think of, not realizing that these reasons do not always capture their true feelings. See Wilson, Hodges, and LaFleur (1995).

14. The studies on dating couples are reported in Wilson and Kraft (1993) and Wilson et al. (1984). The study on art posters is reported in Wilson et al. (1993). Other studies have found that analyzing reasons reduces the accuracy of people's predictions about their own behavior (Wilson and LaFleur 1995), leads to attitudes that correspond less with the opinion of experts (Wilson and Schooler 1991), and reduces the accuracy of predictions about objective, real-world events, such as the outcome of basketball games (Halberstadt and Levine 1999). In a related line of research, Jonathan Schooler and colleagues have found that introspecting about one's memory for stimuli that were stored without words—such as faces or colors—impairs mem-

ory for these stimuli. They argue that trying to put nonverbal memories into words makes it more difficult to recall what cannot be captured with words. See Schooler and Engstler-Schooler (1990); Schooler and Fiore (1997).

15. See Schultheiss and Brunstein (1999); Schultheiss (in press).
16. Lyubomirsky, Caldwell, and Nolen-Hoeksema (1998), pp. 168 and 174. For overviews of the work on rumination see Nolen-Hoeksema (1998, 2000).
17. Pennebaker (1997b), p. 162.
18. For reviews of research on writing about emotional events see Pennebaker (1997a, 1997b) and Smyth (1998).
19. Hawthorne (1850/1996), chap. 11.
20. Pennebaker, Zech, and Rimé (in press).
21. See Wegner (1994).
22. Fels (2001), p. F5.
23. See Sloane et al. (1975); Kelly (1990).

9. Looking Outward to Know Ourselves

1. For reviews of research on subliminal influence, see Moore (1992); Pratkanis (1992); Theus (1994). A review by Dijksterhuis, Aarts, and Smith (2001) is more sanguine about the possibility of subliminal influence, but acknowledges that even effects found under controlled laboratory conditions tend to be small in magnitude.
2. For reviews of the effects of everyday advertising, see Abraham and Lodish (1990); Wells (1997).
3. For more on mental contamination, see Wilson and Brekke (1994); Wilson, Centerbar, and Brekke (in press).
4. For a discussion of changes in measures of prejudice over time, see Dovidio and Gaertner (1986) and McConahay (1986). The housing study is reported in Yinger (1995).
5. For research on automatic versus conscious prejudice see Devine (1989); Devine and Monteith (1999); Fazio (2001); and Banaji (2001). The study with the college students is by Dovidio et al. (1997).
6. See Payne (2001) for more details of this study.
7. See the Implicit Association Test website: http://buster.cs.yale.edu/implicit/)//enottxt/.
8. For research on shyness see Cheek and Melchior (1990) and Cheek and Krasnoperova (1999).

9. For writings on this school of thought, called symbolic interactionism, see Cooley (1902); Mead (1934).

10. Oltmanns, Turkheimer, and Thomas (2000). For a review of similar studies, see Kenny and DePaulo (1993) and Shrauger and Schoeneman (1979).

11. Armor and Taylor (1998); Taylor and Brown (1988).

10. Observing and Changing Our Behavior

Epigraphs: Brontë (1847/1985), chap. 14; Vonnegut (1966), p. v.

1. Muller (2001).
2. Grafton quoted in Waxman (2001), p. C8.
3. Forster (1927/1961), p. 97.
4. See Ryle (1949) and Bem (1972).
5. The study in which people were asked to gather signatures was by Kiesler, Nisbett, and Zanna (1969). For more on the fundamental attribution error, see Ross and Nisbett (1991). For evidence that people in Western cultures are especially prone to the fundamental attribution error, and that people in East Asian cultures are less prone, see Choi, Nisbett, and Norenzayan (1999).
6. For a review of research on this "overjustification effect," see Deci, Koestner, and Ryan (1999); Lepper, Henderlong, and Gingras (1999).
7. Aristotle (1962), p. 34; James (1890), pp. 49–50.
8. Real quoted in Brody (1997), p. F1. For Real's approach to depression, particularly in men, see Real (1997).
9. For a review of the Teen Outreach program, see Allen et al. (1997).
10. Post (1922), chap. 17.
11. David Polonoff (1987) and Dan McAdams (1996) offer useful criteria by which to judge narratives, such as coherence (i.e., that a story be logically consistent) and openness to change. Both also argue that accuracy is a key criterion, but the criterion for accuracy is not well specified.
12. Gergen and Kaye (1992), p. 175.
13. Ibid., pp. 177–178.
14. Brunstein, Schultheiss, and Grässmann (1998).
15. Didion (1979), pp. 12–13.
16. Freud (1937/1976), p. 266.
17. Zajonc quoted in Stephens (1992), p. 40.

Bibliography

Abraham, M. M., and L. M. Lodish. 1990. Getting the most out of advertising and promotion. *Harvard Business Review, 68,* 50–60.

Abrahamson, M. 1980. Sudden wealth, gratification and attainment: Durkheim's anomie of affluence reconsidered. *American Sociological Review, 45,* 49–57.

Adams, H. 1918. *The education of Henry Adams.* Boston: Houghton Mifflin.

Adams, H. E., L. W. J. Wright, and B. A. Lohr. 1996. Is homophobia associated with homosexual arousal? *Journal of Abnormal Psychology, 105,* 440–445.

Allen, J. P., S. Philliber, S. Herrling, and G. P. Kuperminc. 1997. Preventing teen pregnancy and academic failure: Experimental evaluation of a developmentally based approach. *Child Development, 64,* 729–742.

Alloy, L. B., and N. Tabachnik. 1984. Assessment of covariation by humans and animals: Joint influence of prior expectation and current situational information. *Psychological Review, 91,* 112–149.

Allport, G. W. 1961. *Pattern and growth in personality.* New York: Holt, Rinehart and Winston.

Amiel, H. F. 1889/1935. *The private journal of Henri Frédéric Amiel.* New York: Macmillan.

Andersen, S. M., and N. S. Glassman. 1996. Responding to significant others when they are not there: Effects on interpersonal inference, motivation, and affect. In R. M. Sorrentino and E. T. Higgins, eds., *Handbook of motivation and cognition*. Vol. 3, pp. 262–321. New York: Guilford.

Anderson, M. C., and C. Green. 2001. Suppressing unwanted memories by executive control. *Nature, 410,* 366–369.

Aristotle. 1962. *Nicomachean ethics,* trans. M. Ostwald. Indianapolis: Bobbs-Merrill.

Armor, D. A., and S. E. Taylor. 1998. Situated optimism: Specific outcome expectancies and self-regulation. In M. P. Zanna, ed., *Advances in experimental social psychology.* Vol. 30, pp. 309–379. San Diego: Academic.

Armstrong, D. M. 1968. *A materialist theory of the mind.* London: Routledge and Kegan Paul.

Aronson, E., T. D. Wilson, and R. M. Akert. 2002. *Social psychology.* 4th ed. Upper Saddle River, N.J.: Prentice Hall.

Aspinwall, L. G., and S. E. Taylor. 1997. A stitch in time: Self-regulation and proactive coping. *Psychological Bulletin, 121,* 417–436.

Atkinson, J. W. 1964. *An introduction to motivation.* New York: Van Nostrand.

Austen, J. 1713/1966. *Pride and Prejudice.* London: Penguin.

Banaji, M. 2001. Implicit attitudes can be measured. In H. L. I. Roediger and J. S. Nairne, eds., *The nature of remembering: Essays in honor of Robert G. Crowder,* pp. 117–150. Washington, D.C.: American Psychological Association.

Bargh, J. A. 1997. The automaticity of everyday life. In R. S. J. Wyer, ed., *Advances in social cognition.* Vol. 10, pp. 1–61. Mahwah, N.J.: Erlbaum.

Bargh, J. A., R. N. Bond, W. J. Lombardi, and M. E. Tota. 1986. The additive nature of chronic and temporary sources of construct accessibility. *Journal of Personality and Social Psychology, 50,* 869–878.

Bargh, J. A., and T. L. Chartrand. 1999. The unbearable automaticity of being. *American Psychologist, 54,* 462–479.

Bargh, J. A., P. M. Gollwitzer, A. L. Chai, K. Barndollar, and R. Trötschel. 2001. The automated will: Nonconscious activation and pursuit of behavioral goals. *Journal of Personality and Social Psychology, 81,* 1014–27.

Bargh, J. A., and P. Pietromonaco. 1982. Automatic information processing and social perception: The influence of trait information presented outside of conscious awareness on impression formation. *Journal of Personality and Social Psychology, 43,* 437–449.

Bargh, J. A., and P. Raymond. 1995. The naive misuse of power: Nonconscious sources of sexual harassment. *Journal of Social Issues, 51,* 85–96.

Bargh, J. A., and R. D. Thein. 1985. Individual construct accessibility, person memory, and the recall-judgment link: The case of information overload. *Journal of Personality and Social Psychology, 49,* 1129–46.

Barnes, J. 1986. *Staring at the sun.* London: Cape.

——— 2000. The story of Mats Israelson. *New Yorker,* July 24, 62–70.

Bartholomew, K., and P. R. Shaver. 1998. Methods of assessing adult attachment: Do they converge? In J. A. Simpson and W. S. Rholes, eds., *Attachment theory and close relationships,* pp. 25–45. New York: Guilford.

Baumeister, R. F. 1998. The self. In D. T. Gilbert, S. T. Fiske, and G. Lindzey, eds., *Handbook of social psychology.* 4th ed. Vol. 1, pp. 680–740. New York: McGraw-Hill.

Bechara, A., H. Damasio, D. Tranel, and A. R. Damasio. 1997. Deciding advantageously before knowing advantageous strategy. *Science, 275,* 1293–95.

Begley, L. 1992. *The man who was late.* New York: Knopf.

Bem, D. J. 1972. Self-perception theory. In L. Berkowitz, ed., *Advances in experimental social psychology.* Vol. 6, pp. 1–62. New York: Academic.

Bornstein, R. F. 1995. Sex differences in objective and projective dependency tests: A meta-analytic review. *Assessment, 2,* 319–331.

Brickman, P., and D. T. Campbell. 1971. Hedonic relativism and planning the good society. In M. H. Appley, ed., *Adaptation-level theory.* New York: Academic.

Brickman, P., D. Coates, and R. Janoff-Bulman. 1978. Lottery winners and accident victims: Is happiness relative? *Journal of Personality and Social Psychology, 36,* 917–927.

Broadbent, D. E. 1958. *Perception and communication.* London: Pergamon.

Brody, J. 1997. I don't want to talk about it: Overcoming the secret legacy of male depression. *New York Times,* December 30, F1.

Brontë, C. 1847/1984. *Jane Eyre.* New York: Longman.

Bruner, J. S. 1990. *Acts of meaning.* Cambridge, Mass.: Harvard University Press.

Brunstein, J. C., O. C. Schultheiss, and R. Grässmann. 1998. Personal goals and emotional well-being: The moderating role of motive dispositions. *Journal of Personality and Social Psychology, 75,* 494–508.

Cacioppo, J. T., W. L. Gardner, and G. G. Berntson. 1997. Beyond bipolar conceptualization and measures: The case of attitudes and evaluative space. *Personality and Social Psychology Review, 1,* 3–25.

Carpenter, W. B. 1874. *Principles of mental physiology.* New York: D. Appleton.

Cassidy, J., and P. R. E. Shaver, eds. 1999. *Handbook of attachment theory and research: Theory, research, and clinical applications.* New York: Guilford.

Cheek, J. M., and E. N. Krasnoperova. 1999. Varieties of shyness in adolescence and adulthood. In L. A. Schmidt and J. Schulkin, eds., *Extreme fear, shyness, and social phobia: Origins, biological mechanisms, and clinical outcomes,* pp. 224–250. Series in affective science. New York: Oxford University Press.

Cheek, J. M., and L. A. Melchior. 1990. Shyness, self-esteem, and self-consciousness. In H. Leitenberg, ed., *Handbook of social and evaluation anxiety,* pp. 47–82. New York: Plenum.

Chen, S., and S. Andersen. 1999. Relationships from the past in the present: Significant-other representations and transference in interpersonal life. In M. P. Zanna, ed., *Advances in experimental social psychology.* Vol. 31, pp. 123–190. San Diego: Academic.

Choi, I., R. E. Nisbett, and A. Norenzayan. 1999. Causal attribution across cultures: Variation and universality. *Psychological Bulletin, 125,* 47–63.

Claparède, E. 1911/1951. Recognition and "me-ness." In D. Rapaport, ed., *Organization and pathology of thought,* pp. 58–75. New York: Columbia University Press.

Clements, W. A., and J. Perner. 1994. Implicit understanding of belief. *Cognitive Development, 9,* 377–395.

Clore, G. L., K. Gasper, and E. Garvin. 2001. Affect as information. In J. P. Forgas, ed., *Handbook of affect and social cognition,* pp. 121–144. Mahwah, N.J.: Erlbaum.

Cole, J. (1995). *Pride and a daily marathon.* Cambridge, Mass.: MIT Press.

Cooley, C. H. 1902. *Human nature and the social order.* New York: Charles Scribner's Sons.

Crocker, J. 1981. Judgment of covariation by social perceivers. *Psychological Bulletin, 90,* 272–292.

Csikszentmihalyi, M. 1999. If we are so rich, why aren't we happy? *American Psychologist, 54,* 821–827.

Dallas, E. S. 1866. *The gay science.* London: Chapman and Hall.

Damasio, A. 1994. *Descartes's error: Emotion, reason, and the human brain.* New York: Grosset/Putnam.

Darwin, C. 1872. *The expression of emotions in man and animals.* New York: Philosophical Library.

Davidson, R. J. 1995. Cerebral asymmetry, emotion, and affective style. In R. J. Davidson and K. Hugdahl, eds., *Brain asymmetry,* pp. 361–388. Cambridge, Mass.: Bradford.

Davis, C. G., S. Nolen-Hoeksema, and J. Larson. 1998. Making sense of loss and benefitting from the experience: Two construals of meaning. *Journal of Personality and Social Psychology, 75,* 561–574.

Deci, E. L., R. Koestner, and R. M. Ryan. 1999. A meta-analytic review of experiments examining the effects of extrinsic rewards. *Psychological Bulletin, 125,* 627–668.

Deutsch, J. A., and D. Deutsch. 1963. Attention: Some theoretical considerations. *Psychological Review, 70,* 80–90.

Devine, P. G. 1989. Automatic and controlled processes in prejudice: The role of stereotypes and personal beliefs. In A. R. Pratkanis, S. J. Breckler, and A. G. Greenwald, eds., *Attitude structure and function,* pp. 181–212. Hillsdale, N.J.: Erlbaum.

Devine, P. G., and M. Monteith. 1999. Automaticity and control in stereotyping. In S. Chaiken and Y. Trope, eds., *Dual-process theories in social psychology,* pp. 339–360. New York: Guilford.

Didion, J. 1979. *The white album.* New York: Simon and Schuster.

Diener, E. 2000. Subjective well-being: The science of happiness and a proposal for a national index. *American Psychologist, 55,* 34–43.

Dijksterhuis, A., H. Aarts, and P. K. Smith. 2001. The power of the subliminal: On subliminal persuasion and other potential applications. Manuscript, University of Amsterdam.

Dovidio, J. F. 1995. Stereotypes, prejudice, and discrimination: Automatic and controlled processes. Paper presented at the annual meeting of the American Psychological Association, New York, August.

Dovidio, J. F., and S. L. Gaertner. 1986. Prejudice, discrimination, and racism: Historical trends and contemporary approaches. In J. F. Dovidio and S. L. Gaertner, eds., *Prejudice, discrimination, and racism,* pp. 1–34. Orlando, Fla.: Academic.

Dovidio, J. F., K. Kawakami, C. Johnson, B. Johnson, and A. Howard. 1997. On the nature of prejudice: Automatic and controlled processes. *Journal of Experimental Social Psychology, 33,* 510–540.

Draine, S. C., and A. G. Greenwald. 1999. Replicable unconscious semantic priming. *Journal of Experimental Psychology: General, 127,* 286–303.

Dulany, D. E. 1997. Consciousness in the explicit (deliberative) and implicit (evocative). In J. D. Cohen and J. W. Schooler, eds., *Scientific approaches to consciousness,* pp. 179–212. Mahwah, N.J.: Erlbaum.

Dutton, D. G., and A. P. Aron. 1974. Some evidence for heightened sexual attraction under conditions of high anxiety. *Journal of Personality and Social Psychology, 30,* 510–517.

Eisenberg, D. 1994. The girl who left her sock on the floor. *New Yorker,* December 5, 108–124.

Ekman, P. 1992. Facial expressions of emotion: New findings, new questions. *Psychological Science, 3,* 34–38.

Elicker, J., M. Englund, and L. A. Sroufe. 1992. Predicting peer competence and peer relationships in childhood from early parent-child relationships. In R. Parke and G. Ladd, eds., *Family-peer relations: Modes of linkage,* pp. 77–106. Hillsdale, N.J.: Erlbaum.

Ellsworth, P. C. 1994. William James and emotion: Is a century of fame worth a century of misunderstanding? *Psychological Review, 101,* 222–229.

Emmons, R. A. 1986. Personal strivings: An approach to personality and subjective well-being. *Journal of Personality and Social Psychology, 51,* 1058–68.

Epley, N., and D. Dunning. 2000. Feeling "holier than thou": Are self-serving assessments produced by errors in self- or social-prediction? *Journal of Personality and Social Psychology, 79,* 861–875.

Epstein, S. 1973. The self-concept revisited: Or a theory of a theory. *American Psychologist, 28,* 404–416.

Erber, R. 1996. The self-regulation of moods. In L. L. Martin and A. Tesser, eds., *Striving and feeling: Interactions among goals, affect, and self-regulation,* pp. 251–275. Mahwah, N.J.: Erlbaum.

Erdelyi, M. 1985. *Psychoanalysis: Freud's cognitive psychology.* New York: Freeman.

Ericsson, K. A., and H. A. Simon. 1980. Verbal reports as data. *Psychological Review, 87,* 215–251.

Estabrooks, G. H. 1943. *Hypnotism.* New York: E. P. Dutton.

Fazio, R. H. 2001. On the automatic activation of associated evaluations: An overview. *Cognition and Emotion, 15,* 115–141.

Fazio, R. H., J. R. Jackson, B. C. Dunton, and C. J. Williams. 1995. Variability in automatic activation as an unobtrusive measure of racial attitudes. A bona fide pipeline? *Journal of Personality and Social Psychology, 69,* 1013–27.

Fels, A. 2001. An escort into the land of sickness. *New York Times,* July 31, F5.

Flanagan, O. 1992. *Consciousness reconsidered.* Cambridge, Mass.: MIT Press.

Forster, E. M. 1927/1961. *Aspects of the novel.* London: Edward Arnold.

Fredrickson, B. 1998. What good are positive emotions? *Review of General Psychology, 2,* 300–319.

Freud, A. 1966. *The ego and the mechanisms of defense.* New York: International Universities Press.

Freud, S. 1900/1972. *The interpretation of dreams.* New York: Basic Books.

———— 1911/1958. Psychoanalytic notes upon an autobiographical account of a case of paranoia (dementia paranoides). In J. Strachey, ed., *The standard edition of the complete psychological works of Sigmund Freud.* Vol. 12, pp. 9–82. London: Hogarth Press.

———— 1924/1968. *A general introduction to psychoanalysis,* trans. Joan Riviere. New York: Washington Square Press.

———— 1937/1976. Constructions in analysis. In J. Strachey, ed., *The complete psychological works of Sigmund Freud.* Vol. 23. New York: W. W. Norton.

Frijda, N. H. 1994. Emotions are functional, most of the time. In P. Ekman and R. J. Davidson, eds., *The nature of emotion: Fundamental questions,* pp. 112–122. New York: Oxford University Press.

Funder, D. C. 1997. *The personality puzzle.* New York: W. W. Norton.

Gavanski, I., and C. Hoffman. 1987. Awareness of influences on one's own judgments: The roles of covariation detection and attention to the judgment process. *Journal of Personality and Social Psychology, 52,* 453–463.

Gazzaniga, M. S., and J. E. LeDoux. 1978. *The integrated mind.* New York: Plenum.

Gergen, K. J. 1991. *The saturated self: Dilemmas of identity in modern life.* New York: Basic.

Gergen, K. J., and J. Kaye. 1992. Beyond narrative in the negotiation of therapeutic meaning. In S. McNamee and K. J. Gergen, eds., *Therapy as social construction: Inquiries in social construction,* pp. 166–185. London: Sage.

Gilbert, D. T., E. C. Pinel, T. D. Wilson, S. J. Blumberg, and T. P. Wheatley. 1998. Immune neglect: A source of durability bias in affective forecasting. *Journal of Personality and Social Psychology, 75,* 617–638.

Gilbert, D. T., and T. D. Wilson. 2000. Miswanting. In J. Forgas, ed., *Thinking and feeling: The role of affect in social cognition,* pp. 178–197. Cambridge: Cambridge University Press.

Glassman, N. S., and S. M. Andersen. 1999. Activating transference without consciousness: Using significant-other relationships to go beyond the subliminally given information. *Journal of Personality and Social Psychology, 77,* 1146–62.

Goldberg, L. R. 1993. The structure of phenotypic personality traits. *American Psychologist, 48,* 26–34.

Goleman, D. 1995. *Emotional intelligence.* New York: Bantam.

Goodman, N. G. E. 1945. *A Benjamin Franklin reader.* New York: Thomas Y. Crowell.

Greenwald, A. G. 1992. New look 3: Unconscious cognition reclaimed. *American Psychologist, 47,* 766–779.

Griffin, D. W., and L. Ross. 1991. Subjective construal, social inference, and human misunderstanding. In L. Berkowitz, ed., *Advances in experimental social psychology.* Vol. 24, pp. 319–359. San Diego: Academic.

Grünbaum, A. 1984. *The foundations of psychoanalysis: A philosophical critique.* Berkeley: University of California Press.

Güzeldere, G. 1997. The many faces of consciousness: A field guide. In N. Block, O. Flanagan, and G. Güzeldere, eds., *The nature of consciousness: Philosophical debates,* 1–67. Cambridge: MIT Press.

Halberstadt, J. B., and G. M. Levine. 1999. Effects of reasons analysis on the accuracy of predicting basketball games. *Journal of Applied Social Psychology, 29,* 517–530.

Hamilton, W. 1865. *Lectures on metaphysics.* Vol. 1. Boston: Gould and Lincoln.

Hauser, M. 1998. Games primates play. *Discover,* September, 48–57.

Hawthorne, N. 1846/1937. Rappaccini's daughter. In N. H. Pearson, ed., *The complete novels and selected tales of Nathaniel Hawthorne,* 1043–65. New York: Random House.

———— 1850/1996. *The scarlet letter.* London: J. M. Dent.

Hazan, C., and P. Shaver. 1987. Romantic love conceptualized as an attachment process. *Journal of Personality and Social Psychology, 52,* 511–524.

Hebb, D. O. 1946. Emotion in man and animal: An analysis of the intuitive processes of recognition. *Psychological Review, 53,* 88–106.

Heine, S. J., D. R. Lehman, H. R. Markus, and S. Kitayama. 1999. Is there a universal need for positive self-regard? *Psychological Review, 106,* 766–794.

Helson, H. 1964. *Adaptation-level theory.* New York: Harper.

Higgins, E. T. 1987. Self-discrepancy: A theory relating self and affect. *Psychological Review, 94,* 319–340.

———— 1996. The "self-digest": Self-knowledge serving self-regulatory functions. *Journal of Personality and Social Psychology, 71,* 1062–83.

Higgins, E. T., and G. A. King. 1981. Accessibility of social constructs: Information-processing consequences of individual and contextual variability. In N. Cantor and J. F. Kihlstrom, eds., *Personality and social interaction,* pp. 69–121. Hillsdale, N.J.: Erlbaum.

Higgins, E. T., G. A. King, and G. H. Mavin. 1982. Individual construct accessibility and subjective impressions and recall. *Journal of Personality and Social Psychology, 43,* 35–47.

Hochschild, A. R. 1979. Emotion work, feeling rules, and social structure. *American Journal of Sociology, 85,* 551–575.

Hogan, R., J. Johnson, and S. Briggs, eds. 1997. *Handbook of personality psychology.* San Diego: Academic Press.

Holmes, D. S. 1990. The evidence for repression: An examination of sixty years of research. In J. L. Singer, ed., *Repression and dissociation,* pp. 85–102. Chicago: University of Chicago Press.

James, W. 1890. *Principles of psychology.* Vol. 1. New York: Holt.

———— 1894. The physical basis of emotion. *Psychological Review, 1,* 516–529.

Janoff-Bulman, R. 1992. *Shattered assumptions: Toward a new psychology of trauma.* New York: Free Press.

Kaas, J. H., and C. E. Collins. 2001. Evolving ideas of brain evolution. *Nature, 411,* 141.

Kagan, J. 1994. *Galen's prophecy: Temperament in human nature.* New York: Basic.

Kant, I. 1785/1949. *Fundamental principles of the metaphysics of morals,* trans. T. K. Abbott. Indianapolis: Bobbs-Merrill.

Kaplan, H. R. 1978. *Lottery winners: How they won and how winning changed their lives.* New York: Harper and Row.

Kaprio, J., M. Koskenvuo, and H. Rita. 1987. Mortality after bereavement: A prospective study of 95,647 widowed persons. *American Journal of Public Health, 77,* 283–287.

Kelly, G. A. 1955. *The psychology of personal constructs.* New York: W. W. Norton.

Kelly, T. A. 1990. The role of values in psychotherapy: A critical review of process and outcome effects. *Clinical Psychology Review, 10,* 171–186.

Keltner, D., and J. J. Gross. 1999. Functional accounts of emotion. *Cognition and Emotion, 13,* 467–480.

Kenny, D. A. 1994. *Interpersonal perception: A social relations analysis.* New York: Guilford.

Kenny, D. A., and B. M. DePaulo. 1993. Do people know how others view them? An empirical and theoretical account. *Psychological Bulletin, 114,* 145–161.

Kierstead, M. D. 1981. The Shetland pony. *New Yorker,* April 6, 40–48.

Kiesler, C. A., R. E. Nisbett, and M. P. Zanna. 1969. On inferring one's beliefs from one's behavior. *Journal of Personality and Social Psychology, 11,* 321–327.

Kihlstrom, J. F. 1987. The cognitive unconscious. *Science, 237,* 1445–52.

——— 1999. The psychological unconscious. In L. A. Pervin and O. P. John, eds., *Handbook of personality: Theory and research,* pp. 424–442. 2d ed. New York: Guilford.

Kihlstrom, J. F., and D. L. Schacter. 1990. Anesthesia, amnesia, and the cognitive unconscious. In B. Bonke, W. Fitch, and K. Millar, eds., *Memory and awareness in anesthesia,* pp. 21–44. Amsterdam: Swets and Zeitlinger.

Koestler, A. 1978. Introduction. In L. L. Whyte, ed., *The unconscious before Freud,* pp. i–v. New York: St. Martin's.

Kolar, D. W., D. C. Funder, and C. R. Colvin. 1996. Comparing the accuracy of personality judgments by the self and knowledgeable others. *Journal of Personality, 64,* 311–337.

Komatsu, S., M. Naito, and T. Fuke. 1996. Age-related and intelligence-related differences in implicit memory: Effects of generation on a word-fragment completion task. *Journal of Experimental Child Psychology, 62,* 151–172.

Koob, G. F., S. B. Caine, L. Parsons, A. Markou, and F. Weiss. 1997. Opponent process model and psychostimulant addiction. *Pharmacology Biochemistry and Behavior, 57,* 513–521.

Krieger, L. H. 1995. The content of our categories: A cognitive bias approach to discrimination and equal employment opportunity. *Stanford Law Review, 47,* 1161–1248.

Lane, R. D., L. Sechrest, R. Riedel, D. E. Shapiro, and A. W. Kaszniak. 2000. Pervasive emotion recognition deficit common to alexithymia and the repressive coping style. *Psychosomatic Medicine, 62,* 492–501.

Lang, P. J. 1994. The varieties of emotional experience: A meditation on James-Lange theory. *Psychological Review, 101,* 211–221.

Larson, R., M. Csikszentmihalhi, and R. Graef. 1980. Mood variability and the psychosocial adjustment of adolescents. *Journal of Youth and Adolescence, 9,* 469–490.

Laycock, T. 1860. *Mind and brain: The correlations of consciousness and organization.* London: Simpkin, Marschall.

Lazarus, R. S. 1991. *Emotion and adaptation.* Oxford: Oxford University Press.

LeDoux, J. 1996. *The emotional brain: The mysterious underpinnings of emotional life.* New York: Simon and Schuster.

Lehman, D. R., C. B. Wortman, and A. F. Williams. 1987. Long-term effects of losing a spouse or child in a motor vehicle crash. *Journal of Personality and Social Psychology, 52,* 218–231.

Lepper, M. R., D. Greene, and R. E. Nisbett. 1973. Undermining children's intrinsic interest with extrinsic rewards: A test of the overjustification hypothesis. *Journal of Personality and Social Psychology, 28,* 129–137.

Lepper, M. R., J. Henderlong, and I. Gingras. 1999. Understanding the effects of extrinsic rewards on intrinsic motivation–uses and abuses of meta-analysis: Comment on Deci, Koestner, and Ryan (1999). *Psychological Bulletin, 125,* 669–676.

Lewicki, P., T. Hill, and E. Bizot. 1988. Acquisition of procedural knowledge about a pattern of stimuli that cannot be articulated. *Cognitive Psychology, 20,* 24–37.

Linden, W., F. Wen, and D. L. Paulhus. 1995. Measuring alexithymia: Reliability, validity, and prevalence. In J. Butcher et al., eds., *Handbook of personality assessment.* Vol. 10, pp. 51–95. Hillsdale, N.J.: Erlbaum.

Loehlin, J. 1992. *Genes and environment in personality development.* New York: Guilford.

Lund, D. A., M. S. Caserta, and M. F. Dimond. 1989. Impact of spousal bereavement on the subjective well-being of older adults. In D. A. Lund, ed., *Older bereaved spouses: Research with practical implications,* pp. 3–15. New York: Hemisphere.

Lykken, D., and A. Tellegen. 1996. Happiness is a stochastic phenomenon. *Psychological Science, 7,* 186–189.

Lyubomirsky, S., N. D. Caldwell, and S. Nolen-Hoeksema. 1998. Effects of ruminative and distracting responses to depressed mood on retrieval of autobiographical memories. *Journal of Personality and Social Psychology, 75,* 166–177.

Mahoney, M. J. 1995. The cognitive and constructive psychotherapies: Contexts and challenges. In M. J. Mahoney, ed., *Cognitive and constructive psychotherapies: Theory, research, and practice,* pp. 195–208. New York: Springer.

Main, M., N. Kaplan, and J. Cassidy. 1985. Security in infancy, childhood, and adulthood: A move to the level of representation. In I. Bretherton and E. Waters, eds., *Monographs of the Society for Research in Child Development, 50,* pp. 66–106.

Malcolm, J. 1981. *Psychoanalysis: The impossible profession.* New York: Knopf.

Mandler, G. 1997. Consciousness redux. In J. D. Cohen and J. W. Schooler, eds., *Scientific approaches to consciousness,* pp. 479–498. Mahwah, N.J.: Erlbaum.

Marcel, A. J. 1983. Conscious and unconscious perception: Experiments on visual masking and word recognition. *Cognitive Psychology, 15,* 197–237.

Margolis, H. 1987. *Patterns, thinking, and cognition: A theory of judgment.* Chicago: University of Chicago Press.

Markus, H. R. 1977. Self-schemata and processing information about the self. *Journal of Personality and Social Psychology, 35,* 63–78.

Markus, H. R., and S. Kitayama. 1991. Culture and the self: Implications for cognition, emotion, and motivation. *Psychological Review, 98,* 224–253.

Markus, H. R., and P. Nurius. 1986. Possible selves. *American Psychologist, 41,* 954–969.

McAdams, D. P. 1994. *The stories we live by: Personal myths and the making of the self.* New York: Morrow.

———— 1996. Personality, modernity, and the storied self: A contemporary framework for studying persons. *Psychological Inquiry, 7,* 295–321.

———— 1999. Personal narratives and the life story. In L. A. Pervin and O. P. John, eds., *Handbook of personality: Theory and research,* pp. 443–476. 2d ed. New York: Guilford.

McClelland, D. C. 1985. How motives, skills and values determine what people do. *American Psychologist, 40,* 812–825.

McClelland, D. C., R. Koestner, and J. Weinberger. 1992. How do self-attributed and implicit motives differ? In C. P. Smith, ed., *Motivation and personality: Handbook of thematic content analysis,* pp. 49–72. Cambridge: Cambridge University Press.

McClelland, D. C., and D. A. Pilon. 1983. Sources of adult motives in patterns of parent behavior in early childhood. *Journal of Personality and Social Psychology, 44,* 564–574.

McConahay, J. B. 1986. Modern racism, ambivalence, and the Modern Racism Scale. In J. F. Dovidio and S. L. Gaertner, eds., *Prejudice, discrimination, and racism,* pp. 91–125. Orlando, Fla.: Academic.

McCrae, R. R. 1996. Integrating the levels of personality. *Psychological Inquiry, 7,* 353–356.

McCrae, R. R., and P. T. J. Costa. 1990. *Personality in adulthood.* New York: Guilford.

McGuire, W. J., and A. Padawer-Singer. 1976. Trait salience in the spontaneous self-concept. *Journal of Personality and Social Psychology, 33,* 743–754.

Mead, G. H. 1934. *Mind, self, and society.* Chicago: University of Chicago Press.

Milgram, S. 1974. *Obedience to authority: An experimental view.* New York: Harper and Row.

Miller, J. 1995. Going unconscious. *New York Review of Books,* April 20, 59–65.

Miller, J. G. 1942. *Unconsciousness.* London: Chapman and Hall.

Millward, R. B., and A. S. Reber. 1972. Probability learning: Contingent-event sequences with lags. *American Journal of Psychology, 85,* 81–98.

Mischel, W. 1968. *Personality and assessment.* New York: Wiley.

———— 1973. Toward a cognitive social learning reconceptualization of personality. *Psychological Review, 80,* 252–283.

Mischel, W., and Y. Shoda. 1995. A cognitive-affective system theory of personality: Reconceptualizing the situations, dispositions, dynamics, and invariance in personality structure. *Psychological Review, 102,* 246–268.

———— 1999. Integrating dispositions and processing dynamics within a unified theory of personality: The cognitive-affective personality system. In L. A. Pervin and O. P. John, eds., *Handbook of personality: Theory and research,* pp. 197–218. 2d ed. New York: Guilford.

Moore, T. E. 1992. Subliminal perception: Facts and fallacies. *Skeptical Inquirer, 16,* 273–281.

Moray, N. 1959. Attention in dichotic listening: Affective cues and the influence of instructions. *Quarterly Journal of Experimental Psychology, 11,* 56–60.

Muller, M. 2001. The novelist's life is altered by a confident alter ego. *New York Times,* August 13, pp. B1, B2.

Murray, H. A. 1938. *Explorations in personality.* New York: Oxford University Press.

Nisbett, R. E. 1980. The trait construct in lay and professional psychology. In L. Festinger, ed., *Retrospections on social psychology,* pp. 109–130. New York: Oxford University Press.

Nisbett, R. E., and L. Ross. 1980. *Human inference: Strategies and shortcomings of social judgment.* Englewood Cliffs, N.J.: Prentice-Hall.

Nisbett, R. E., and T. D. Wilson. 1977. Telling more than we can know: Verbal reports on mental processes. *Psychological Review, 84,* 231–259.

Nolen-Hoeksema, S. 1998. The other end of the continuum: The costs of rumination. *Psychological Inquiry, 9,* 216–219.

———— 2000. The role of rumination in depressive disorders and mixed anxiety/depressive symptoms. *Journal of Abnormal Psychology, 109,* 504–511.

Norman, D. A. 1968. Toward a theory of memory and attention. *Psychological Review, 75,* 522–536.

Nørretranders, T. 1998. *The user illusion,* trans. J. Sydenham. New York: Viking.

Oltmanns, T. F., E. Turkheimer, and C. Thomas. 2000. Perceptions of the self and others in relation to personality disorders. Paper presented at the American Psychological Society, Miami, June 9.

Palmer, D. 1975. Unfelt pains. *American Philosophical Quarterly, 12,* 289–298.

Parducci, A. 1995. *Happiness, pleasure, and judgment: The contextual theory and its applications.* Mahwah, N.J.: Erlbaum.

Payne, B. K. 2001. Prejudice and perception: The role of automatic and controlled processes in misperceiving a weapon. *Journal of Personality and Social Psychology, 81,* 181–192.

Pennebaker, J. W. 1997a. *Opening up: The healing power of expressing emotions.* Rev. ed. New York: Guilford.

——— 1997b. Writing about emotional experiences as a therapeutic process. *Psychological Science, 8,* 162–166.

Pennebaker, J. W., E. Zech, and B. Rimé. In press. Disclosing and sharing emotion: Psychological, social, and health consequences. In M. S. Stroebe, R. O. Hansson, W. Stroebe, and H. Schut, eds., *Handbook of bereavement research: Consequences, coping, and care.* Washington, D.C.: American Psychological Association.

Perner, J., and W. A. Clements. 2000. From an implicit to an explicit "theory of mind." In Y. Rossetti and A. Revonsuo, eds., *Beyond dissociation: Interaction between dissociated implicit and explicit processing,* pp. 273–294. Amsterdam: John Benjamins.

Plomin, R. 1994. *Genetics and experience: The developmental interplay between nature and nurture.* Newbury Park, Calif.: Sage.

Polonoff, D. 1987. Self-deception. *Social Research, 54,* 45–53.

Post, E. 1922. *Etiquette in society, in business, in politics and at home.* New York: Funk and Wagnalls.

Pratkanis, A. 1992. The cargo-cult science of subliminal persuasion. *Skeptical Inquirer, 16,* 260–272.

Proffitt, D. R., M. Bhalla, R. Gossweiler, and J. Midgett. 1995. Perceiving geographical slant. *Psychonomic Bulletin and Review, 2,* 409–428.

Proust, M. 1934. *Remembrance of things past,* trans. C. K. Scott-Moncrieff. New York: Random House.

Real, T. 1998. *I don't want to talk about it: Overcoming the secret legacy of male depression.* New York: Simon and Schuster.

Reber, A. S. 1992. The cognitive unconscious: An evolutionary perspective. *Consciousness and Cognition, 1,* 93–133.

——— 1993. *Implicit learning and tacit knowledge: An essay on the cognitive unconscious.* New York: Oxford University Press.

——— 1997. How to differentiate implicit and explicit modes of acquisition. In J. D. Cohen and J. W. Schooler, eds., *Scientific approaches to consciousness,* pp. 137–159. Mahwah, N.J.: Erlbaum.

Richburg, K. B. 1993. Reaching the end of a pot o' gold. *Washington Post,* October 10, A1, A28.

Rock, I., ed. 1997. *Indirect perception.* Cambridge, Mass.: MIT Press.

Roediger, H. L., and K. B. McDermott. 1993. Implicit memory in normal human subjects. In F. Boller and J. Grafman, eds., *Handbook of Neuropsychology.* Vol. 8, pp. 63–131. Amsterdam: Elsevier.

Roethke, R. 1975. *The collected poems of Theodore Roethke.* Garden City, N.Y.: Anchor.

Rosenthal, R., and L. Jacobson. 1968. *Pygmalion in the classroom: Teacher expectation and student intellectual development.* New York: Holt, Rinehart and Winston.

Ross, L., and R. E. Nisbett. 1991. *The person and the situation.* New York: McGraw-Hill.

Rovee-Collier, C. 1997. Dissociations in infant memory: Rethinking the development of implicit and explicit memory. *Psychological Review, 104,* 467–498.

Russell, J. A., and L. F. Barrett. 1999. Core affect, prototypical emotional episodes, and other things called emotion: Dissecting the elephant. *Journal of Personality and Social Psychology, 76,* 805–819.

Russo, R. 1997. *Straight Man.* New York: Random House.

Ruvolo, A. P., and H. R. Markus. 1992. Possible selves and performance: The power of self-relevant imagery. *Social Cognition, 10,* 95–124.

Ryan, R. M., K. M. Sheldon, T. Kasser, and E. L. Deci. 1996. All goals are not created equal. In J. A. Bargh and P. M. Gollwitzer, eds., *The psychology of action: Linking cognition and motivation to behavior,* pp. 7–26. New York: Guilford.

Ryle, G. 1949. *The concept of mind.* London: Hutchinson.

Sacks, O. 1987. *The man who mistook his wife for a hat and other clinical tales.* New York: Harper and Row.

Sadker, M., and D. Sadker. 1994. *Failing at fairness: How America's schools cheat girls.* New York: Charles Scribner's Sons.

Salovey, P., C. K. Hsee, and J. D. Mayer. 1993. Emotional intelligence and the self-regulation of affect. In D. M. Wegner and J. W. Pennebaker, eds., *Handbook of mental control,* pp. 258–277. Englewood Cliffs, N.J.: Prentice-Hall.

Salovey, P., and J. D. Mayer. 1990. Emotional intelligence. *Imagination, Cognition, and Personality, 9,* 185–211.

Sampson, E. E. 1989. The challenge of social change for psychology: Globalization and psychology's theory of the person. *American Psychologist, 44,* 914–921.

Sandvik, E., E. Diener, and R. J. Larson. 1985. The opponent process theory and affective reactions. *Motivation and Emotion, 94,* 407–418.

Schachter, S., and J. E. Singer. 1962. Cognitive, social, and physiological determinants of emotion. *Psychological Review, 69,* 379–399.

Schachter, S., and L. Wheeler. 1962. Epinephrine, chlorpromazine, and amusement. *Journal of Abnormal and Social Psychology, 65,* 121–128.

Schacter, D. L. 1996. *Searching for memory: The brain, the mind, and the past.* New York: Basic.

Schafer, R. 1976. *A new language for psychoanalysis.* New Haven: Yale University Press.

Schkade, D. A., and D. Kahneman. 1998. Would you be happy if you lived in California? A focusing illusion in judgments of well-being. *Psychological Science, 9,* 340–346.

Schneider, B. H., L. Atkinson, and C. Tardif. 2001. Child-parent attachment and children's peer relations: A quantitative review. *Developmental Psychology, 37,* 86–100.

Schooler, J. W., and T. Y. Engstler-Schooler. 1990. Verbal overshadowing of visual memories: Some things are better left unsaid. *Cognitive Psychology, 22,* 36–71.

Schooler, J. W., and S. M. Fiore. 1997. Consciousness and the limits of language: You can't always say what you think or think what you say. In J. D. Cohen and J. W. Schooler, eds., *Scientific approaches to consciousness: Carnegie Mellon Symposia on cognition,* pp. 241–257. Mahwah, N.J.: Erlbaum.

Schultheiss, O. In press. An information processing account of implicit motive arousal. In M. L. Maehr and P. Pintrich, eds., *Advances in motivation and achievement.* Vol. 12. Greenwich, Conn.: JAI Press.

Schultheiss, O. C., and J. C. Brunstein. 1999. Goal imagery: Bridging the gap between implicit motives and explicit goals. *Journal of Personality, 67,* 1–38.

Shaw, G. B. 1913/1979. *Pygmalion.* New York: Penguin.

Shenk, D. 2001. *The forgetting Alzheimer's: Portrait of an epidemic.* New York: Doubleday.

Sheridan, G. 1969. The electroencephalogram argument against incorrigibility. *American Philosophical Quarterly, 6,* 62–70.

Shoda, Y., W. Mischel, and J. C. Wright. 1994. Intraindividual stability in the organization and patterning of behavior: Incorporating psychological situations into the idiographic analysis of personality. *Journal of Personality and Social Psychology, 67,* 674–687.

Shrauger, J. S., and T. J. Schoeneman. 1979. Symbolic interactionist view of self-concept: Through the looking glass darkly. *Psychological Bulletin, 86,* 549–573.

Silvia, P. J., and G. H. E. Gendolla. 2001. On introspection and self-perception: Does self-focused attention enable accurate self-knowledge? *Review of General Psychology, 5,* 241–269.

Simon, H. 1997. Scientific approaches to the question of consciousness. In J. D. Cohen and J. W. Schooler, eds., *Scientific approaches to consciousness,* pp. 513–520. Mahwah, N.J.: Erlbaum.

Sloane, R. B., F. R. Staples, A. H. Cristol, N. J. Yorkston, and K. Whipple. 1975. *Psychotherapy versus behavior therapy.* Cambridge, Mass.: Harvard University Press.

Smith, A. 1759/1853. *The theory of moral sentiments.* London: H. G. Bohn.

Smith, C. P., ed. 1992. *Motivation and personality: Handbook of thematic content analysis.* Cambridge: Cambridge University Press.

Smith, E. R., and F. D. Miller. 1978. Limits on perception of cognitive processes: A reply to Nisbett and Wilson. *Psychological Review, 85,* 355–382.

Smyth, J. M. 1998. Written emotional expression: Effect sizes, outcome types, and moderating variables. *Journal of Consulting and Clinical Psychology, 66,* 174–184.

Solomon, R. L. 1980. The opponent-process theory of acquired motivation. *American Psychologist, 35,* 691–712.

Spain, J. S., L. G. Eaton, and D. C. Funder. 2000. Perspectives on personality: The relative accuracy of self versus others for the prediction of emotion and behavior. *Journal of Personality, 68,* 837–867.

Spence, D. P. 1982. *Narrative truth and historical truth.* New York: W. W. Norton.

Stephens, M. 1992. To thine own selves be true. *Los Angeles Times,* August 23, 40.

Suh, E., E. Diener, and F. Fujita. 1996. Events and subjective well-being: Only recent events matter. *Journal of Personality and Social Psychology, 70,* 1091–1102.

Sullivan, H. S. 1953. *The interpersonal theory of psychiatry.* New York: W. W. Norton.

Swann, W. B., Jr. 1996. *Self-traps: The elusive quest for higher self-esteem.* New York: Freeman.

Tatarkiewicz, W. 1976. *Analysis of happiness,* trans. E. Rothert and D. Zielińska. Warszawa: PWN/Polish Scientific. Original work published 1962.

Taylor, C. 1989. *Sources of the self: The making of the modern identity.* Cambridge, Mass.: Harvard University Press.

Taylor, S. E., and J. D. Brown. 1988a. Illusions and well-being: A social-psychological perspective on mental health. *Psychological Bulletin, 103,* 193–210.

——— 1988b. Positive illusions and well-being revisited: Separating fact from fiction. *Psychological Bulletin, 116,* 21–27.

Tellegen, A., D. T. Lykken, T. J. J. Bouchard, K. J. Wilcox, N. L. Segal, and S. Rich. 1988. Personality similarity in twins reared apart and together. *Journal of Personality and Social Psychology, 40,* 885–898.

Theus, K. T. 1994. Subliminal advertising and the psychology of processing unconscious stimuli: A review. *Psychology and Marketing, 11,* 271–290.

Tidwell, M. O., H. T. Reiss, and P. R. Shaver. 1966. Attachment, attractiveness, and social interaction: A diary study. *Journal of Personality and Social Psychology, 71,* 729–745.

Tooby, J., and L. Cosmides. 1990. The past explains the present: Emotional adaptations and the structure of ancestral environments. *Ethology and Sociobiology, 11,* 375–424.

Treisman, A. M. 1964. Monitoring and storage of irrelevant messages and selective attention. *Journal of Verbal Learning and Verbal Behavior, 3,* 449–459.

———— 1993. The perception of features and objects. In A. Baddeley and L. Weiskrantz, eds., *Attention: Selection, awareness, and control,* pp. 5–35. Oxford: Clarendon Press.

Triandis, H. C. 1989. The self and social behavior in differing cultural contexts. *Psychological Review, 93,* 506–520.

Vaillant, G. E. 1993. *The wisdom of the ego.* Cambridge, Mass.: Harvard University Press.

Vargas Llosa, M. 1986. My son the Rastafarian. *New York Times Magazine,* February 16, 20–28, 30, 41–43, 67.

Velmans, M. 1991. Is human information processing conscious? *Behavioral and Brain Sciences, 14,* 651–726.

Vonnegut, K. 1966. *Mother night.* New York: Delacorte.

Warnes, H. 1986. Alexithymia, clinical and therapeutic aspects. *Psychotherapy and Psychosomatics, 46,* 96–104.

Waxman, S. 2001. Mystery writer in the mirror. *Washington Post,* November 1, C1, C8.

Wegner, D. M. 1994. Ironic processes of mental control. *Psychological Review, 101,* 34–52.

———— 2002. *The illusion of conscious will.* Cambridge, Mass.: MIT Press.

Wegner, D. M., and R. R. Vallacher. 1981. Common-sense psychology. In J. P. Forgas, ed., *Social cognition: Perspectives in everyday understanding,* pp. 224–246. London: Academic.

Wegner, D. M., and T. Wheatley. 1999. Apparent mental causation: Sources of the experience of will. *American Psychologist, 54,* 480–492.

Weiss, J., and P. Brown. 1977. Self-insight error in the explanation of mood. Manuscript, Harvard University.

Wellman, H. M., D. Cross, and J. Watson. 2001. Meta-analysis of theory-of-mind development: The truth about false belief. *Child Development, 72,* 655–684.

Wells, W. D., ed. 1997. *Measuring advertising effectiveness.* Mahwah, N.J.: Erlbaum.

Westen, D. 1998. The scientific legacy of Sigmund Freud: Toward a psychodynamically informed psychological science. *Psychological Bulletin, 124,* 333–371.

Whyte, L. L. 1978. *The unconscious before Freud.* New York: St. Martin's.

Willingham, D. B., and L. Preuss. 1995. The death of implicit of implicit memory. *PSYCHE, 2,* http://psyche.cs.monash.edu.au/volume2-1/psyche-95-2-15-implicit-1-willingham.html.

Wilson, T. D. 1985. Strangers to ourselves: The origins and accuracy of beliefs about one's own mental states. In J. H. Harvey and G. Weary, eds., *Attribution: Basic issues and applications,* pp. 9–35. Orlando, Fla.: Academic.

Wilson, T. D., and N. Brekke. 1994. Mental contamination and mental correction: Unwanted influences on judgments and evaluations. *Psychological Bulletin, 116,* 117–142.

Wilson, T. D., D. B. Centerbar, and N. Brekke. In press. Mental contamination and the debiasing problem. In T. Gilovich, D. W. Griffin, and D. Kahneman, eds., *The psychology of judgment: Heuristics and biases.* New York: Cambridge University Press.

Wilson, T. D., and D. S. Dunn. 1986. Effects of introspection on attitude-behavior consistency: Analyzing reasons versus focusing on feelings. *Journal of Experimental Social Psychology, 22,* 249–263.

Wilson, T. D., D. S. Dunn, J. A. Bybee, D. B. Hyman, and J. A. Rotondo. 1984. Effects of analyzing reasons on attitude-behavior consistency. *Journal of Personality and Social Psychology, 47,* 5–16.

Wilson, T. D., S. D. Hodges, and S. J. LaFleur. 1995. Effects of introspecting about reasons: Inferring attitudes from accessible thoughts. *Journal of Personality and Social Psychology, 69,* 16–28.

Wilson, T. D., J. Hull, and J. Johnson. 1981. Awareness and self-perception: Verbal reports on internal states. *Journal of Personality and Social Psychology, 40,* 53–71.

Wilson, T. D., and D. Kraft. 1993. Why do I love thee? Effects of repeated introspections on attitudes toward the relationship. *Personality and Social Psychology Bulletin, 19,* 409–418.

Wilson, T. D., and S. J. LaFleur. 1995. Knowing what you'll do: Effects of analyzing reasons on self-prediction. *Journal of Personality and Social Psychology, 68,* 21–35.

Wilson, T. D., P. S. Laser, and J. I. Stone. 1982. Judging the predictors of one's own mood: Accuracy and the use of shared theories. *Journal of Experimental Social Psychology, 18,* 537–556.

Wilson, T. D., S. Lindsey, and T. Y. Schooler. 2000. A model of dual attitudes. *Psychological Review, 107,* 101–126.

Wilson, T. D., D. Lisle, J. Schooler, S. D. Hodges, K. J. Klaaren, and S. J. LaFleur. 1993. Introspecting about reasons can reduce post-choice satisfaction. *Personality and Social Psychology Bulletin, 19,* 331–339.

Wilson, T. D., and J. W. Schooler. 1991. Thinking too much: Introspection can reduce the quality of preferences and decisions. *Journal of Personality and Social Psychology, 60,* 181–192.

Wilson, T. D., and J. I. Stone. 1985. Limitations of self-knowledge: More on telling more than we can know. In P. Shaver, ed., *Review of personality and social psychology.* Vol. 6, pp. 167–183. Beverly Hills: Sage.

Wilson, T. D., T. P. Wheatley, J. M. Meyers, D. T. Gilbert, and D. Axsom. 2000. Focalism: A Source of durability bias in affective forecasting. *Journal of Personality and Social Psychology, 78,* 821–836.

Winter, D. G. 1992. Power motivation revisited. In C. P. Smith, ed., *Motivation and personality: Handbook of thematic content analysis,* pp. 301–311. Cambridge: Cambridge University Press.

Winter, D. G., O. P. John, A. J. Stewart, E. C. Klohnen, and L. E. Duncan. 1998. Traits and motives: Toward an integration of two traditions in personality research. *Psychological Review, 105,* 230–250.

Wortman, C. B., R. C. Silver, and R. C. Kessler. 1993. The meaning of loss and adjustment to bereavement. In M. S. Stroebe, W. Stroebe, and R. O. Hansson, eds., *Handbook of bereavement: Theory, research, and intervention,* pp. 349–366. New York: Cambridge University Press.

Yinger, J. 1995. *Closed doors, opportunities lost: The continuing costs of housing discrimination.* New York: Russell Sage Foundation.

Zajonc, R. B. 1980. Feeling and thinking: Preferences need no inferences. *American Psychologist, 35,* 151–175.

Zillmann, D. 1978. Attribution and misattribution of excitatory reaction. In J. H. Harvey, W. Ickes, and R. F. Kidd, eds., *New directions in attribution research.* Vol. 2, pp. 335–368. Hillsdale, N.J.: Erlbaum.

Index